FOOL'S
HILL

THE MEANING "WHY" (TMW)

Ron Cubit Ed.D, MBA, BS, AA, AS

PAGE PUBLISHING, INC.
Conneaut Lake, PA

First originally published by Page Publishing 2019

ISBN 978-1-64628-053-7 (pbk)
ISBN 978-1-64628-039-1 (digital)

Printed in the United States of America

Dedicated to

Aiden
Baron
Levant
Kayden
Maurice
Nalani
Orion
Souvignon

Leishan, Lealani, Lahina

You Changed My Life!

The two most important days in your life are
the day you are born and
the day you find out why.

—Mark Twain

INTRODUCTION

I sit in a shabby hotel room in the early morning, wondering what happened in my life. The carpet is filthy, and the walls have the essence of food from previous guests. I can't leave the hot water on for too long, for the pipes begin to vibrate as if to sing. The room smells like cigarettes and a combination of other odors, and the two containers of Febreze and Glade carpet deodorant doesn't eliminate the smell. In fear of attracting a fungus, I decide my shoes should remain on my feet. The bathroom-how grotesque! I want to vomit, and I fear taking a shower in that shabby motel.

Today, my thoughts begin to wander. I achieved the highest education in the land from a prestigious school. I read motivational books and listened to similar tapes and CDs. As the authors in the books and speakers in the tapes and CDs professed, set goals, and never quit. At one time, I studied the Scriptures fervently under an exceptional, God-fearing pastor. Every morning, I say my affirmations. I strived to live outside of my comfort zone. For a period, I refrained from using controlled substances and abstained from drinking alcohol, and I do believe I mastered most of my demons. I've written my goals and review them periodically.

I took risks in order to achieve success with business ventures and employment. I alleviated the fear of public speaking, of writing, of transitioning myself from a fearful individual, and beat shyness, and the lack of confidence, I hope. I derailed a troubled childhood that transcended to my adult life sometimes. I overcame thinking that African American males are inferior. I addressed a challenge of questioning my manhood. I raised three beautiful children that have morals. At this time, I'm single, and after my failed relationships, I ask, "Why try?" Although at my detriment, I sacrificed family to achieve goals.

As I sit at a desk in that shabby hotel room, I wonder about the next advent in my life. Where will I live next week? My health becomes an issue; I now have allergies. I'm thirty pounds overweight, and my back hurts from sleeping in my car sometimes, and I always fear a mental breakdown. I have high blood pressure and have been warned about changing my diet and my doctor suggest that I take medication to control my cholesterol, which is incomprehensible for me.

All my personal belongings fit into a ten-by-fifteen-foot storage unit. My car is aging and filled with my essential possessions. I'm not lazy. I've fervently worked to create a life opposite from the afore-mentioned; however, the current condition prevails. I look into the mirror and ask, "What happened?" I realize that drinking alcohol is a part of my life. I'm not a drunk, though! *Who is at fault?* I ponder. God, my parents, individuals of other races, employers, me? As I look into the mirror, my tears begin to flow. However, I have aspirations.

The last night in the shabby motel, I dreamed of meeting at that time First Lady Michelle Obama and President Barack Obama at Air Force One. Nervously, I give the president and first lady a tour of San Diego. I show them my favorite restaurant, the Barbeque Pit. We drive by Jerry's Market, where I used to buy pickled pigs' feet delicious at that time. My mouth begins to water as I describe the hot link sandwiches and dill pickles I ate as a child from that same market. We then dine at Huffman's Barbeque, a place where one could buy chitterlings. I begin to describe to the president and the first lady the challenges I've faced, and I cry as if life has no meaning. I awake in tears.

Now it is 4:00 a.m., and I begin to pack my clothes for the last day in that shabby motel. I begin to wonder at what point in my life the dilemma described here actually began. More so, I wonder what lies ahead. I remember my grandmother's comment: "That boy will be all right once he gets over fool's hill." Currently, I wonder about my placement on that hill, and it is now I start to write about my journey. I begin…

Chapter 1

THE BEGINNING

Both of my parents were from the great state of Oklahoma. They lived in small rural towns. My father had a fourth-grade education, and he could barely read or write, let alone pronounce some words correctly. I remember my eldest sister reading for my father. He was a country boy and he helped my grandfather support the acreage, including the livestock that consisted of chickens, cows, pigs, a smokehouse, and other necessities to sustain the family.

His great-grandparents were slaves and that instilled the ethics of hard work into my grandfather, which resonated in my father. My grandfather believed that hard work was necessary for survival. He cut down trees on the family property and started a firewood business. My grandfather, father, and uncles drove a buckboard to town and sold the firewood. Often, times were rough, and my father and uncles had to hunt rabbits and food for supper. I remember visiting Oklahoma with my father when I was about nine years old. While visiting a relative one day, my father accidentally hit a rabbit with the car. Immediately he ran to the roadkill and threw it in the back of the car. "Good 'nuf to eat, only in da winter, no worms in dis meat," he said in his fourth-grade manner of speaking.

My father was handsome in some respect. He wanted to serve his country in whatever capacity he could. During the war, he served in the army and was a truck driver. He remembered his harsh days growing up and the separation of the blacks and whites, including in the military. Wanting to be an army man when I grew up, I asked my father why few blacks participated in combat during the war.

In his fourth-grade manner of speaking, he said, "Because niggars not allowed to carry guns. White man scared of niggars. They might shoot 'em in da back. White man thought niggars might be scared and run too. Good 'nuf more white peoples killed in da war, good for niggars." Pop scratched his head in disbelief and added, "Don't un'stand dem white folks. Good chance to get rid of sum niggars."

On occasion, for family reasons, my father drove from California to Oklahoma. Later in life, I asked him why my mother always fried chicken when he made the journey. He mentioned that "niggars couldn't stop and stay in hotels and had to drive all the way through and be careful goin' through dem small towns" when buying ethyl, their version of what is now known as high-octane gasoline. My brother and I sometimes chuckled when my father spoke, and he threatened to spank us. Our laughter was probably learned behavior from my mother and aunts as they sat, discussed, and laughed at black men. The sessions were entertaining. Moreover, my father could barely read or write and pronouncing some words was a challenge; however, he was smart enough to manage without those tools. My father wasn't ignorant. He was able to retire from a civil service job and build a retirement home in Oklahoma.

After his retirement, I visited my father several times in Oklahoma, and by then he had remarried. When visiting, we sat outside near a forested area, a family time to relax and converse. All of a sudden, in midspeech, with a flyswatter in hand to ward off the mosquitoes and other flying insects, my stepmother hesitated then said that she smelled a snake. That was interesting, and those sitting with us promised that if she smelled a snake, then one was in the vicinity. Probably a survival instinct developed while living in heavily forested areas in the Southern states as a youth. My stepmother then told a story about a young person who was picking berries in the woods. While she was picking berries, a snake lunged from the patch and became stuck in her braces, which she wore to straighten her teeth. She then said that the girl died not from the snake's venom but from a heart attack at an early age. I enjoyed sitting in my father's yard and listening to stories on those hot humid summer days.

My birth mother was born and raised in a small town approximately thirty-five miles from where my father was born. She was an elegant and beautiful female. Some believed she had some Native American blood, but I researched our lineage on her father's side of the family, and in the bloodline I couldn't find evidence of this. However, some on my mother's father's side were Choctaw freedmen and owned by the tribe. I've yet to research the lineage on my maternal grandmother's side of the family, but at that time I do remember seeing my great-grandfather, who was as white as a sheet. He was senile and had one leg.

I took a DNA test, and the results revealed that my bloodline is mostly of African descent. To confirm this, I'm often approached by individuals of Ethiopian ancestry. Once I was at the airport in Sacramento, and an individual approached me and began talking in his Ethiopian tongue. Being from San Diego, a city with a heavy Hispanic influence, all I could say was "No hablo," which is a Spanish phrase, but I do believe he got the point and he walked away. In another incident in my travels, I was approached while walking around in Washington, DC, of all places. A female approached me and asked if I was from Ethiopia. Of course, I said that I was from the hood in San Diego. She said that I was mistaken and that, if visiting the homeland in Africa, individuals could automatically communicate who my people were. I was thinking, *Maybe I should attempt to visit the country one day. Besides, those Ethiopian women are fine.* (*Fine* means "attractive" in layman's terms.) I might visit one day and never come back. Just recently, I went to an Ethiopian restaurant, and the female who owned the establishment encouraged me to research my lineage and take that DNA test.

Nevertheless, my mother was an excellent writer and a dynamic speaker. I still remember some of her clichés: "Everything will come out in the wash" and "They come out of the woodworks" and "You make your bed hard, you have to sleep on it" and, most importantly, "Only the strong survive." In addition, my mother told me something about a woman's facial feature and if the female has it, a certain trait prevailed. To this date, my mother was right and that facial feature is something I look for when dating someone or considering a partner for life.

My mother graduated from high school and aspired to be a movie star. However, in her youth, she faced challenging circumstances as a beautiful black female. I speculate that dilemmas affected her psychologically and was a reason for her transient nature and the many moves back and forth from California to Ohio. However, with limited means, she was able to survive the challenges of rearing two daughters, one mentally challenged, and two sons who were destined for challenging lives themselves, especially me.

Both parents had aspirations for a better life. While my mother was pregnant with my eldest sister, my parents decided to move from Oklahoma to "Daygo," which is local slang for San Diego, California. They had no roots in California, but they did have a desire for a better life for themselves and the family. On the way to California, my eldest sister was born in Hugo, Oklahoma. After they arrived in California, my father took odd jobs. He washed dishes and was a janitor as well. He finally landed a federal job, and at that time, an African American male without a high school diploma, especially a veteran, could do so. Sometimes my father worked three jobs to make ends meet.

Soon after their arrival in California, my second eldest sister was born. Later in my adult life, my eldest sister told me that my second eldest sister wasn't from my father. I find it interesting, because my father had a child by another woman, my stepsister. Sleeping around, or infidelity, seemed to be prevalent in those days. Perhaps the music of the time influenced this. I remember songs blasting from the living room walls while I was in bed when my mother was partying at night. Some of the songs were "Cheatin' in the Next Room," "Breaking Up Somebody's Home," "Slip Away," and "I Can't Leave Your Love Alone," and others.

Alternatively, my mom was a stay-at-home mother for some time, and public assistance was the income source. However, she was a party animal. My mother spent time in the local bars, and sometimes she wasn't at home. Sometimes my eldest sister took care of things while my mother was away. God bless her heart, and I'll stop here describing my mother, for some things that we encountered shouldn't be mentioned.

Soon after, I was born, and I assume my parents were divorced at that time. Then my younger brother was born almost a year to the day after my birthday, which means my mother was impregnated with my brother approximately three months after I was born.

I don't remember my father staying in the house with us. If visiting for a night he slept in the room with my brother and me. I remember that when my father visited, he parked his car around the corner from the house. "So the county don't find out and cut off my check," my mother said. My birth parents attempted to reconcile several times and lived together for short stints. They had plans to buy a house and raise their four children.

At that time, San Diego was a military and sailor's town, and nightclubs were everywhere. Before I was born, my mother met a sailor in a bar in San Diego. He was from Ohio. My mother and the sailor began seeing each other regularly. After I was born, at one time, my mother visited the sailor in Ohio with me in tow, leaving behind the other children. My mother stayed with the sailor for some time, knowing that she had three children in California. I do believe that during this time, my mother suffered from postpartum depression. Perhaps the scars from her childhood trauma gave reason for my mother's actions as well. My mother decided to leave Ohio and gravitated to Oklahoma for a while, but I broke out in an uncontrollable rash, that caused my mother to return to California.

However, my mother was destined to be with the sailor. One day, during one of the short live-in stints, my father came home from work to find the house empty. She left my father without so much as leaving a note. I speculate that my father was dumbfounded. This would be the first of many moves in which my mother left my father and or stepfather without a warning. They came home to find the house empty, children and wife (or ex-wife) gone. We made many moves as children back and forth between California and Ohio. My mother and the sailor eventually married.

Chapter 2

ITS ELEMENTARY

I was born on a winter day in January in beautiful San Diego, California. For the sake of living in diverse communities, I thank God that my parents decided to leave Oklahoma and move to San Diego. I was born a healthy baby and weighed about eight pounds. I'm the first son and the fourth of five children for my father and the third of four children for my mother.

In reviewing my elementary photos, I realized my classes were diverse, and I remember students of Polynesian descent, some Hispanics, not many Caucasians, and predominantly African American. By the time I was briefly in junior high school, the neighborhood in which I lived in Southeast San Diego was predominantly African American.

My birthday is the same day (but not year) as that of Dr. Martin Luther King, Jr. A birthday on the same day as one of the most influential and dynamic martyrs provided an inspiration for me. Later in life, knowing that my birthday is on the same day as Dr. Martin Luther King Jr.'s influenced some decisions I made. I'm honored to share the same birthday with someone who died for his beliefs, especially since his goal was to create equality for all human beings. More so than having the same birthday as Dr. Martin Luther King Jr., I've always believed that life was going to be special for me.

In my preteens, I might describe myself as a cute and happy-go-lucky child; however, I was also mischievous and I could make others laugh. I had a curious side to me as well. One day, my father

14

was driving down a busy street, and I wanted to know what would happen if I pulled the handle that opened the car door. Well, I did and out the door I fell. There I was, sitting on the busy street in my striped short pants, near the line in the middle of the road with my covadis haircut. Thank God there were no cars behind us! My father stopped the Oldsmobile, and I can still hear the tires screeching and the smell of the rubber. My father threw me in the car, and off we went. I didn't grasp the gravity of what just took place. However, my father was angry and, in his fourth-grade manner of speaking, commenced hollering at me. Looking back at my mischievousness, it's too bad my parents couldn't have assisted me in channeling that energy into something constructive.

At that time, I remember, on occasion, communicating to my mother that I was proud to live in America and proud to be black. My environment helped create those beliefs. Sometimes teachers said that I was smart, but I look in the mirror today and ask, "What happened to Ronnie, that happy-go-lucky smart boy without inhibitions?"

At that time I wasn't fond of the opposite sex and somehow obtained the belief that boys weren't supposed to like girls. Today I wonder why. While I was living in San Diego, a female who lived next door had the hots for me, a crush, I guess. She was kind of cute but a big girl and much older. One day, I was playing in the garage while my parents were away. I was about five years old, and the girl next door trapped me in the garage and began kissing me. She stuck her tongue in my mouth. I didn't know what to do. This happened more than once, and each time the girl's breath smelled like pickled beets. I never told anyone about the kissing but the events reinforced my wondering about the opposite sex, and questioning about why they existed.

Early in life, I acquired blemishes all over my body. Some of the dark brown blemishes were the size of a quarter. My mother took me to the doctor, and he prescribed a special diet; one item was pickled beets. Don't ask me why. The blemishes increased during the times my father stayed with us. He used to yell at me and, one day, kicked me twice in the rear, hard, right in the middle, because the dog licked me in the face. I believed my father thought I wasn't the boy he wanted me to be and assumed I was just different. When my father was away, the blemishes diminished. Today, if I'm faced with prolonged highly stressful situations, the blemishes appear but on a smaller scale. Concerning the comment about my father and me being different, I need to mention here that today I strive to be different, or dissimilar, and refuse to accept the status quo. For example, I dated a female who lived by a park, and individuals, for exercise, walked or ran around the track in the same direction. No, I wasn't going to follow the masses. I completed my trek in the opposite direction.

We spent the early years moving back and forth from California to Ohio. I thought riding the train was fun, and I'll never forget the station smell. Today, visiting a train station brings back memories, for as a child, we spent a vast amount of time in them. I remember riding the train to Ohio one time, and we had a layover in Chicago. My mother began walking the streets to find something to eat. A taxicab stopped, and the driver asked her where she was going. The taxicab driver said it wasn't a good idea to be walking the streets near the train station in Chicago at that time of the night with three children straggling. He took us back to the train station without charging a fare.

When riding the trains, I thought the conductors were cool. They carried what I thought was a hole puncher that was attached to a chain on their belt. The conductor hollered "Tickets!" then went from seat to seat rapidly punching tickets. I wanted one of those ticket punchers, and while in elementary school, I asked my mother for a paper-hole puncher, which she provided. While alone one day with nothing to do, I happened upon one of my elementary class pictures. I took that hole puncher and rapidly punched out eyes of students in that elementary class picture like the train conductor. My mother happened upon the pictures; in fact, I showed it to her among many in the folder. All she could do was shake her head in disbelief, and that was her first comment about me seeing a psychiatrist. I still have that picture.

At one time in Southeast San Diego, we lived on West Street across from Saxony Arms (the apartment complex was called that at that time). We lived in a house on the corner. In our front yard, we had a banana tree, and we had citrus trees in the backyard. Jerry's Market was right behind us. The market had the best dill pickles, pickled pigs' feet, and a scrumptious hot link sandwich. Today, because of my health consciousness, I limit myself to a dill pickle now and then. Some time ago when in San Diego, I visited Jerry's Market, but the hot link sandwiches didn't have the same scrumptious taste as they did when I lived in the hood. Memorable times.

In my preteen days, starting in San Diego, California, we must've relocated more than eight times within the city. What makes it interesting is, besides other streets, we lived on three that I remember, Delta, Alpha, and Beta. At one time, we lived in a low-income old navy housing in Point Loma, California. When the city, and perhaps developers, realized the value of that property, which was near the ocean, they forced the low-income residents out, demolished the housing complex, and redeveloped the property.

In addition, as mentioned in the last paragraph, we must've relocated a similar number of times from San Diego to Ohio. The moves started before I was in kindergarten in California. By the sixth grade, we lived in several neighborhoods. We were constantly on the move. In analysis, I find that I follow similar patterns as an adult-always on the move-and today, a transient nature is concentric to aspects of my life.

Most of the time we were on public assistance (called "welfare" at that time) and picked up commodities or government surplus food from various locations, such as a church, school, or county social service entity. In our house, we pronounced the food "camadee" (ca-ma-dee), for *commodity*, especially the camadee meat. Sometimes in the hood, folks, especially the children, rename things or mispronounce words they can't spell.

My mother knew all the locations for acquiring camadees. I loved the luncheon meat, which looked and tasted like Spam. The shredded beef mixed with mayonnaise (mayo) and onions was delicious. The cheese was the best of all the camadees. The powdered eggs and powdered milk were compliments as well. I used to eat a thick slice of the luncheon meat. I'd fry it and put a behemoth slice of that delicious government cheese between two slices of white bread. Don't forget the onions and mayo. If I wanted toast using the white bread, I'd slap a dab of camadee butter on the cast iron skillet, wait until it was hot, lay the bread on that hot camadee butter, and turn it over a few times. When the burn marks appeared around the perimeter, it was ready to consume. Who needed a toaster? The skillet was more than a protection implement. To explain, in the hood, some (mostly females) used a cast-iron skillet for protection and wielding one was necessary incase C-dale came by and started acting out. Other protection implements were hot grits, lye, boiling water and the deadly high hill shoe. Every time I hear the remake of the song "High-Heel Sneakers" by Tommy Tucker (1964), it reminds me of those times. Anyway, today my skillet serves as an important cooking utensil in the place where I live and can be used otherwise.

After consuming a camadee meat sandwich, I wanted to drink a gallon of water. Probably because of the sodium content in that camadee meat sandwich slathered with the government cheese. Here I note the importance of initiatives such as healthy eating and active living especially for individuals living in the hood. Imagine eating one of those camadee meat sandwiches and or other high-sodium foods before going to school. While sitting in class, all an individual probably thought about was a drink of water instead of listening to the teacher. Today, when I see a person of color constantly licking his or her lips, I believe the act is a learned habit from kinfolk because someone in their lineage probably ate an enormous amount of camadee meat sandwiches or other high-sodium government surplus foods.

Anyway, we were creative, and one could devise what we thought was a decent meal with the camadee meat in addition to the other items previously mentioned. Although not a camadee, another delicacy was the bologna, and I don't care about the official spelling. In the hood, we called it baloney. I used to take a dab of lard and fry the baloney, and to eliminate the hump in the middle, I cut an X in the meat concoction. The aroma of the fried baloney drifted throughout the house. Later, I found that because of the fat content, I could fry the baloney without lard. I placed that fried baloney between two pieces of white bread with mustard, and sometimes government cheese, then pour a large cup of Kool-Aid. Sometimes I'd eat a dill pickle with it. I was in heaven. Pickled pigs' feet and the pork rinds were delicacies of that time as well.

If someone shouted, "Havers!" especially at school, the cardinal rule was to share without hesitation. I always complied with the rule, but to circumvent sharing at home after making a meal consisting of two to three baloney or camadee meat sandwiches with other fixings, I hid in the house so no one would ask for some. Sometimes I hid behind the couch or under the kitchen table, which had a long table-cloth. When I hid under the kitchen table, no one knew I was under there, but they could smell the aroma from the kitchen. However, I knew who was in the kitchen while I was under the table, because I could see their feet. I was especially quiet if it was my eldest sister, and I'll explain why later. Importantly, today, if facing stressful situations, I have to watch myself, for sometimes I gravitate toward salty foods and snacks, perhaps because what was ingrained from my childhood resurfaces in my subconscious. Please know, today, my diet is 180 degrees from what I thought were delicacies in the days of old. However, I'll confess, I indulge in a turkey baloney sandwich sometimes.

A friend of the family gave us fishing poles, and I decided to go fishing for cats out of the back window of the two-story place where we lived. I used the camadee meat as bait. I thought, *fishing poles and no water, so why not fish for cats?* I hated cats. To emphasize the dislike for cats, for Christmas, my mother bought me a Johnny Seven OMA. The OMA stood for "One-Man Army." The Johnny Seven was just that, seven weapons in one. I used to lock the cat in the garage and practice hitting the animal with the plastic bullets and other projectiles from the Johnny Seven. I laughed when the cat jumped while arching its back. Anyway, concerning fishing for cats and sometimes birds with the fishing poles I had just acquired, I often scrounged a roach from somewhere in the house to use as bait to catch birds. I positioned the bait on the hooks and threw the line out of the back window. Of course, I wasn't successful catching cats or birds, thank God. Please know that today I believe all animals have a right to life and should be treated accordingly. In addition, the first movie during which I cried in my youth was *Old Yeller*, a Disney movie about a young boy and his dog. My goal today is to have mated pairs of Rhodesian ridgebacks.

Because we were constantly on the move, I was sometimes the new kid on the block or in school. I had to adapt constantly to changing situations and new environments. I remember, on one occasion we'd just left San Diego, California, and typically, the temperature during that time of the year was sixty-five degrees. We arrived in Ohio, and the snow was knee-high. I had to walk to school in the snow. My mother bought me some snow boots to wear to school. I walked to school, and the teacher asked me to take off my boots. All I had on were socks and no shoes. Some of the students in the classroom laughed. Others said, "Pewww," and the teacher asked where my shoes were. Of course, I said, "At home." I was the only student in the class without shoes on. The aforementioned serves as an example of one of many situations I experienced because of the transient nature of my family.

Most often, I was the tallest student in the class and didn't have to worry about others picking on me. In Ohio, sometimes they made fun of me, though. I remember students laughing at me because I had corduroy pants on in the summer and was wearing wing-tip shoes. Except for the wing-tip shoes, which we thought weren't cool, we wore we wanted anytime when living in Daygo.

One day in Ohio, my stepfather took us to get a haircut, and back then, a soup-bowl haircut wasn't popular. A soup-bowl haircut means that someone placed a soup bowl on the boy's head then cut off all the hair below the rim, sometimes unevenly. I was a new student at one school and entered the class with that soup-bowl haircut. I can still hear that laughter today. The event did little for my ability to overcome shyness.

After a while as I became comfortable in junior high school, my revenge was that if someone in class had a soup-bowl haircut, I slapped him in the back of the head, and the whole class could hear the sound. I thought the slapping sound was hilarious. However, a soup-bowl haircut or a facsimile of it is widely accepted today.

I hated facing the challenges of constantly being the new kid on the block and in the classroom, especially the times in Ohio when the teacher introduced me as the kid from California. Adjusting was constantly a challenge, and I developed a loner mentality, learning to be self-sufficient.

One day, I was involved in an altercation with another boy in the neighborhood. His name was Stephen. Previously, my parents had purchased BB guns for us. In Daygo the juicy berries that grew on bushes were a delicacy. At that time of the year, the berries were unripe, green, and not fully formed. I ran out of BBs for my gun and figured out how to use the unripe berries in place of the BBs. Stephen already pissed me off that day, so I loaded my BB gun with the immature berries and shot him in the ass at close range.

Stephen told my father what had happened with tears in his eyes. My father made me go to my room. Later that day, I was playing tackle football in the front yard. I experienced an elbow in the mouth that almost dislodged a tooth. Nonetheless, later that day, in pain, I approached my mother and explained the situation.

She said, "Boy, get away from me. Nothing is wrong with you." I suffered with that tooth until I was about thirty years old when my dentist performed surgery twice and finally removed the tooth. On another occasion as a child, I hurt my elbow playing baseball, same response: "Boy get away from me" and "Nothing is wrong with you." Today, I wear a brace on that elbow on occasion. Connected with the two incidences I just described, I developed a mentality to never ask anyone for anything and, in addition to being a loner and self-sufficient, to suck it up. I thought no one cared and sometimes I had thoughts of committing suicide.

While in my loner state, I often fantasized about being a submarine captain, and my reference point was the television show *Voyage to the Bottom of the Sea*, or a captain of a spaceship like Captain Kirk of the starship *Enterprise*. Some mornings, especially on the weekends, I hid under my bedcovers for hours and pretended to be a submarine or starship captain. I killed Klingons, especially those damn Romulans, which I don't think I ever saw on the show, and sank ships while maneuvering the starship or the submarine out of challenges. I fought space monsters and every kind of sea creature imaginable.

In San Diego, while I was in elementary school, teachers said that I was a smart kid and, some might say, a good boy. At night, I remember reading pages of the dictionary before going to bed. I practiced this well into my teens. However, I thought school was boring. During school, I daydreamed about slaying sea creatures or space monsters. I was shy, and while living in Ohio, I remember one student commenting, "Can he talk?" to ask if I had the ability to speak. What didn't help was my parents constantly reinforced that I was too shy. To compensate for the shyness and boredom, sometimes I acted out in school or reverted to my comedian acts and that good-boy image began to revert to one who was mischievous. I don't remember completing any schoolwork.

Although we moved to different neighborhoods from the second to sixth grade in San Diego, I attended the same school, which provided a sense of stability. At school, students and teachers called me Pig-Pen, after the Peanuts character, because I always managed to find a dirt pile. I was always dirty.

Because I was bigger than most of my classmates, some mentioned that I was the king of the school. I never fought anyone for that title and didn't know how I earned it; however, I was comfortable with the perception. I remember, on one occasion, an individual hit my younger brother. We found the individual, and I told my brother to hit him back. He did so, and I was so happy the individual didn't retaliate. One day, I bullied the same individual in the classroom, and he hit me in the jaw. Before I could retaliate, the teacher separated us. Believe me, though the kill switch was on. From that point on, I learned something about bullying, and I don't know what would have happened if the teacher hadn't separated us. I believe I lost my "king of the school" title that day, and it didn't matter, because we were at the end of the school year. Anyway, my mother bought me an autograph book. Circumventing my shyness, on the last day of school, I asked my sixth-grade classmates to sign the book. Their comments were interesting, and I still have that book today.

While in elementary school in San Diego, to extend friendships, I stole money from my mother's purse and treated the fellows after school. I believed they hung out with me because of the treats. Back then, an individual could buy a bag of potato chips, a candy bar, and a soda for about fifty cents. Taking money from my mother's purse became habitual. At home, I remember all of us sitting at the dinner table and my mother saying that she couldn't buy milk because of the money missing from her purse. My father wasn't around at that time. I didn't feel guilty because I wanted to please my friends. Sometimes I took more than one or two dollars and decided to have a banquet with friends. I once took a ten-dollar bill, which I later found out to be part of the rent money.

One day, my mother, while my father was visiting, left her purse in an inconspicuous place, and I struck. Later that day, my mother and father confronted me and said that they knew I'd taken the money. They explained how they'd accomplished the stakeout, and I knew I was busted. Of course, I denied the accusations. However, my father tore my ass up-a spanking that I remember. Back then, when my parents spanked us, they gave us a lecture during the act. Did that change the error of my ways? Perhaps not!

While in elementary school, I went to the principal's office maybe once or twice. Sometimes the teachers gave me a note to give to my parents. I had to return the note the next day. I remember those long treks across the park on the way home with that note in my hand. I knew I was going to get a spanking, but at some point, those didn't matter and were just a formality.

While spanked, mostly by my mother, I yelled and hollered as if the world were ending. Afterward, I went into the bedroom and laughed. Sometimes, when both my brother and I were spanked, we compared notes afterward and teased each other while laughing. For example, we mimicked how each of us hollered while being spanked and made silly gestures about how the other had gyrated. The goal in mimicking was to outperform the other and determine who could generate the loudest laugh between us. When mimicking each other, we almost looked like break-dancers, and we took turns with our acts. Each started with "So what? You sounded like this and almost stood on your head when you was on the ground." Then it was the other's turn, which started with "So what? You…" We were two clowns, and what a sight to see, especially for anyone stumbling upon the semi-break-dancing scenes. To keep ourselves entertained, sometimes the charades went on for hours-at least we weren't getting into trouble. Next, we gravitated toward trying to outdo each other, calling each other nonsensical names prefaced with bald-headed. For example, "You bald-headed jellyfish with…" We laughed for hours, trying to determine who had the most hilarious bald-headed joke. "Shut up, you bald-headed parrot," or something similar is what one of us ended the session with, and then on to the next adventure. Today, if someone saw a text message between my brother and me, the person might think that we needed psychological counseling. Nonetheless, I bet my mother aged several years, and spanking both of us, one after the other was an exhausting experience.

As previously stated, my mother spanked both my brother and me, and sometimes consecutively. Often, my mother told us that my father was going to spank us sometime during the next week or when he visited. Often, the spankings never happened, and we managed to push the envelope. For example, my parents bought us orange life jackets because my father promised to take us fishing. In those days, the life jackets weren't as streamlined as they are today. My mother sent my brother and me to our room because we'd done something wrong. We were in the room for a period, and when my mother heard a commotion, I could hear her saying, "What are the hard-headed Negroes doing in this room?" When she opened the door, we were at the top of a two-section closet, jumping out with the life jackets on pretending that we were parachuting from the top of the closet with the life jackets on to mimic a television show at that time, *Ripcord*. The television show was about individuals parachuting out of an airplane to rescue someone or to solve crimes.

When entering the room and discovering one of us in midair with the life jacket on, all she could do was shake her head in disgust and say, "Just wait until your father gets here. Just wait until your father gets here. He is going to tear your asses up." I think she was angry with us because I broke the bed when "parachuting."

In anticipation of my father's spankings, we placed newspaper and magazines in our clothes sometimes for days, which did no good when my father spanked us. After removing the newspapers or magazines while lecturing at the same time, he spanked us harder.

During elementary school, I aspired to be a patrol boy; they were usually sixth graders. They carried signs and stopped traffic so students and parents could cross the street. The patrol boy with the whistle was in charge, and I thought they were so cool. The patrol boy in charge blew a whistle, and the other two from opposite sides of the street extended signs to stop the traffic. Patrol boys wore white pants and red jackets. They marched to their stations in unison with signs in a port arms position, to use a military reference. I asked my teacher if I could be a patrol boy.

To champion my cause to be a patrol boy, I began doing good deeds at school. I gained the teacher's trust and he appointed me the audiovisual monitor. If the teacher needed a movie projector, filmstrip, or any audiovisual material or equipment, I left the class to obtain what was needed from a storeroom. *My first real responsibility on the way to becoming a patrol boy,* I thought. One day, the teacher asked me to return the projector to the storeroom, which was on a chest-high cart with wheels. On the way to the storeroom was a small hill, and I decided to ride the cart down the hill. While riding the cart with the projector, I lost control, and all I remember is the loud sound of my ass and the projector hitting the ground. The movie projector shattered in pieces. If one remembers those projectors that had the two arms that the teacher extended to put the film in place, well, both of those arms looked like mangled octopus tentacles. My opportunity to be a patrol boy ended that day. My first career aspiration shattered. As I was walking across the park on my way home after school, I wondered if a spanking was in order, which was a minor concern.

Upon my return to school, I asked my teacher about being a patrol-boy. My teacher explained the reasons that I couldn't be patrol-boy, and how disappointing my act was, lecturing me about choices. However, the incident did little to change my ways. Because of my mischievous ways, it was probably a good thing I didn't become a patrol boy. It was a tremendous responsibility stopping automobiles so students could cross the street; no telling what might've happened. Soon after, it was time to attend camp in the mountains.

Before promotion to junior high school, sixth graders had an opportunity to attend camp for a week. The reasons for attending camp was to give inner-city students exposure to the wilderness. Yes, there was a cost, and my mother couldn't afford to send me. Because we were on public assistance, the school gave us a break, and I was allowed to attend camp. For one week, I was going to be away from home and experience the wilderness. No family for five days.

I was apprehensive about attending camp. A few years prior, my father took us to Oklahoma during the winter. My mother bought us suede pointed-toe dress shoes in which one could see the thick stitching that held together the front part of the shoe that met the flat part of the toe. I called the shoes "roach-in-the-corner killers." Because the shoes had pointed-toe tips, one could kill a roach in the corner of the house. We thought we were cool. After we arrived in Oklahoma, my cousins, country boys at that time, took us on an adventure into the woods. Of course, I decided to wear my "roach-in-the-corner killers." As we traversed the woods, we stopped to drink from a creek, which was the most refreshing water I ever tasted.

After a while, we stopped at what I eventually learned was a cousin's house, and at that time, a lone female was in the shanty. She let us in, and for some reason, we started misbehaving. She brandished a shotgun, and we took off running and laughing.

After a while, it was time to head back, and I thought my route was the best way. On the other hand, my cousins knew the way back, but I insisted my way was the best. Go figure. They went their way, and alone, I went mine. The dog that accompanied us decided to follow me. After a few hours, cold and hungry, I realized I was lost in the woods. There I was, a kid from the hood with suede "roach-in-the-corner killers," lost in the woods. It started to get dark and cold. The dog started walking, and I followed. Just before dark, the dog led me to the road, and I followed it for miles, which finally led me to my grandparents' house.

My father was enraged and threatened to spank me. He asked in his fourth grade language what had possessed me to think I could find my way back without the others. I could hardly understand him, not only because of his fourth-grade manner of speaking, but also because he was angry. Head down, I said, "I don't know." Others were happy to see me, and if it hadn't been for the dog, I don't know if I'd have made it. What further made my father mad were those suede shoes that were destroyed. My cousin, whose birthday is a few days after mine, always reminds me of the event when we see each other. And his description of my father's reaction to the destruction of the "roach-in-the-corner killers" warrants an academy award for comedy. I do state here that the hero of the lost-in-the-woods dilemma was the dog. However, I didn't learn the error of my ways, and because I had a my-way-is-the-best-way mentality, I found myself lost in the woods two more times, which I'll explain later.

Based on my shenanigans in elementary school and the event when I was lost in the woods, looking back, I'm surprised my parents and the school allowed me to attend camp. However, I was off to camp. I thought camp was so cool, and I had an opportunity to see trees other than those in the hood and the banana tree in the front yard. While we were in camp, the counselors taught us about conservation, and we planted trees. I was having the time of my life. I was enamored with the beauty of the outdoors, which is consistent with my love for nature today. I wanted to stay in camp forever.

Another summer, as part of a federal government subsidized program for disadvantaged youth, I returned to camp in the wilderness, and again, the camp counselors taught us about conservation, and I was excited at the beauty of the outdoors. I'd only brought two sets of clothes, and those were filthy the first two days, and I was able to maintain my Pig-Pen mode. One night, I was dirty and didn't want to take a shower, and I took my pants off before getting into the bunk. That day, one of the male students played a joke on me, and I decided to pay him back. He was in another log cabin. That night, in my underwear, no shirt, no shoes, I ran across a dirt path to that log cabin and began punching individuals and laughing as they lay in their bunks trying to get some sleep. The next morning, during breakfast, one of the camp counselors asked if it was fun running around in my underwear last night. I was speechless.

While in elementary school, I asked my mother if I could play the trumpet. She rented one, and I began practicing and then signed up for the school band and I had to learn how to play "Taps," which is usually accomplished with a bugle. The music teacher made all the trumpet players learn "Taps," which I later learned was a difficult task. At home, I practiced and practiced but couldn't master playing "Taps." In my frustration and lack of patience, I gave the trumpet several whacks against the side of the house. The trumpet was dented, and one of the valves was missing the key. That trumpet was pretty much destroyed I decided to place a large nail in the valve. I placed the trumpet in the case and hoped for the best. My mother asked why I hadn't attended band practice for some time. I told her that I'd return on Monday, hoping that she wouldn't open the trumpet case.

That Monday, I returned to the band and sat in the back with my damaged trumpet and did the best I could. In fact, the teacher said that she was impressed with my ability to play, especially since I'd been absent for some time. I went home and didn't play the trumpet for some time. Definitely not "Taps." My mother asked why and found the trumpet case under my bed. She opened the case, and I remember the look on her face as she took a small step back. All she could say was "Oh, Jesus." That was the last time I saw the trumpet that she'd rented.

While living in Ohio, I wanted to play the guitar. My mother bought me one and a small amplifier from a pawnshop. To enhance my ability to play the guitar, she paid for lessons, and I rode the bus downtown for the sessions. I wanted to play the guitar right then. Damn the lessons. I also purchased Glen Campbell's course (a country singer before he became famous) that promised one could learn how to play a guitar in seven days. I became frustrated with the instrument and thought back to the cartoon *Quick Draw McGraw*. I remembered El Kabong and someone getting hit over the head with a guitar. Well, El Kabong was my chant as I smashed the guitar on the basement floor. That was the end of my musical-instrument playing interventions. My mother asked what had happened to the guitar and amplifier, and my answer was, "Traded for some comic books," which was an often-used response.

Back in elementary school, I was told that two girls were fighting over me and wanted to be my girlfriend. One day, a female classmate rode her bike across town, knocked on the door, and asked if I was home. My mother asked who she was. "His girlfriend," she replied. When it came to girls, I was shy and hid in the house somewhere. All I could think of was, *Did her breath smell like pickled beets? Stay away from me.* After several attempts, she finally stopped visiting. All I remember is that her name started with an *M* and she was tall. I always thought I was an ugly kid, for that was what was programmed. Eventually, I began to get past my dislike for girls. I had a crush on a Samoan female. *She is stacked* ("voluptuous" in layman's terms), I thought. We called her Fia Mama because she had a long last name that began with Fia. Eventually, she moved away. And then there was Lavonnette.

Lavonnette-I believed I'd found the love of my life. She never knew that I had an overwhelming crush on her. I thought of Lavonnette every waking moment and thought she was my life partner. She was a beautiful Nubian queen. I needed to find a way to ask her to be my woman. I prayed that her breath didn't smell like pickled beets. *But for her, bring on the smell,* I thought. I dreamed of our life together. A house together. A barking dog in the yard and a wife of a submarine captain or astronaut. I practiced in the boys' bathroom how I would ask her to be my girlfriend. I practiced at home as well.

The day arrived when I decided I would ask Lavonnette to be my girlfriend. As a conversation piece, I took a prize from a Cracker Jack box and was going to give it to her, which I knew would seal the deal. In those days, the prizes in the Cracker Jacks were better than the cheap ones today. Anyway, I was going to explain to Lavonnette my aspirations about being a patrol boy and someday selling real estate. While we were walking to school, Lavonnette was with a group of girls. While walking past, they all shouted, "Hi, Ronnie!" I don't know what came over me, but I took a rock and threw it toward the girls. The rock struck Lavonnette in the eye. She fell to the ground, and blood was gushing. The girls started screaming. The ambulance came and took Lavonnette away. I walked to class and sat down. The principal called me to his office, and I was suspended. I took my time walking across the park this time, baby steps. I was scared, but I didn't fully understand the consequences of my actions, and the greater distress was that I lost the love of my life.

Here I examine what possessed me to pick up a rock and throw it toward another individual. Did I not understand the consequences? Apparently not. Relating to a current incident in 2014, for my side of the family, we had a family picnic, a camping trip. My grandson picked up a plastic baseball-shaped bottle full of water and haphazardly threw it across a street. We were in a secluded campsite. I was furious and asked him what had possessed him to take a plastic bottle full of water and throw it across the street. *Darn, kids these days,* I thought.

After some time, I thought back to the situation with Lavonnette, which gave me a reference. Nonetheless, I commanded that my eldest grandson retrieve the bottle and place it near the fence. The grandson who threw the bottle had to take it and throw it in the trash. He couldn't give me a reason why he'd thrown the bottle across the street. Next, he received a lecture about the appreciation for the outdoors and how choices present positive or negative consequences. As I ponder, perhaps the bottle wasn't so bad. At least he didn't almost put someone's eye out. However, if a car had been approaching, the consequences could've been dire. I thought, how soon we forget.

Back to Lavonnette. On occasion, my mother visited her while she was bedridden at home. My mother couldn't grasp how I could've performed such an act and again said that I needed to see a psychiatrist, as she often said. After the psychiatrist comment, one day upon awakening, she noticed there were several dead kittens hanging from a noose in the backyard. Eventually, she did take me to see a psychiatrist, and I'll comment on that experience later.

I returned to school, but it didn't matter because we were off to Ohio again. When I returned to California in junior high school, Lavonnette made a comment to me, and insensitively, I referred back to the incident about the rock. Her comment was, "I'm going to tell my mama." That was the last day I saw her. At that time and even a few years later, she was the love of my life. What brought this situation to life was that I had finished writing my memoir and was about to submit the manuscript for review. I was in the garage, looking for pictures for my website (www.foolshillthemeaningwhy.com) and happened upon my elementary school photos. Behold, I found the elementary school pictures, the one when Lavonnette and I had been in the same class, and there she was, as beautiful as ever. What brought the situation to light was that her picture was close to mine, very close. In viewing both pictures, I did believe we'd have made an attractive couple. But for me, we remain connected through the annals of time by my actions, the elementary school picture, and the writing here.

Back then, the Black Panthers were prevalent in Northern California, and sometimes I saw them on television. They wore black leather jackets, black boots, and a black tam, which I thought was cool. I wanted to be one. At that time, the civil rights movement was emerging. Sometimes there were riots in San Diego, and one time, my mother said that we had to participate in a walkout in protest. I didn't know why. So at noon most of us walked peacefully from school to Ocean View Park, where there were rallies. While at the park, I remember, there were roaches on the ground, the essence of remaining marijuana joints.

I wanted to be a part of the civil unrest at that time and decided to learn how to make a Molotov cocktail. On television, while watching the news during a broadcast about a riot, I saw individuals throwing the cocktail, and I wanted to know how to make one. At a friend's house by what was then the Granny Goose potato chip factory, as we called it, my first try was a mason jar with the lid on and a small hole for the rag. Didn't work. Next, my friend and I learned that the cocktail works best using gasoline, a beverage bottle (Coke, Bubble Up, Pepsi, etc.) without the cap, and a rag-success. I threw the cocktail, and it burst into flames near the potato chip factory. We took off running in fear of burning the factory down.

I never used a cocktail again, but I did set fires in canyons and then took off running. One time, another individual, Smithy, and I, while walking home from school, set a fire that burned several acres. We could hear the fire engines, and thinking back, that act could've cost lives in addition to burning an area in my neighborhood, and setting it aflame served no purpose.

Those were interesting times in San Diego, and an important time in American history, which included the Motown Experience, Black Panthers, the civil rights movement, civil unrest, Dr. Martin Luther King Jr., Muhammad Ali, Malcom X, James Brown, Aretha Franklin, and the Four Tops. I could go on and on, the whole experience forever etched in my memory and the embodiment of history, especially for African Americans, I believe. It was a time of social change like none before and perpetuated by some violent and non-violent events (walkouts, riots, boycotts, etc.) orchestrated by African Americans and their communities, as well as others outside the African American communities who contributed. I have yet to experience a culmination of social change in the same amount of time in America since. Today, others benefit from the toll African Americans paid during the civil rights movement and the events leading to this globally.

Every time I hear songs from that era, they take me back to an important time, and I'm happy to experience this. At that time, I had, of all things, a portable record player that worked on D-size batteries. I took that device to the park and jammed, playing the songs of the time, the LP 33 1/3 versions of some albums. However, the 45 rpms were jamming as well. I still have many of each today, including several eight-track tapes, which I keep as mementos. I need to interject here; in the 1960s, I remember the first instances of low-rider vehicles and African Americans in Southeast San Diego. They cruised the main streets of Logan Heights and other areas of the Black communities in Daygo playing the songs of the time, and most cars with the female riding (p-some know what this means) blasted slow songs.

I recall when the Temptations and other African American artists began recording the long versions of some songs, which sometimes remind me of the smooth jazz cuts today. Then came some of the Caucasian artists, such as Rare Earth, who recorded music like that of the Temptations, the long version of some songs. Some of the successful smooth jazz artists of today are influenced by African American musicians from that era. Music from that era, rock and roll, and hard rock can be traced to slaves singing in the fields. I recently saw a documentary on the National Geographic channel about Daygo, but the show failed to mention anything about the African American influences that contribute to the diversity in that city. Others cultures were mentioned. What about the many African American athletes and musicians who were born and lived in Daygo? Anyway, I love my birth city, which is always in my heart.

My father started us in Little League, and one day, I threw the baseball from the outfield impressing the coach with my ability to throw. That ability came from throwing rocks in the hood. Rock throwing was a favorite pastime, and one could develop a reputation for rock throwing. "Don't mess with that n-word. He can throw rocks." Because I could effectively throw a baseball from center field, I was made a pitcher. I had a screaming fastball. However, I pitched the ball sidearm. My coaches attempted to correct me and wanted me to pitch overhand. I developed the ability to throw sidearm when practicing baseball with my brother.

During one important game, while I was pitching, my coach wanted me to throw overhand. He kept screaming at me, although I had several strikes when pitching sidearm. However, while pitching overhand, I hit one player in the helmet. One pitch almost went over the backstop. Another pitch made a rival player hit a home run, and the ball went not only over the home run fence but also over the parking lot, and the ball was on the side of a hill. I was devastated. However, the next sidearm pitch was a strike. After that game, they eventually moved me to first base, and I excelled at that position.

One of my favorite players in the National Football League was a quarterback of the San Diego Chargers. Some might say that his throwing motion is unorthodox. However, he continues to excel in the NFL with that unorthodox throwing motion. I wonder about my fate as a pitcher in Little League if I'd had the opportunity to pitch the ball in a manner that I felt was natural.

I won't forget the day Dr. Martin Luther King Jr. was assassinated. I was on the baseball field. I remember my father approaching the baseball field in a rage. In his fourth-grade manner of speaking, I could hardly understand my father as he shouted, "They killed him! They killed him!" I remember that day when the individual with whom I share my birthday was assassinated. I didn't understand much at that time, but I eventually understood the gravity of the moment and situation.

At that time, I was able to attend the same school for two years (fifth and sixth grades). Although we moved to a new location in San Diego before junior high school, we attended schools in the same neighborhood in which we used to live. We walked what seemed like miles to school to keep the close ties with individuals in the old neighborhood.

I finally finished elementary school and was promoted to junior high (seventh grade) in California. I began playing baseball again. Sports were a social outlet, and it seemed to keep me occupied. My brother and I practiced playing baseball for hours. He was better than me, mostly because of confidence. However, physically I probably had the advantage. Together we spent hours pitching and hitting the baseball in our driveway. I finally felt as though I had established roots in California this time.

Shortly after school started in my junior high years, my mother pulled up roots and moved back to Ohio. The move was devastating. No more baseball, no more sports, and it was time to make new friends again. I was gaining confidence in life in addition to playing baseball, and I was hitting the ball better than in the past, eventually hitting my first home run. Some thought, if my brother and I continued playing baseball, perhaps the game would be an outlet for us and lead to the professional leagues.

Chapter 3

JUNIOR HIGH SCHOOL-
THE CHANGE

I was now in junior high school in Ohio and facing another adjustment. Now I was approaching my teens, and it was important that I fit in, so I reverted to my class clown activities. My favorite joke was to put thumbtacks in chairs and watch students jump after sitting on them. I thought that was hilarious, and I often had to restrain myself from laughing. The act was funny until someone put a thumbtack in my chair. Therefore, I started to step up my game. Behind the school was a semiforested area, which is now Dunbar High School, or at least it was the last time I checked. During early spring, garter snakes were abundant, and I remember that smell from the concentration of snakes in the lightly forested area. I took some snakes to school in my lunch pail. The goal was to take the snakes and put them in someone's lunch pail or in the pocket of a coat or jacket that was stored in a closet during the day. The day I decided to strike and complete my heinous act, I was almost caught by the teacher. She entered the class as I was in the process of committing the act.

That was the end of that escapade. I ended up killing the snakes and skinned two. Today I have a fear of snakes and have had bad dreams about them. Soon after writing my first draft here about those snakes, I was on a long hike in Colorado, and on the trail was a large bull snake. The first snake that I'd encountered in Colorado after hiking the trails for four years. Talk about karma!

The next mischievous act I did in junior high was opening stink bombs at school. To accomplish this, I soaked chicken bones in water for about a week or two. Someone in the school had relayed the information about making the stinky liquid. After the chicken bones had been soaked, because of the smell, transferring the concoction from a larger container to a smaller one was sometimes overwhelming. Between classes, I'd open a vial of the obnoxious liquid. I thought the reactions of students were hilarious.

The students in Ohio were different from those in California. On one occasion, I was in a cutup situation with another student. "Cutup" means that someone makes a joke about another, whether the comments were true or not. Sometimes when an individual made jokes about someone's parents, we called it the dozens. Talking about another's mother was taboo. The same didn't apply to someone's father. A reason could be that, at that time, mothers were the lifeblood of some African American families in the hood. Often fathers were despondent or not around, to put things bluntly. However, talking negatively about someone's mother was fighting words. I was good at it and could enter a cutup situation whether the content was about someone's mother, father, or the individual him or herself. Nevertheless, people listening laughed at the jokes, which angered the receiver of my comments.

Anyway, I learned to best others in a cutup session. I learned how to accomplish the act by listening to my mother and aunt's negative comments about black males. I also had plenty of practice while trying to best my brother in those spanking shenanigans or those bald-headed joke escapades. Then there was Uncle J, who seemed to be always drunk when visiting. At a family function, he could always make us laugh. Uncle J could make a clown laugh, and his black humor was hilarious. Those in the African American community know what I'm talking about, and I believe most families have an Uncle J. He was about five-foot-five with fair skin, a stocky, muscular build, and male pattern baldness prevailed.

After my teenage years, one time, Uncle J visited my father. My brother and I stopped by to say hello on our way to a business meeting. I thought I was dressed to the nines. Uncle J said, "Where ya'll going with those cheap suits? If it rains, we have to cut it off y'all, cut it off of y'all." He repeated this as he raised the inflection in his gruff voice, bringing the point home. Then he displayed that Uncle J smirk with his high cheekbones. "Remember, when washing those cheap suits, use the low tumble dry if you want to get that thang back on," Uncle J said. At the meeting, I was self-conscious about my suit. Looking at pictures from that era, I admit that suit looked cheap. Dang, at that time, I didn't have a clue about how to dress until associates in the business recommended that I read the book *Dress for Success* by John T. Molloy. However, Uncle J brought that point home, and his shenanigans served as another reference point for my ability to make someone laugh. Therefore, in the cutup sessions while in junior high, I could be brutal, and those listening would be cracking up (which means "laughter," for some of you). This angered some.

On one occasion in junior high school, I was in a cutup session with an individual I thought was a friend. In fact, later on, we stole cars together. Everyone was laughing about the comments I made, and the individual was angered. Keep in mind, most of my comments weren't true; however, the greater problem probably was that other students laughed at my jokes but not at the other individual's jokes. Was he angry! Instead of provoking a fight with me, he gathered some friends to jump me (gang up on me). Because the event happened during the day, teachers were able to defuse the situation.

In another situation, an individual received the same punishment from the barrage of my words. The next day after school, his older brother met me. He was older and stronger than me. He threatened me and punched me on the side of the head. Keep in mind I was fairly the new kid on the block. From that day on-I don't know where I found it-I carried a large Bowie knife to school and dared anyone to jump me or try to gang up on me. After that, no one bothered me, and I felt I'd resumed an unwritten title as the king of the campus like in elementary school, whether or not others in the junior high school knew it to be so. At that time, my goal was to take anyone out who attempted to harm me. Eventually, I became bored with putting tacks in chairs, and after the failed attempt to put snakes in lunch pails or coat pockets, I reverted to throwing books in class at others and sometimes in the direction of the teacher when his or her back was turned.

In continuing the error of my ways, one day, another student and I threw books in a science class, sometimes toward the teacher. A student in class and I were friends, and I visited his house many times. Keep in mind that the teacher didn't know who was throwing the books, and other students didn't snitch. The science teacher was an African American male who stood well over six feet. He wore a suit coat every day and had teeth that grew on top of one another.

One day, someone threw a book in the direction of the science teacher, and we began to laugh. The science teacher asked the individual, whose house I'd visited several times, who had thrown the book and approached my friend in an aggressive manner. My friend was trying to stand up as if he wanted to throw down (fight). However, the science teacher pushed the desk on him and began punching. That tall science teacher was all over him, throwing blows before my friend had a chance to respond. My friend was beaten to a pulp, and the teacher got the best of him. Someone called the principal, and there was much commotion. My friend was out of school and had what appeared to be a broken jaw and some swelling in his face. I tried to visit him at home, but no one answered the door. That day in the class was the last I saw of him.

I thought the school was going to fire the teacher. But the following Monday he was still teaching the class. I began to throw books in the same class in retaliation for my friend's beating. The teacher approached me and attempted to push the desk on me. I was too fast for him. I stood up, and the teacher saw the large Bowie knife tucked in my trousers. The teacher quietly walked to the front of the class. He didn't say anything, nor did he approach the intercom to call the principal. From that point on, there was an unwritten rule in that class. I didn't complete any work nor did I act out in the teacher's class. On the other hand, the teacher didn't confront me. From that day on, there was peace in the class. I don't know what would have happened the day of the altercation if the teacher had called the principal or attempted to confront me. Perhaps he saved me from a serious altercation. I didn't care though. I vowed that nobody was going to take advantage of me, and I continued to carry the Bowie knife to school. I was fortunate that I never used that knife in school or in any situation. However, today, as some will realize later in this book, sometimes it's a blessing to have African American males teaching in public school. I just hope I didn't thwart the science teacher's effort.

Junior high continued to be a troubled time for me. About halfway through the year, I had a new friend. He was from a well-rounded respected family, and I visited his house often. I admired his home, and the yard was always well maintained. He and I ventured everywhere together. His parents bought him a bike, and I didn't have one. I devised a scheme to acquire one, though, because I was tired of riding on my friend's handlebars. During this time, Stingray bikes were popular, especially those with a sissy bar that extended from the back seat vertically. One day, my friend and I were on another escapade, and a kid was riding his bike. This bike had all the amenities: a sissy bar, brakes operated from the handlebars, streamers protruding from the handlebars, and a banana seat. The bike was new and bright orange. I just had to have it, and in a strong-arm move, I took the kid's bike. I rode the bike everywhere. While I was putting the bike in the basement, my mother asked where it had come from. I said, "Keeping it for a friend while he reads some of my comic books." Yes, I used the comic book excuse again.

I thought I was king of the neighborhood with my new bike. In about two weeks, a car pulled up in front of me and slammed on the brakes. I assumed it was the father of the kid from whom I'd stolen the bike. He started cursing. I took off running, and the man put the bike in the trunk while constantly cursing, using F-bombs. Sad to say, I wasn't afraid, but I didn't have a bike anymore. Back to the handlebars on my friend's bike.

On another escapade during a hot summer day, my friend and I ventured to the school we'd attended. I began checking the windows and found one open. I entered the school through the window and opened the door for my friend. In the school, we created some havoc. But my goal was to find VCRs and movie projectors, like the one I had destroyed when riding the cart in sixth grade. I looked for a small reel-to-reel tape recorder as well. I began to position content in the hallway to come back and collect my goods. Upon one attempt to position the goods, I looked out the window and saw police cars on the school grounds. I yelled to my friend, and he must've panicked, because he took off running out the door and jumped on his bike and tried to outrun the police. While they were preoccupied with my friend, I took the liberty of slipping out a door and hiding in a dumpster. Meanwhile, they took my friend away, and while I was in the dumpster, I could hear the commotion as they handcuffed him and put his bike in the trunk. The police checked the building unaware that I was in the dumpster.

Later, I slithered out of the dumpster and walked home. On the way, I saw the police car outside my friend's house. Fortunately, he didn't snitch on me. I would have denied everything anyway; after all, they hadn't seen or caught me. A few days later, I had the nerve to knock on my friend's door to find out what happened and to see if he wanted to go on another escapade. I knew someone was home, because there were cars in the driveway. No one answered the door, just like the house of the student who was beaten in the science class.

I became friends with the individual I used to demoralize in cutup sessions, the one who'd gathered his friends to gang up on me. We buried our differences. One day, we saw a freezer railcar and busted the seal. Inside was a shitload of frozen pizzas. We helped ourselves to as many as we could carry. That night at home, I stuffed myself with pizza. We told others; however, they said that the railcar was no longer there.

My brother mentioned that he had a friend who spent some time around the rail yards and in the parking lots of dairies where they actually made products, such as pasteurized milk and ice cream. For my brother's friend, his escapades lent to survival and a meal for the day, perhaps. Nonetheless, for my friend and I, the dairies were places where we could access the delivery trucks and take whatever was available, especially the chocolate milk or ice cream sandwich bars.

Sometimes my friend and I walked around the rail yards looking for mischief. We forced our way into the cabooses to look for what we could steal. Sometimes the train engineers left their pants in the unlocked caboose. We took wallets or cigarettes or anything we could find. I also took the engineer's keys and started a collection. Most of the keys were for automobiles.

The town in Ohio was mostly industrial, and in addition to dairies and rail yards, there were factories. In the parking lots was an abundant supply of parked automobiles. The key collection I generated from breaking into the cabooses in the rail yards (or other means) came in handy. Back then, the Chevrolet B10 or B11 were interchangeable and fit the ignition of some cars. Sometimes the keys fit the doors, or the workers who parked their cars in the lot forgot to lock them or left the keys inside. After accessing the cars, we tried some of the ignition keys and jiggled them, and sometimes the cars started. Time for a joyride. We drove the cars all over the city, sometimes laughing our asses off. I couldn't drive, but my friend could. However, my first time attempting to drive a car was with a stolen one. We ended up in a ditch and left the car. Sometimes I attempted to steal the cars alone and ended hitting a fence or driving for some time and then abandoning the car. For some cars, I couldn't get the damn things out of first gear. We were never caught for the car-stealing escapades. At this stage in my life, one could infer that the mischievousness escalated to criminal activity and, sometimes, to unfathomable acts.

There was a drainage tunnel right by the school. My brother and I walked as far as we could in that tunnel. Good thing the tunnel never flooded. Sometimes there were bats in the tunnel, and we doused them with gasoline and set them on fire. One time, a cousin from California came to visit, and we took him to the drainage tunnel, the one with the bats. We walked in quite a way and then turned off the lights. All my cousin could hear was us laughing after we took off running, and he was left alone. He still reminds me of the event some forty years later. Anyway, after junior high, we moved to another neighborhood, and it was time to make new friends again.

At that time, I remember the constant implications that I wouldn't make it past my sixteenth birthday. "I'm going to take you to see a psychiatrist," my mother constantly said. Another comment was that I would never amount to anything and I was a dope addict. I didn't know what dope was then. Interesting comments from adults who were part of my life. However, I remember my grandmother saying, "He'll be all right once he gets over fool's hill."

Chapter 4

THE HIGH SCHOOL YEARS

I n high school, I found myself in an unfamiliar situation again. We moved to Residence Park in Ohio, which was approximately ten miles from the old neighborhood. Far enough that I didn't keep ties with individuals in the old hood. Now I found my body maturing, and I had hair on my face. I appeared older than my age. I could buy cigarettes or booze in most stores in the hood, yet I was underage.

I was shy when I started high school, and I had to find a way to fit in. At home, I lived in seclusion in the basement, my preference. Soon after the start of school, winter arrived, and all I remember was the cold weather. Constantly, I thought about the warmer winter days when we lived in San Diego. One day, while walking to school in Ohio, I decided to wear street shoes that had been saved from my days in California. The shoes were like the "roach-in-the-corner killers" I'd worn when I was lost in the woods in Oklahoma. Living in Ohio for about eighteen months, I should've known that after one step on the frozen pavement I'd look like would result, and then I'd look like the dog in the *Scooby-Doo* cartoon as the mutt slips and slides, limbs flying everywhere. That was the last day I wore street shoes with heel plates (taps) when the ground was covered with snow and ice. I hated the cold weather in Ohio and that dislike exists today.

During the winter, I spent most of my time in the basement and not in the room with my brother. I was cold all the time. I reverted to my submarine or spaceship fantasies. At this time, I figured that solitude was my way of life. However, when I did spend time with my brother, mostly, we watched army shows, as we called them. I said, "Someday I'll be an army man." Sometimes I hated watching television with my brother. He asked a question every second, and one can expect that from a younger sibling. "How come this and how come that?" Today, I find myself anxious when someone asks me what I believe are too many questions, especially those from significant others. As with my brother, I can hide my irritation when someone asks what I believe are too many questions to a point. Love ya, bro.

In the new neighborhood, there was Deborah. She lived next door, and I saw her occasionally. She was another beautiful Nubian queen and close to trumping Lavonnette. Rarely did she come outside, and I wanted to marry her. However, shyness overcame me. Definitely, the thoughts of the situation with Lavonnette crossed my mind, and I didn't want the same result.

One day, nervously, I asked Deborah for a picture and phone number and she gave me both. Eventually, she moved away, but I still had the picture and phone number. After Deborah moved away, two songs by the Chi-Lites, "Have You Seen Her" and "Write a Letter to Myself," in addition to the song "Just My Imagination" by the Temptations were all hits on the airwaves. I thought of Lavonnette and Deborah, but my imagination was just that. Still, today when I hear and sing those songs, I recall those times and what I experienced during that era. Another song by the Temptations was the hit "I Wish It Would Rain." Later in life, I discovered why the songwriter had penned the song and that, soon after writing it, he had committed suicide. Sometimes I wished it would rain because of losing the loves of my life. What took place during that time concerning Lavonnette and Deborah were sentimental times in my life that resonate today. Later in life, before my enlistment in the Marine Corps and while I was in San Diego, my sister asked why I had an affinity for love songs. I didn't say, but Lavonnette and Deborah contributed to that.

In the ninth grade, I tried out for the freshman football team and, at first, was afraid. Athletically, I had the potential to be a good player, but I lacked confidence. I made the team as the first-string receiver, although I had never watched a football game in my life. After football practice, I remember lighting up my cigarette and walking home. I carried my shoulder pads, which were placed over my helmet, when walking home, smoking. Cars passed by, but I didn't care. I felt my reward for football practice was a drag on a Salem cigarette. One day, my coach pulled me aside and, in a sarcastic voice, asked if I enjoyed smoking those damn cigarettes on the way home. In a sarcastic voice, I said, "Yup." Coach said, "Probably why you can't catch those damn passes." For two weeks, I didn't smoke a cigarette.

One day on my way home, I thought back and asked myself why I smoked. I first started with Salems and then shifted to Kools and then Newports. I thought smoking was cool, a way to fit in. By the time I was in high school, I smoked cigarettes on and off for about four years. I started while living in San Diego and found the cigarettes my mother hid in the closet. I took two or three. I sometimes gave my brother a smoke, and I regret that today. He eventually became a chain-smoker. Once I diminished the supply of smokes, I stole the silver dollars my mother hid in the same closet as well as the cigarettes. I wondered why the store owner was happy to see me coming to buy cigarettes. Those silver dollars today might be worth something. My mother was furious when she found the silver dollars missing. Of course, I denied everything.

The football season was near the end. I gained some confidence. I actually scored four touchdowns like Al Bundy in the television show *Married...with Children*. My coach said that the hole I'd run through was big enough to drive a truck. "Thanks, Coach," I said, "Maybe it's the cigarettes." "Five laps for you during the next practice, Cubit!"

While we played football, some players commented on my improvement. One day, the coach saw me kick the football and assigned me to be the team's punter. Thinking back, the same had happened when I played baseball. The coach had seen me throw the ball and made me a starting pitcher. I had a fantastic fastball, and that was it. Anyway, I liked punting the ball and playing wide receiver. Besides scoring the four touchdowns in one game, my greatest memory as a punter didn't fare so well. However, one day, when playing Dunbar High School, I needed to punt the ball to pin the opposing team to the end zone. The long snapper made a bad snap, and I had to field the ball. The snapper backed into me. Instead of punting the ball, I kicked him square in the ass, right in the middle. Served him right. The laughter from those attending the game was deafening and overshadowed the coach yelling at us from the sideline.

It was the last game of the football season, and we only won one game, as I recall. We played another rival in the hood, Roosevelt High School. The reputation was that if a school beat Roosevelt, the folks attending the game would rock the bus (throw rocks at the bus). It was rumored that players had to fight their way to the bus as well. We were worried about beating Roosevelt. The other wide receiver for the opposite end of the offensive line thought he was a better player, and we didn't like each other.

Two petty boys. Eventually, we buried our differences and respected each other. While playing Roosevelt, we were in the fourth quarter then, and a touchdown would win the game for us. It was the last game of the year. If we won, it would be win number two for the season. Time was running out, and the quarterback called an audible. The other wide receiver and I ran down the field to catch a Hail Mary. The quarterback threw the ball, and the other wide receiver and I were the only ones who could catch it. It was a perfect pass, and the ball dropped between both of us. Either of us could've caught the ball. I purposely didn't catch the ball, and I believed the other wide receiver did the same. It was an easy catch. To tell you the truth, I had visions of rocks crashing through the glass on the bus, and that was my excuse for not catching the football. We could've won the game and beat an intercity rival.

The coach was furious, and I had an opportunity to blame my lapse in catching the ball on the cigarettes. On the bus ride back to the school, the coach and the other wide receiver started arguing. I had enough sense to keep my mouth shut; after all, I didn't catch the ball. The argument between the coach and the other wide receiver escalated into a fight. The coach won, and it was my second experience of a student and a teacher fighting. Times were challenging in both junior high school and high school in Ohio. One day, the head varsity football coach met me in the hall and said that he couldn't wait until I tried out for the team the next year. Nonetheless, that was the end of my football-playing days.

During high school, a Caucasian science teacher aspired to introduce inner-city African American youth to golf. I had some experience, and in my old neighborhood, I used to hang around the golf course, attempting to make money caddying. Sometimes individuals hired me to shag golf balls. The teacher who'd introduced me to golf taught science, which was a favorite class of mine. As in the fifth grade class. I was among the smartest in the science class. The teacher took us to his house which I thought was on a farm. He had a bunch of neat stuff that and what amazed me was an old beat-up car that looked like a spaceship. In my experience this was the second time a Caucasian teacher accepted African American students in their home.

The first time was with my fifth-grade teacher, a Caucasian female. One day, she took several of us to her house for a formal dinner, and we didn't know how to act, grabbing food when we wanted, and one individual licked the ketchup bottle. She lived in an affluent area, and her husband was an attorney. She eventually divorced him and married an African American gentleman. That fifth-grade teacher wrote a letter to me, which I still have today. In that letter, she mentioned how I liked working with science projects, which was similar to other comments made by my high school science teacher. She also commented on my ability to make others laugh and my charm.

Concerning golf, I tried out, became the captain of the team, and was the best player. We sucked and didn't win a tournament. Our opponents were from predominantly Caucasian high schools. In two years, I came close to winning one game. I earned a letter for playing golf. The letter was a purple *R* with golf clubs. Today, I regret misplacing that letter.

Eventually, I became bored with sports, and the mischief began. I needed to be accepted and find some friends. I didn't want to deal with crowds in the lunchroom, therefore I hung out at the end of a hallway. I couldn't wait for lunch to end, because I hated the dead time. Also several older boys not enrolled in the school were on the school grounds. They found their way to my hangout and took my lunch money. One time, a gang of them took my cap. So enough of that. I carried my knife to school.

I don't know how we met, but I became friends with an individual, and some thought we were brothers. We hung out and ventured everywhere. Both of us had dogs from the same litter. Where we went, so did our dogs. For the most part, I managed to stay out of trouble. Soon I began to affiliate with other boys in the neighborhood. The goal was always to be accepted. I was then introduced to RK by my brother. RK was a big young man and was on the varsity football team, something of a star. He was a natural-born leader. RK could fight. RK started a gang, and there wasn't an initiation. All one had to do was hang around.

We were a lively bunch and managed to find ways to cause trouble. A favorite was going to Westtown Shopping Center and causing havoc. We walked through the stores and threw groceries at one another, including frozen chickens, cans of soup, fruits and vegetables, and anything else we could find. If we needed some food, we took it and sometimes consumed goods in the store. Our favorite was ham sandwiches made with white bread. Some of us carried weapons and dared anyone to stop us. After raiding the supermarket one time, we walked to the drugstore and stole Robitussin DM cough syrup, which had a high alcohol content. At that time, Robitussin DM was sold from the shelf and not over the counter. A favorite drink was a quart of Country Club beer and Robitussin DM. Sometimes we switched to Spañada wine. Another was Acadama wine, different from the Japanese Akadama, and our favorite phrase mimicking the commercial on television was "Pass the Acadama Mama" as each of us took a swig from the bottle. We spent the rest of the day sobering up from our drunken stupor. On some Fridays, my mother gave my brother and me an allowance, which was about one dollar. She used to clean houses and was paid cash. One time, she took my brother and me with her, and all I could think about was finding a gun in that house. When she was paid on Fridays, after receiving our allowance, we couldn't wait to go to the local liquor store and buy a bottle, either the Acadama, Spañada, or a quart of the Country Club beer to drink with the cough syrup or a bottle of Thunderbird wine mixed with Kool Aid.

Hanging out with the guys was becoming routine. I convinced my parents to buy me a Levi's jacket. I cut the sleeves off the jacket and placed metal studs in distinct locations. I then put my gang name on the jacket under the colors. Those colors were red and traced in white. We used cloth tape for all the lettering. I wore the jacket only once or twice to the skating rink, which was a local hangout on Saturday night, where we often wreaked havoc.

Often, there were fights at the rink, and when the police arrived, I threw rocks at them from the wooded area across the street and then took off running. Sometimes the fire truck arrived, for whatever reason. I remember throwing rocks at the truck as well. One time, a group of individuals turned over a car and set it aflame.

In one incident at the skating rink, there was much turmoil. The fire truck was there, and I was across the street, in a wooded area, throwing rocks. I started running up an alley nearby, and all of a sudden, LC was in the bushes with a shotgun. Stood on end, the shotgun was taller than LC, and he was from a neighboring country town. Rumor had it that LC had been to prison for killing someone as a minor. LC pointed the shotgun at me. Our eyes connected, and LC took off and ran the other way. I believe my life was spared that day.

Shoplifting was a pastime as well, especially in the stores downtown. Although I hated riding the bus, it beat walking in the winter, so I found a way to pay my fare. If I didn't have enough money for the bus, I closely followed a person paying the fare. As the person ahead of me deposited their fare and before the individual removed their hand from the box, I deposited my coins. The bus driver couldn't decipher who'd paid what.

In winter, while wearing heavy coats, we stole mostly albums or backlight posters. Back then, it was easy to slide the albums under the coat and hold them with both hands in the coat pocket. To get downtown, sometimes I walked for fear of getting on the bus.

One day, my mother took me to a new mall; she was going to do some shopping in one of the large department stores. I wasn't familiar with that part of town, but I put on my coat and was happy about a new shoplifting opportunity. As my mother shopped, I went on my stealing escapade. While I walked out with my mother, my hands in my pocket, a plainclothes detective stopped me and asked if I could open my coat. Of course, I became belligerent, and he showed me his badge. I opened my coat, a long brown one with fur around the collar, and what seemed like a convenience store full of merchandise fell to the ground, right in front of my mother. They took my mother and me to a small room in the back, and she was in tears. "I just don't know what to do with him." I began to break out in a cold sweat, and I had to sit down. They processed some paperwork, and my mother and I walked out of the store. All the while, she reinforced the need for me to see a psychiatrist. "I don't know what to do with you," she said. Dang, I thought I was doing things I was supposed to do. I was grounded, but I didn't care because I could sneak out the basement window if I wanted to be with my friends.

My mother finally took me to see a shrink, and all I did was stare at him. I didn't say a word. He was a goofy-looking young Caucasian man, and I was thinking that he became a shrink to overcome his goofiness and the inner challenges he faced. I thought that what he learned in his shrink classes would help him sustain life. Nonetheless, after my silent treatment, there were no more visits to see a shrink.

A group of us often wreaked havoc in the neighborhood at night. Sometimes we canvassed the neighborhood, looking for houses to break into. To find out if anyone was home, we first threw rocks at the house. One night, after we had thrown rocks, an individual yelled out a window, "Come on in!" We proceeded to another house. The next house we broke in to, there were two women sleeping in the bedroom, and they were donning hairnets. Despite the commotion, they didn't appear to be awake. They never moved a muscle, and I don't blame them. We gathered our goods and left. I remember someone shouting, "People sleeping in here!" I dived out the window and took off running.

Most of the individuals I hung with carried guns. I wanted a gun badly, and I continued to break into houses to find one. An individual who ran with us had a sawed-off .22-caliber rifle that he let me borrow sometimes. He acquired a pistol from somewhere, and I traded him a pack of cigarettes for the sawed-off .22. I'd finally arrived. One night, I was at a party in Westwood, carrying my sawed-off .22 rifle that fired when it wanted to. I was in a state from the Country Club beer and Robitussin cough syrup. My rifle was loaded. We were in a rival gang's territory and what we thought was the Black Masters. An individual arrived, and I thought he was a Black Master. I challenged him. I pointed the gun .22 rifle point-blank at his head. All he wanted to do was go to the party. Other individuals of our gang stopped me, and it's a good thing I never fired the rifle, for I might not be writing this exposé now. The individual whom I pointed the rifle at went to the same high school as me and was either a junior or senior. He liked my sister. I saw him in the hall one day and apologized. He said it was a good thing, for he was planning to ambush me with a weapon in my backyard one day.

On another occasion, while in Black Master territory, another individual and I were walking down an alley late one night. At that time, I had run away from home for the third time. While we walked through the alley, some individuals called out, and we started mouthing off at them. They started shooting, and I remember the bullets splitting the wood just above my head. Another narrow escape from death.

We ran to a house a few blocks away, and the person I was with knew someone in the neighborhood who had a car. We jumped in the car and went back to that alley where we thought the rival Black Masters were shooting at us. The individual I was with had a .38 Special with a long barrel under his colors. He fired at the individuals in the alley until his pistol was empty. The next day, I heard from someone that an individual in an alley was shot in the foot but didn't know if that was because of the incident the night before.

On one memorable night, the police brought my brother home, beaten beyond recognition. Individuals in the neighborhood claimed that he broke into their house. At that time, my brother had two guns with him, and from that night he inherited the name Two Pistol Pete. I don't know what really happened that night, but I was pissed. I vowed to seek revenge on those who'd beaten my brother. RK was going to seek revenge as well.

Previously, I wanted a handgun so I could feel equal to others I ran with in our gang. I wasn't satisfied with the sawed-off .22-caliber rifle, which fired when it wanted. I yearned to have a handgun. Breaking into houses hadn't paid off, so I devised a plan to get a handgun. My step-grandfather, the individual who said that I wouldn't amount to anything and might not make it past my sixteenth birthday, kept a handgun under his pillow. He was bedridden and had emphysema. During one visit, while my step-grandfather went to the bathroom, I took the gun and walked home. Noticing that the pistol was missing, my step-grandfather called my mother, and I denied everything.

Eventually, I ran away from home and stayed in the basement of the individual who'd emptied the pistol while shooting at individuals in the alley. I went to Westtown and stole some white bread and ham for sandwiches. I vowed to get revenge on the individuals who'd beaten my brother. That night, I mentioned that I knew where we could score some minibikes. A *minibike* is a small motorized bike.

The individual who emptied the pistol in the alley and I decided to go for it. One night, he had the family's station wagon. We drove across town to where I knew the minibikes were. We had bolt cutters, and we cut the lock where the minibikes and a go-kart were stored. All the while, I thought about the individual living there. I knew him, and I thought he was going to wake up and shoot the both of us. The individual was someone I knew from the old neighborhood. We used to hang out in an alley, and he had two sons. They allowed us to ride their minibikes sometimes. My mother eventually bought us minibikes, and the individual we stole the minibikes from took ours and his son's minibikes, including a go-kart, to the stadium so we could have a fun of riding. However, our minibikes didn't last long. I destroyed my brother's while running into the back of him with that go-kart. My mother and stepfather had my brother's bike repaired. My punishment for destroying my brother's minibike was to pay for the repairs, and I didn't get anything for Christmas. I didn't care, for if I needed something, I found a way to steal it.

Anyway, we stole both minibikes from the garage and loaded them into the station wagon. I went back for the go-kart, but it was too heavy. Off, we went with the bikes. I eventually went back home with the minibike, and my mother asked where it had come from. I said I was holding it for a friend, and you guessed it he was reading some of my comic books.

One day, I was trying to ride the stolen minibike, and I saw the police. Individuals less than sixteen years of age needed a permit or something to ride a minibike in the city. The police saw me and started chasing me, and I thought I could outrun them in first gear. Eventually, the bike sputtered. I believe the police were laughing at me for trying to outrun them, and instead of arresting me, they loaded the minibike in the car and took me home. They never checked if the bike was stolen. I was on restriction again but could sneak out through the basement window and hang out with friends if I wanted to. I hated restriction. One summer we couldn't even leave the house.

We rode those stolen bikes until they were inoperable. I didn't know how to ride one bike, for it had gears, and I didn't know how to shift them. Finally, I blew the motor and ditched the minibike. About a week later, one of the individuals from whom we'd stolen the minibikes knocked on our front door and asked if I'd seen their minibikes in the neighborhood. The police had recovered the bike and must've notified the individual. As I reminisce about the act, I admit that stealing those minibikes from that family in the old neighborhood was betrayal.

Eventually, I ran away again. One night, another individual and I broke into another house. Jackpot-we scored a rifle, a pistol, and a shotgun. My intent was to make it a sawed-off shotgun. Soon I went back home and hid the weapons, including the .38-caliber revolver stolen from my step-grandfather. I hid several weapons in the backyard and one of the pistols under the mattress in the basement. I also scored a small color TV.

After I had returned home, my mother tried to counsel me, and my stepfather, much smaller in stature, was supposed to spank me. I said, "You just try, and I'll kill you all. Besides, you aren't my father. You just try." Again, in an argument with my mother, she pulled a gun on me. She cocked the hammer and said, "I brought you into this world, and I can take you out." This was the first of two times she would pull a gun on me. I went to pout in the basement. At that time, I hated my mother, my stepfather, my father, my grandparents, and I wanted everyone to die. Keep in mind, I had the firepower hidden in the backyard and basement to accomplish this.

Few days later, my mother asked me to come upstairs. The police were waiting for me. They handcuffed me and away to juvenile hall (juvie) I went. There wasn't an explanation, they just took me away. I spent what seemed like an eternity in juvenile hall. I was angry and I hated everyone. I believed my parents never loved me. I wondered why my parents never told me they loved me or never gave me a hug. I was angry. I wanted them dead. From juvie I wanted to escape but I went outside in the yard only a few times. My brother was in juvie as well.

While we were in juvie, my brother and I were separated, and the only time I saw him was in the dining facility. I couldn't wait to be released so I could hang out with my friends. I hated the single cells, the food, and the incarceration, and no one came to visit, not even my parents. I didn't blame them, though.

One day, a guard appeared and asked me to come with him. They took my brother and me in handcuffs to a courtroom. The judge spouted legal terms, and one I heard was "incorrigible." He said that we couldn't return to the state until we were adults. After the judge ruled and pounded his gavel, sheriffs placed handcuffs on my brother and me. Two sheriffs drove my brother and me to the airport. They escorted us to the plane, took off the handcuffs, and watched us walk up to the ramp. We were the only passengers on the aircraft. The sheriffs waited until the door was closed, and off we went to live with my father in California. *Unbelievable,* I thought. I felt cheated. *You all took me away from my friends.* The only sense of connection to anything. *They, my friends, seemed like family,* I thought. *I hate everyone for this.*

My brother and I were now living in a one-bedroom apartment with my father in San Diego. Sometimes my father spent nights at his girlfriend's house. This gave my brother and me time to continue the error of our ways. During that summer, we spent most of the time drinking, smoking Mary Jane, and playing music. At that time, I was still a minor. We didn't have any friends, and we kept to ourselves. Thinking back, I'd created much havoc in that three to four-year stint in Ohio. I vowed to return to Ohio someday to live. However, returning at that time wasn't in my control.

My father enrolled me in school at Lincoln High, which was in the old neighborhood. Lincoln High was adjacent to the elementary school I'd attended and, at that time, was John F. Kennedy and previously Ocean View elementary. The junior high school, Samuel Gompers, I attended briefly was about a mile away. We were in our old stomping grounds, but things had changed since the last time we lived in Daygo.

High school in San Diego was foreign to me, and I wanted to be back in Ohio with my friends. All the new faces in class again. Most of the time, I was quiet and sat in the back of the class but did nothing. I couldn't pull any of my shenanigans like I'd done in Ohio; at most, I didn't have the audience to accomplish this. I survived the first week in class. During the second week, I started ditching school. I hated my new surroundings. I was still upset, and I felt as if my life had abruptly taken a turn for the worse. Although I was from San Diego and had lived there most of my life, I wanted to go back to Ohio and be with my friends. But that was the last time I lived in Ohio.

Nevertheless, in San Diego, instead of going to school, I hung out at Southcrest Park, the same place I'd played Little League baseball. I smoked weed instead of going to school. Whenever I could, I scored a lid of Mary Jane, which was ten dollars at that time. I smoked two or three joints and spaced out. Once at the park, after smoking a doobie or two, I was standing up in a corner and sleeping at the gym entrance. An individual walked by and saw me. I opened one eye and said, "What the shuck you lookin' at?" (Replacing "shuck" for the actual word used.) Anyway, he took off running. At that time, every third word in my vocabulary was a curse word, and one wouldn't suspect that I was someone who read pages of the dictionary every night before going to bed. Cursing, or the ability to curse at someone effectively, was a survival mechanism in the hood. Today, I can still hold my own when cursing, but I prefer to use more sophisticated means to communicate. Sometimes I do slip with a word or two. Southcrest park and smoking marijuana were my refuges.

Eventually, unofficially, I dropped out of high school because I hated going to classes. I said that I would never return to school; I thought it was for idiots. Go figure. The latter was an excuse because I was shy and uncomfortable sitting in classrooms where I didn't know anybody. I didn't want to make new friends again; besides, the students in California were different from those in Ohio. I wanted to be in comfortable surroundings with my friends in Ohio, but I knew that wasn't possible.

I heard about applying for employment through another job-training program different from the one in Ohio, which I explain in the next chapter. I thought perhaps I could apply. After all, I already had my social security card. I wasn't going to return to high school at any cost, and I wondered if I could find a job and support myself.

I didn't give much thought to my grandmother's comment and my placement on fool's hill. Her comment was somewhere, lost in the back of my mind, and didn't make sense to me at that time.

Chapter 5

TIME TO GO TO WORK

I started my first job while living in Ohio. One summer, when I was confined to the house, my mother enrolled me in a summer youth job-training program. I applied for my social security card, and my number indicated that I lived in a Mideastern state instead of California. Remember: at that time, I was a minor from the hood and hadn't achieved anything. My only accomplishment was playing baseball and creating havoc in the neighborhood.

In Ohio, for my first job, I was an assistant, and I helped counselors at a camp for individuals with severe disabilities. Imagine that. Some couldn't talk or walk and were in wheelchairs. A counselor asked that I take one individual to the bathroom and help him empty his urine sack. I didn't have a clue what a urine sack was or how to empty one. I told one of the counselors that I didn't know what to do, and he said, "Push the individual into the bathroom stall and figure it out. He'll help you." My first stint with on-the-job training. Not only was I scared, but I was also dumbfounded. I left the individual in the bathroom stall, got on the bus, and never returned. I swore to never work in a job like that again.

While still in Ohio, I responded to a newspaper advertisement for a sales job. The advertisement displayed that the product was easy to sell and I could make money instantly. The job was for door-to-door selling cleaning brushes and other household goods. I arrived the next day with a partially ironed white shirt, slacks, shoes, and a tie I'd borrowed from my stepfather. We jumped in a van that took us to an affluent Caucasian neighborhood. The team leader gave me some tips and said that I was responsible for selling brushes door-to-door on two streets. All the youth in the van were Caucasian, and it appeared they had been selling brushes for some time. My first customer, I knocked on the door and said, "You wanna buy some brushes, muther[shuckers]?" Just kidding. But that was what I felt like saying, because that was the extent of my vocabulary and was what I knew in terms of speaking. Although I read the dictionary before going to bed, those words didn't translate into communicating a sentence.

The customers asked me to come in. Nervously, I showed them the catalog, but didn't know what to say. They looked like a couple that might hit me over the head, put me in the freezer, and then cut off portions of my body periodically to serve with some fava beans or black-eyed peas and rice. Anyway, I could barely pronounce any words, and I was scared *shitless*. They probably thought I was from a foreign country and still learning English as I stuttered, but they ordered a few things from me, I believe out of sympathy. I waited on the corner for the van to return and pick me up without going to another house. I never returned to that company.

While I was back in San Diego, my mother and sister moved from Ohio, and I stayed with my mom sometimes. The arguments with my mother continued, and she promised to throw my ass out of the house when I turned eighteen. Eventually, I applied for the Neighborhood Youth Corps, one of the local job-training programs for disadvantaged youth funded by the federal government. My first job while in the program in San Diego was part-time, supposedly after school, and eight hours on Saturday. I was a janitor's helper at a local Catholic school. My pay at that time was $1.56 per hour. I was a good worker, and I was proud when I learned how to use a buffer to shine the floors. I got along with my supervisor, the school's janitor, Henry, who spoke a little English. He always wore a Dickies uniform; the shirt and pants matched. He had all the keys to the rooms dangling from his belt, and he sometimes gave me the keys to some doors. His uniform was always immaculate. Most times, he showed me what to do and then left me alone to do the work. Now I had a job, great, I now had funds to buy beer and marijuana. One day, he asked me to do something that I believed I shouldn't be doing. I was angry at him for asking me. The next week, I left that job and had nothing to do.

Summertime was upon me, and prior to that, I hadn't attended school and was dishonest with my father. He thought I attended school every day until someone from the school called. Nonetheless, the end of the school year was approaching. At that time, I went back to the Neighborhood Youth Corps and asked for another job for the summer. I applied for a job at Southcrest Park and was hired. Here I learned about changing sprinklers, watering plants, and performing outside maintenance. I was also picking up trash on the same hill the player on the opposing team had hit the baseball when my coach was yelling at me to pitch overhand. I liked the job. And I had an opportunity to work in isolation, and sometimes I even hid from my supervisor. I worked full-time, and the money was great, which gave me the opportunity to buy albums, beer, and weed.

My job continued after the summer, and eventually, I became a good worker. I remember a commercial on TV at that time that said, "To get a good job, get an education." Then my sister recommended that I attend adult school. Because of the time out of high school, I enrolled in adult school to get my high school diploma. While I was in class, most of the individuals slept, and I assume they were vets returning from Vietnam. Again, I was too shy to continue going to school. I hated riding the bus, for fear someone would laugh at me, so I walked what seemed like miles to the school and to and from work. I continued working full-time.

Through the Neighborhood Youth Corps, I'd obtained a job with the City of San Diego. The Neighborhood Youth Corps paid my salary, and I still have the paycheck stubs now. I worked with a street-striping crew, and the job was fun. The street-striping crew, painted the lines in the middle of the road and some on the side near the shoulder. We didn't physically paint the lines; we rode in a truck, and in front of the vehicle was a street-striper. The street striper resembled a hot rod sand rail. I rode on the back of the truck and placed cones while the striper painted the lines. When I was first hired, the crew supervisor explained what I needed to do, and I thought this was the easiest job in the world.

Now it was time to lay the cones during my first outing, and I thought I was cool, riding on the back of the truck. I had a real job. The objective was to place the cones so that cars didn't run over the newly applied paint. The crew supervisor yelled, "Paint coming on!" meaning to start striping. As the truck moved, I placed the cones, and during my first outing, cones were everywhere except where they needed to be. I couldn't keep up. Cars were running over the cones, and I was upset, for I knew everyone saw the cones lying everywhere. Placing the cones properly made it easier to pick them up while the truck was moving. We had to stop and pick up the cones individually, which took time. Finally, one of the crew members, an African American, showed me how to place the cones. He also explained the importance of setting the cones to prevent accidents. I understood and became the best cone-setter on the crew. I was proud of this job, and everyone complimented me on my accomplishments. I liked the job because I had an opportunity to see parts of the city besides Southeast San Diego. I remembered the affluent neighborhoods, and this fifteen-year-old teenager wondered if he would own a home in a neighborhood like those.

Next, a friend of the family came by the house to visit often and tried to encourage me to excel in life. Often, he took my brother and me to do odd jobs. He was a hard worker, and he managed to make a decent living in the construction industry as a supervisor. Working with him was a challenge, for he was a construction supervisor, and he made us work hard. While we worked for him, he was a different person compared to his friend-of-the-family demeanor. However, he rewarded us with sweets and any hamburger we wanted. I believe his gestures were sympathetic. He'd suffered from polio as a youth, which caused him to walk with a limp, and one arm and hand were malformed.

The individual was an encouragement to me, and I thought I should pursue sports. He also bought me my first fishing pole, the same one I attempted to use to catch cats and birds from a second-story window. While I was in woodshop in the seventh grade, I was given a project to build a small boat that floated. I entered that boat in a regatta in San Diego and was amazed when it floated, and I retrieved it from the other side of the bay. As a gesture of my gratitude, when departing to Ohio on one trip, I gave him that boat. After we returned to California years later, I noticed that boat was still in his garage.

Anyway, one day, he picked me up so I could help him with a construction job. I had to operate what felt like a ninety-pound jackhammer to break up a slab of concrete. All I knew was the jackhammer was heavy, the work was strenuous, and that night in bed, I could still feel the vibrations from that jackhammer. At that point, I decided that jobs in the construction industry weren't for me. I continued working for the paint-striping crew, and one day, the same friend of the family asked if I wanted to make some extra money. An acquaintance of his was building a house in an affluent neighborhood. Of course, I said yes; the extra income would provide an opportunity to buy more albums, beer, and weed.

I was employed full-time with the Neighborhood Youth Corps job and, on the weekends, worked at the side job as a laborer. The pay was all cash. The work site was about forty miles away from home. TB, a Caucasian carpenter, picked me up and then stopped to pick up another Caucasian teenager who lived near the San Diego Chargers stadium, Jack Murphy, as it was called at that time. The neighborhood where I lived and where the other person lived were quite different.

I believe TB, the individual who gave us the ride, was thankful that where I lived was close to the freeway. The less time in the hood, the better off he'd be. I could tell that he wasn't used to driving in the hood, for he looked nervous when picking me up and dropping me off.

I really enjoyed working my weekend side job. I gained valuable house-building experience. Besides digging ditches, I helped add a roof on the house and liked helping the electrician and bricklayer. Little did I know, the skills I learned would come in handy later.

I continued working both jobs; however, I was constantly partying. Several times, the individual picking me up on the weekend had to wait while I gathered myself. During lunchtime on the weekend job, I slept most of the time. The person who helped me get the job came by one day to talk to me about life and the direction I was heading. He wanted me to save part of my earnings and find a way to get my high school diploma, but I had my own agenda. Finally, after a futile effort to talk to me, the individual who helped me obtain the weekend gig went to the person I was helping build the house and recommended that he let me go. The next Saturday, at the end of day, the homeowner whose house we were building said that my services were no longer needed. I was somewhat happy because now I could enjoy my weekends. I continued working full-time for the City of San Diego. I enjoyed the job, and the only challenge was that I walked about five miles to get there not because I didn't have the money but because I didn't want to deal with riding the bus.

I lived with my mother sometimes, but I lived mostly with my father. My mother and I didn't get along. She often repeated her promise that she was going to throw me out of the house when I turned eighteen. At that time, I didn't mind because I knew I could live with my father. *He lives closer to my job, anyway,* I thought. One day, I was at my mother's house and was going to stay the night. Although I was underage, my mother bought me a six-pack of beer, and after several, I began talking to my mother, and the conversation went awry. I mentioned that she was crazy moving us around when we were children. She said that dealing with someone like me would drive a person crazy. She became angry, and that was the second time she pulled a gun on me and put it in my face. I was upset because I was having problems with her mother and couldn't stay in her house. I had to make some decisions.

My father said that he was going to Oklahoma to get married. *Cool,* I thought. I stayed at his place and went to work every day for the City of San Diego. After his trip to Oklahoma, he arrived home not only with his wife but also with two daughters in tow. A ready-made family. I wasn't expecting the addition of two stepsisters living in the house. I was shy and didn't know how to interact and, most of the time, stayed in my room I believe one of the daughters had a crush on me. Aside from Lavonnette, I was still dealing with the aroma of pickled beets on a female's breath. I had yet to realize the value of a girlfriend. We went to the movies and conversed on the porch on hot summer days. However, I do believe her mother was uncomfortable with her daughter's actions, and eventually, I experienced the same. One day, I overheard the mother communicating her displeasure with the situation as she spanked her grown daughter. Now I was faced with an uncomfortable situation living with my father and experienced unfavorable situations when staying with my mother.

Remember: I have an older sister who had been born when my mother and father were on their way to California. I looked up to my sister and really liked her female friends. They were so much older, though. However, I still had memories of the girl who lived next door and the pickled beet breath. As noted throughout these writings, my sister was and is instrumental to my development as a person.

However, the quintessential sibling rivalries existed, and the relationship with my sister was typical, but these situations require mentioning. As I've said, my sister was older than I was, and she was responsible for the house when my mother was away. My brother and I often teased my sister because she was skinny, and we made her angry. What got to her wasn't what we said but how we said it. Remember: we had plenty of comical influences: my mother and aunts in their cantankerous episodes when cutting up black males; my brother and I and our silly spanking shenanigans, including the episodes about bald-headed jokes; and of course, Uncle J. We called my sister names, such as Spider, and I revised the name and called her Spydarrr to tease her about how skinny she was. In a low, monotone voice like Freddy Krueger, the character from the movie *Nightmare on Elm Street*, I spouted "Spydarrr," which made her mad. While my mother was away, I found ways to get next to her, and she chased me, and I locked myself in the room and behind a closed door. All she heard was that low, monotone voice, "Spydarrr" over and over, which angered her, because she couldn't get to me. In her frustration, skinny, with braids standing on her head and wearing glasses, she beat on the door and tried to pry it open while shouting, "I'm going to get you!"

"Spydarrr," I teased. "I'm going to get you, Spydarrr," I murmured. "I'M GOING TO KILL YOU." From me, in that voice, I said "Spydarrrrrrr" over and over. Please know that her room was next to the one I shared with my brother, and she liked to read. While locked in the room, I took a break and read comic books or played with plastic soldiers and, every few minutes, reminded my sister about the spider. I might comment, "Wonder what the spider is doing in the next room." I said, "Probably playing with daddy longlegs." Then she heard laughter. A few minutes passed while I read a comic book, then I cracked another joke about a spider. Sometimes I might comment, "I wonder how spiders dance." If in the room with me, my brother or I did a stupid dance and laughed aloud so my sister could hear. A few minutes passed, we made another joke about a spider so she could hear, then started laughing. Our shenanigans were worse than the Chinese water torture. When my mother came home, my brother and I emerged from the room with one last "Spydarrr" under my breath in that voice. I then welcomed my mother home with a big smile on my face. "Hi, Mama."

No wonder individuals in junior high school wanted to kick my ass after those cutup sessions. I might add that an individual might now understand why I hid under the table while eating those camadee meat or baloney sandwiches.

I used similar tactics to anger my brother as well, and I had a special name devised from a textbook I read in school. A character in that textbook was Ribsy, whom I remember to be a dog. I devised a name for him, "Ribbaeyyy," noting how skinny he was. In a low, monotone voice, I spouted, "Ribbaeyyy, Ribbaeyyy," over and over, which made him mad as well. However, with my brother, he was younger and had to endure the constant name-calling by his older brother. I might add that the harassment my brother endured from his older brother made him tough, and he didn't take crap from anybody except from his older brother. It eventually helped my brother while playing defense on the football field. I didn't have the luxury of an older brother, and my two sisters were born before me. Perhaps an older brother beating my ass would have made me tougher.

One night, my brother and I had to take a bath together, as we often did, and looked at my toothbrush and foreign objects were present. My brother did the same, and we washed it off and brushed our teeth, noting the interesting taste. In later years, my sister confessed and told me about her revenge tactic. All I have to say about this is, if sibling rivalries exist, keep your toothbrush in your bedroom. *I love you, sis!* As I became older and stronger, naturally, the days running from my older sister passed. Fortunately, our relationship evolved into something that is positive. My sister influenced many aspects of my life.

My sister was aware of the challenges I faced. I sometimes hung out at the park and ventured to my sister's house. One time, my sister dated a marine, and recommended that I enlist. At that time, I was in my late teens, and the Vietnam conflict was in session. I remembered looking at my sister's school yearbook and viewing the photographs of the young men who had died in the war. However, I had to make some decisions about life.

One day, I was walking past a local shopping center to buy some record albums. I took a shortcut through someone's yard and proceeded down a long blacktop surface. I looked to my right and saw an armed forces recruitment center. In fact, that center is still there today.

First I approached the navy recruiter. I inquired about enlisting in the navy first because they were numerous in San Diego, and I could be stationed at home. In hindsight, stationed at a location far from home might've been my best option. Furthermore, I said to the navy recruiter that I saw an advertisement on television that conveyed I could be trained in electronics. I thought, he did a good job restraining himself from laughing. I envisioned him thinking, "The [N-word] from the hood with a goatee, no high school diploma, underage, wants electronics. Perhaps infantry on the front line would suit him well." Next, the recruiter asked me to take a test. *All right,* I thought and breezed through the test. I had a sense of urgency because my mother promised to throw me out of the house at the age of eighteen. Later, I found how important that test was.

The navy recruiter mentioned that maybe I could earn a good trade instead of pursuing electronics. I said nope, I wanted electronics or radar. Because I thought the navy had wimpy uniforms and the hats looked ridiculous, I decided to try the army. Based on the time spent with my brother watching movies, I wanted to be an army man anyway. The army recruiter looked at my test scores and said that electronics was out of the question. Because I didn't have a high school diploma I took the GED test and failed one section and began studying to increase my score. The Army recruiter explained that if I raised my score substantially, I could acquire a good trade as well. I enrolled in remedial GED study classes, based on the recruiter's recommendation.

In the meantime I talked to a marine recruiter and he reviewed my military entrance test scores. He asked, "How soon can you leave?" However, I had one obstacle; I wasn't eighteen. I had been watching television and asked for a guarantee, and I wanted electronics or radar. He chuckled. The recruiter said that my GTC scores (don't ask me what that acronym means—a form of intelligence test, I assume) were high enough to give me a guarantee other than infantry. I later found my scores were high for someone from the hood without a high school diploma, and several individuals in administration at the bases at which I was stationed commented on my high GTC score as well. I might add that I asked the air force recruiter about enlisting but from his reaction I believe the answer wasn't no, but hell no.

Anyway, I talked to my father, and he was supportive but didn't know I was serious. I think part of his motivation for support was that he wouldn't have to pay child support anymore. My mother was hysterical. "What do you mean enlisting in the marines! Do you know there is a war going on? Plus, you're not old enough. Them white folks will let you get killed over there." I thought, *After the last time you pulled a gun on me and said that you were about to throw me out of the house when I was eighteen, now you give me grief about enlisting in the marines.* She finally signed. Years later, I talked to my father, and he mentioned that after a few weeks of not seeing me while I was in boot camp, he asked where I was. Finally, someone told him I was in boot camp, and I guess he paid child support for a few more months anyway. Before leaving for boot camp, I told my sister, and she was happy. I gave her credit for the advice about volunteering to enlist in the marines.

At that time, the Vietnam War was just about over, and the United States military ended the draft, thank God; therefore, I volunteered to enlist. The day finally arrived when I had to report to the marines. I was somewhat apprehensive because I was about to leave home and be on my own. On that day, not one recruiter came to the house, but two. Both were Caucasian and probably scared. The recruiters were dressed in their green fatigues, as if they were going to war. Both of them looked at me and asked if I was ready to go, acting as if they would take adverse action if I resisted. The thought was never on my mind. I was in the recruiter's car and whisked away. I wondered if I was going to be someone like those service members who were in my sister's high school yearbook.

The recruiters put me on a bus that took me to a hotel in Los Angeles. While on the bus, I sat next to a Caucasian teenager. We came to know each other, and he had some weed. That night was our last day as civilians, and we smoked weed on the hotel roof in downtown Los Angeles. Soon a police helicopter began to hover; after all, we were near downtown Los Angeles. We ran to our room, stoned.

The next day, I went to my physical, was sworn in, and went back to the hotel. While we were at AFES, which I believe stands for the Armed Forces Evaluation System at that time, all the people were nice. We ate a good lunch but didn't know what to expect in boot camp. At AFES were hundreds of young men. They divided us into our military groups. Someone was shouting, "army over here, navy over there, air force over by the wall, and the marines outside." *Oh, shucks,* I thought.

They herded us on buses again for the long ride to San Diego Marine Corps Recruit Depot. It was about a two-hour ride, and most of us were talking and laughing on the bus. Some were silent, and one individual was crying. "I didn't know what to expect." *Duh, you enlisted in the marines.* I wondered what was happening at home.

We finally arrived, and the bus driver opened the door with a smirk on his face. As soon as he opened the door, three marines in their Smokey hats were yelling and screaming. "Get off the bus, you maggots! Hurry up, you girls! Slimy pieces of shit." There was chaos and pandemonium. One individual took off running, and I was told they found him trying to climb the fence near the San Diego Airport, which was next door. The military police found one individual in a tree. The drill instructors kept screaming, "Maggots, you civilian slime, get on the yellow footprints!" There were rows of yellow footprints painted on the blacktop, and the imprints were angled at forty-five degrees. Every time I go to the airport and see those yellow footprints in the scanning machine, I have flashbacks about boot camp, and sometimes I chuckle.

Another DI yelled, "Girls, you had better get those feet at a forty-five-degree angle on the yellow footprints!" After I had placed my feet on the painted footprints, I realized my feet were larger than the yellow representations. I looked at a drill instructor to confirm my correctness and perhaps to gain some sympathy. He yelled in my face, "Sweetheart, you better stop eyeballing me!" I thought, *Shit, I should shuck this muthershucker up.* "You wanna try me, maggot?" he shouted in my face. "You are now in my United States Marine Corps." And he reinforced *maggot.*

That night, I didn't sleep. Instead I watched the planes fly by as they landed and took off from San Diego International Airport. I still remember the smell from the aircraft's exhaust in addition to the aroma from that cold night in the barracks. I lay in my bunk and said to myself, *Oh, shit, what have I got myself into now? Mama, mama, I want my mama.* The badass punk from the hood!

Chapter 6

YOU'RE IN THE (ARMY) MARINES NOW

Boot camp certified that I was officially a United States Marine. I felt as though I'd lost control of my life. A few days ago, I could go where I wanted, could eat when and where I wanted, and had the liberty to sleep anytime. All that had changed. The Marine Corps was a drastic adjustment. From my first night in boot camp, I was confused about the unknown. However, I knew boot camp was going to be a challenge, and I understood that they couldn't deliberately kill me.

The next morning, after the yellow-footprint incident, which seemed like three hours before, I heard some ruckus and saw a trash can rolling down the middle of the barracks. The same idiots I thought who'd been yelling the night before were screaming, "Get on your feet, girls!" I wondered if they went to bed the night before or sat somewhere and waited for the witching hour to throw the trash cans down the middle of the barracks. After all, their uniforms were neatly pressed. "Hurry up, you slimeball, civilian pukes!" After some time, in the background, I heard a tape of a bugle playing "Reveille." "You have five minutes to get on those yellow footprints!" I said to myself, *Damn, not those things again.* Folks were running out of the barracks half-dressed, shirts on backward, shoes on the wrong feet. One individual urinated on himself. I guess he didn't have the opportunity to take that morning piss. Another was throwing up amid all the chaos.

That morning, after breakfast, they took us to get our haircuts. They gave us uniforms and toiletries then took our civilian clothes. Our newly acquired uniforms smelled as if they came right out of a box. We didn't know how to march, so the drill instructors said, "Okay, herd, march!" The first day was busy, and soon it was time for lunch.

We made it to the mess hall and waited in line to eat. We had to hold our trays in a port arms position, which means hands clasped on both sides while the arm displayed ninety-degree angles. While in line, I saw a drill instructor from another platoon explaining how the recruits must eat their food. In his military DI voice he said, "Today, this is another square meal in my mess hall, you maggots." He proceeded to describe how to eat a square meal. The recruits' motions had to represent a square. Scooping food, hand straight up then at a right angle, ninety-degree motion to one's mouth, and back in reverse.

All the overweight recruits in the weight management platoon and those who looked like "beach balls with lips" (as the DIs called them) were served a portion that even I couldn't survive on. After the recruits in the weight management platoon obtained their food, they had to stand and sit down at the same time. One of the fat recruits couldn't wait and was probably exhausted from all the activities. He sat down and started filling his face. I didn't understand why he was scarfing his food when hardly anything was on his plate. Soon after, three drill instructors were yelling at him in his ear. "What are you doing, Porky, you slimeball?" one said. "Did I tell you to feed your face?" By this time, Porky had a few scraps hanging from his mouth and was looking at another recruit's plate, as if he was going to snatch some food.

"Outside, you fat civilian, slimeball, maggot!" the drill instructor commanded. Now, one of the DIs escorted him out. For the rest of the recruits in that platoon, the other drill instructor gave the command: "READY?" Everyone said, "Yes, sir."

He gave the command: "EAT!" As I was approaching the door, I saw one of the DIs yelling at Porky. He had him doing push-ups, and as the DI commanded, "Up!" Porky chanted, "Loyalty, sir!" The DI commanded, "Down!" Porky shouted, "Discipline, sir!" until Porky barely completed about five push-ups. Porky still had a few scraps of food on his face and looked like a stuffed pig while doing push-ups. It appeared that there was an impression of food in his back pocket, supposedly a biscuit, and perhaps food given to him from a sympathetic recruit. Finally, the DI of the weight management platoon commanded, "Everyone outside," and off they marched to the next event.

After viewing the antics in the other platoon, I wondered if I was going to complete boot camp and further questioned if I had made the right choice to enlist in the marines. Little did I know the events here were important to traversing fool's hill and the why.

Finally, we made it to the chow line and had a different experience than the platoon before us. In what seemed to be about ten minutes, the DI commanded everyone out. "Hurry up, you maggots!" I shoved the last of the food in my mouth and ran outside. "Okay, you maggots, now you had a square meal and ate some of the taxpayers' chow and filled your worthless guts. March! Left, right, left, right." At that time, I still had my walk from the hood; the DIs called it ditty bopping. We in the hood called it pimping (for the layman, pimp walking). The drill instructor yelled, "Tree, stop ditty bopping." I had a problem marching in formation for I had long legs and big feet; therefore, ditty bopping was what I knew and helped me continue marching. Otherwise, I stepped on the heels of the individual in front of me and marching was difficult. The drill instructor yelled, "Cover down!" When I'd received my uniforms the DI said that my cap was a cover; therefore, I commenced to pull it down. "Cover down" actually meant staying in alignment with the individual in front of me. But I was confused. I kept pulling my cover down. The DI broke through the formation and yelled in my face, "Cover down, you maggot!" Finally, the DI yelled, "Stop! Here we go again. We have an undisciplined maggot that doesn't know how to follow directions."

Besides the first night, getting on the yellow footprints and reviewing the Porky scenario finally, I said *Damn, I didn't know that being an army man or marine was going to be this much of a challenge.*

This was tough, and I wished I had studied for a higher test score and enlisted in the United States Navy. *Regardless of what I felt about the uniforms and what I thought was a stupid hat, life would be easier right now,* I thought.

The next day was the same routine, trash cans, and this time seemed like we had only ten minutes to shit, shower, and shave. Most didn't shower, but shaving was mandatory. Some of the sinks had blood in them, for some individuals cut themselves shaving. Some shaved the night before, but in the marines, it was forbidden to have stubble on your face. In approximately fifteen minutes, someone yelled again, "Get on the yellow footprints! Hurry up, ladies! We don't have all day!" Recruits were scrambling, some trying to put on their pants and some tripping as they scrambled to make it to the yellow footprints. After a while, someone yelled, "Attention!" Almost everyone didn't know what standing at attention was but faked it like what they saw on television, me included.

Several were late getting to the yellow footprints, and one of them was the individual whom I'd smoked weed with at AFES. This made him a marked man. Those who were late weren't allowed to get on the yellow footprints and had to stand in front of us. One drill instructor said, "You see, we have some individuals here who don't understand what I meant when I said 'Shit, shower, and shave, and on the yellow footprints.' You see, we have a failure to communicate" he said, as if he had been watching *Cool Hand Luke* the night before. He continued, "You see, these individuals are slimeballs and would get you killed in combat. They aren't loyal and think they are still civilian pukes. Everybody, get down and give me twenty while the slimeball watches." That was a sight to see, for some individuals were out of shape, including me. Another recruit took off running as if to head for the airport to go home. No one took off after him. Soon after, the military police returned him, and he looked like he had been beaten. It was rumored that they'd found him hiding in a tree as well. The DIs finally marched us to morning chow.

It was almost daylight, and the DI started counting cadence slowly, left, right, left, right. "Stop!" the DI commanded. "You maggots look like a herd of animals. Okay, you cows, let us try it again slowly." He then said, "Left, right, left, right, left, right. Okay, herd, stop." And we all did. We were near a road, and a formation of recruits that were about to graduate passed while marching. What a sight to see. They all marched together like a well-oiled machine. The drill instructor for the other platoon was calling cadence, left, right, left, right, almost like he was singing. I couldn't help but to turn my head in amazement, and what did I do that for? One of the drill instructors yelled at me, "What are you looking at, you undisciplined maggot? Did I tell you to turn your head? From that point on, I was a marked recruit and perhaps deservingly so.

As previously stated, the individual with whom I smoked weed with prior to AFES faced a challenge. One of the first nights, the drill instructors called him into the office. The DIs called him by his last name and commanded that he enter their house, or hooch, meaning the office. The rest of us were sitting in an area near the DI's office, designated the classroom. Suddenly, there was much noise from the office, and the recruit finally emerged and appeared as if he was beaten. Perhaps this served as a message to all of us sitting in the classroom that the DIs had the power to do what they wished and a means to degrade the civilian part of us and make us United States Marines. For me, the strategy was beginning to work, especially after I realized that running away wasn't possible.

Finally, the individual with whom I smoked weed was assigned to be the house mouse, and whenever the DIs needed something, he fetched it for them. The DIs yelled, "House mouse!" and he ran to the hooch. However, that individual was privy to inside information from the DIs, and he was a good person to befriend.

After processing in boot camp, all of us were assigned platoons, and the next challenge was physical training. Prior to enlisting, I'd begun an exercise routine that didn't compare to the rigorous boot camp training. Before enlisting, I knew about the requirement to run three miles. I appeared to be buff, but I had unhealthy eating habits. Before boot camp, while playing baseball at a function, I bragged about eating ten hot dogs and didn't have a clue about the effects it had on the body. I could eat more than enough then, and most of the food wasn't healthy, including the salty camadee meat and that delicious government cheese. At that time, there wasn't a model for eating healthy, and I figure that some who live in the inner city suffer the same today. Here I note the importance of helping individuals in the hood, or those experiencing poverty, understand the importance of nutrition. Those who receive public assistance for food should be required to attend and participate in classes for nutrition. Anyway, to prepare for boot camp, I did some jogging at night. Keep in mind, at that time, I was a smoker (cigarettes and sometimes weed).

Moments before the first run in formation in boot camp, all the recruits stood outside getting ready. I thought the run was going to be a piece of cake. The first run was about one mile. During the end of the run, those hot dogs, baloney sandwiches, pickled pigs' feet, pork rinds, beer, cigarettes, camadees, and other delicacies of the hood started to ooze out of my pores. I finally dropped out. My entire thoughts ventured back to Porky at the mess hall, and I worried about suffering the same fate.

Two drill instructors yelled at me, "You maggot, you slimeball, quitter, puke!" At that time, I needed moral support, but not in the Corps. I did my best and walked and ran slowly the rest of the way and eventually paid the price. In succession, the DIs gathered all the recruits who'd quit on the run. The DIs yelled that we'd failed the Marine Corps and the United States and commanded, "On your belly, you slime!" We were separated from the rest of the platoon. The instructions were to wiggle on our stomachs in a fishlike motion to resemble slime. "Slime, you slimeballs!" the DI commanded. Here I was, approximately six feet, two inches tall, big feet, an individual from the hood, on his belly, doing fishlike motions. The DI continued to yell, "Slime, to your left and your right, and let me hear you say, 'Loyalty, sir. Discipline, sir.'" I felt the grit of the dirt as it lined on my teeth.

After a period that didn't come fast enough for me, the DI yelled, "On your feet, slimeballs!" We yelled, "On your feet, yes, sir." The DI, with his hands behind his back, yelled, "Bends and thrusts, ready!" "YES, SIR." "Begin one." "Loyalty, sir." "Two." "Discipline, sir." It was difficult to recognize those next to me, for sweat and dirt were all over our bodies. I had never seen so much sweat ooze from my body, which I feared would turn to mud or grease from my afore-mentioned diet. Next were push-ups, running in place, and a host of other calisthenics.

Finally, the DI yelled, "On your feet, maggots!" With his hands behind his back, Smokey hat partly covering his eyes, he began to lecture us about quitting and failing the United States government and *his* United States Marine Corps. Then he commanded us to align ourselves in a marching formation. "Double time, hut!" We ran back to the squad bay. We entered, and I believe our appearance was reg-istered by all the recruits viewing the incident and probably had a lasting effect on some. However, the DI looked as though his uni-form was directly from the cleaners. Since the incident described, as a recruit, I never dropped out or quit a run again.

Next was the marching and rifle drills. Marching was an art, and recruits had to be disciplined and proficient in order to execute a good march, as a team and in unison. Keep in mind, from day one, we marched as a unit everywhere. While marching and standing in formation, disciplined marines looked straight ahead.

Our platoon was ready to emerge from the first phase to the sec-ond phase of training. To do this, the platoon had to pass a test and effectively execute drill movements with a rifle both while marching and while stationary. One of the drills was to transfer a rifle from one shoulder to another while marching or standing in formation. We were ready for our marching and rifle test. During the test, marine officers and others were present and critiquing our drills. Toward the end of the test, we were standing in formation, conducting stationary rifle drills. We were at parade rest, which is a position in which one arm is behind the back, and the butt of the rifle is on the ground and held by an extended arm. While conducting the drill, one DI com-manded, "While standing in formation, you better let those gnats stand on your nose, and don't move unless ordered." We went from parade rest to attention and then to port arms, which means posi-tion the rifle diagonally across your chess, and remember: we had to accomplish the maneuver in unison.

While I was in port arms, my nose started itching. I knew the evaluation team was behind us. My nose itch was becoming unbearable. At that time, we looked good in front of the graders. Prior to one of the rifle drills, an officer inspected each recruit, face-to-face. Part of the inspection included an examination of our uniforms, hygiene, and fingernails. To prevent our breath from smelling bad, the DIs made us gargle with Listerine and then swallow it. I'm hesitant to mention that if using a mouthwash today, sometimes I swallow it. Anyway, the itch in my nose was becoming unbearable, and I knew we were toward the end of the exercise. As soon as the DI walked past, I just had to satisfy the itch in my nose and went for it and thought I was quick about it; however, I wasn't quick enough. The DI saw me and lost it, and I believe his antics provided the raters more attention than my quickly scratching my nose. He broke through the ranks, for I was in second column, and ran toward me. "You undisciplined slime!" he hollered and shouted all kinds of degrading comments in my face. By the way, his breath smelled worse than pickled beets.

The DI commanded port arms, and then we marched back to the barracks. I was then called into the classroom. "Private Cubit to the classroom," he commanded. Bends and thrusts forever. I could see the other recruits watching while I was getting my freshly cleaned uniform sweaty. The DI paced back and forth in front of me, hands behind him, and said every degrading comment possible-no curse words, though. The event reminded me of the movie *An Officer and a Gentleman*, when Lou Gossett was disciplining Mayo. I was hoarse from yelling "Loyalty, sir! Discipline, sir!" as commanded. The DI sometimes commanded "Louder, louder!" I believe I lost five pounds during that episode.

The platoon and I made it past the first phase, and the nose-scratching incident didn't hold us back. When transitioning from the first to the second phase, the platoon earned the right to wear boot blouses. Those are the rubber bands placed at the bottom of one's pant legs so the trousers appear tucked as opposed to placing the bottom of the pant legs inside one's boots. I was proud then. The platoon made the transition from first to second phase, an important success in my military life.

Now, we were in the second phase, and it was time for the rifle range. All marines must be able to fire a rifle effectively. At that time, part or our creed was that a marine's best friend was his rifle. For the past six weeks, we'd carried our rifles, and now was the time to use them. Periodically, we cleaned and lubricated them, especially after times in the dirt when being punished for doing something wrong. Because of the many incidents, my rifle was dirtier than the others were at times.

The rifle range was about forty miles north of the Marine Corps Recruit Depot in San Diego. Before we transitioned to the rifle range, the DIs' attitude toward us changed dramatically. They were now very nice to us. I believe their disposition had something to do with the fact that the recruits they yelled at for six weeks were going to have loaded rifles. We finally arrived at the range and began training to fire the rifle effectively. During the first week at the rifle range, we learned more about the rifle. We learned how to calculate the wind when shooting, how to adjust our aim, and the different positions from which to fire the rifle. These include standing, sitting, and lying on our stomach, or the prone position. Boy, did I have some practice from sliming on my stomach after I dropped out of the first run! Sometimes I had trouble sitting in some positions because of my long legs and big feet. Prior to shooting a rifle at the range, the only weapon I'd fired previously was the sawed-off .22-caliber rifle when I was a teenager. The .22-caliber rifle had a mind of its own when fired. I couldn't wait until it was time to shoot a real rifle, an M14. I thought shooting an M14 was the same as shooting the sawed-off .22-caliber rifle. *Wrong.*

At the rifle range, I had to pull guard duty around the weapon's armory. While I was on guard duty, the DIs ordered me to march around the armory as if I were in formation and to practice saying my general orders, which were twelve at that time. I had to memorize each order because sometimes the DIs gave us pop quizzes, asking us to repeat a general order at random. While I pranced around the armory like a soldier in a foreign army repeating my general orders, two military policemen (MPs) approached me. They asked me to stick my head inside the truck. One of the MPs was African American. After I had stuck my head inside the truck, they began to give loud commands toward my face. The African American MP shouted what a dumb shuck I was. They said that if I didn't walk faster, they would shoot me. They drove away laughing. I thought, if this were a different situation, I would be the one walking away laughing. *Cowards.*

Finally, it was Thursday, prequalification day. The shooting score obtained that day indicated how a marine might score on qualification day, the following Friday. On prequalification day, I scored 210 out of 250 points and was confident that I would qualify the next day. I was nervous, but I understood the importance of qualifying with my rifle.

On qualification day, I blew my score at the two-hundred-yard line while firing from the standing position. I fired better at the three-hundred-yard line sitting, regardless of my long legs and big feet. I was now at the five-hundred-yard line and struggled. I was down to my last round in hand and needed at least five points to qualify. I took a deep breath, relaxed, aimed, and squeezed the trigger as instructed during prequalifying practices the week before. Up came a red flag indicating that I had completely missed the target. I was upset and knew if I'd had my sawed-off .22 rifle, I could've hit that target. The failure here reminded me of my days playing baseball and pitching. I threw a fastball, and the individual hit the ball, not only over the home run fence, but he also hit the ball over the outer fence as well. That hit cost us the game. The feeling was about the same as when I kicked the individual in the ass when punting the football or refraining from catching the pass in my last football game as a freshman in high school. Not only was I upset, but the DIs were furious as well. After qualification day, as we cleaned our rifles, the DIs began to revert to their harassing ways. The marines who were successful at the rifle range strutted and marched with pride because they qualified. However, I didn't experience the same feelings.

Once we were back at the barracks, the DIs dismissed everyone except all those who didn't qualify, approximately six of us. Everyone ran upstairs, yelling as they never had before, sounds of joy. Those of us who didn't qualify marched to the dirt pit. The DI commanded bends and thrusts, forever and a day. For a long time those in the barracks could hear, "One," "Loyalty, sir," "Two," "Discipline, sir." Now and then, he commanded us to stop and lectured us about taking pride in *his* United States Marine Corps.

Out of nervousness and sympathy, as I typically did then, I smiled, and the DI grabbed me by the collar and shook my head back and forth as his fist met my face several times. I was furious and was going to make a report to the commanding officer. I was angry and started to retaliate but refrained and swore instead that if I saw him again outside boot camp, I would kick his ass. Finally, I was able to get past the incident as I progressed as an individual, but it took me a few years after boot camp. I realized the mental challenges wanting revenge caused me. Anyway, back to the bends and thrusts. It seemed like we were in the dirt forever. While performing the grueling task, I looked to my left, and there was the Caucasian person I'd smoked weed with while at AFES. In addition, unfortunately, I struggled at the rifle range during my entire enlistment in the Marine Corps. Fortunately, my military occupational specialty (MOS) sometimes required that I carry and use a shotgun or a .45-caliber pistol instead of a rifle.

A few years into my enlistment, I needed to qualify with the M16 rifle. After boot camp and because of the Vietnam War, the marines used the M16 rifle, which was lighter and better suited for jungle warfare. Then the drugs of choice for some were speed, a hallucinogen, weed, or alcohol. At that time, I experimented with speed, the white crosses, and a form of hallucinogen called purple microdot. During the prequalification day at the rifle range, I took a purple microdot, and for me, the effect was more like speed. That day, I shot 235 out of 250 for prequalification day. Back then, the military didn't have effective drug-testing methods like they do today. The next day, I had nothing in my system other than the residue from the drug the day before, and I almost didn't qualify, which expresses my challenge while on the rifle range, among other issues.

In another incident on the rifle range during practice, drug-free this time, I fired a few rounds. Then I pulled the trigger, and smoke flowed from the chamber. I called the range coach, and he pulled the charging handle back and expended the empty cartridge case. The range coach, an African American male, told me to fire again.

However, I knew that the projectile was still lodged in the barrel. I raised my hand to exit from the firing line. I cleared my weapon, and as I had speculated when firing, the round was a cook-off, meaning that black powder in the cartridge ignited and burned, but it wasn't powerful enough to send the projectile downrange. Therefore, the projectile was still lodged in the barrel. Had I fired, the explosion would have caused serious injury and perhaps death. I didn't care that the range coach outranked me; I gave that dumb ass a piece of my mind. He had a dumbfounded look on his face. I cleared my rifle, returned to the line, and continued firing. Another brush with death averted.

After the military, firing a weapon still challenges me. While in Oklahoma visiting my father once, I wanted my wife at that time and my son to become familiar with weapons. I had a .38-caliber pistol and was target-shooting in my father's backyard. I placed some targets for my wife and son to shoot. I explained to my wife how to handle and shoot the pistol. While I handed the pistol to her, for some reason, she pulled the trigger and almost shot me in the leg, perhaps by accident, of course. My fault for handing her a loaded weapon. My son was able to hit all the targets with amazing accuracy. However, it was my turn, and I reverted to my Marine Corps days and missed all the targets. A shotgun works best for me.

Anyway, the next day in boot camp was a forest march from the rifle range to infantry training school. I was still disappointed about not qualifying at the rifle range. I and the other rifle range "unquals" were in the back of the formation. In front of us were three platoons, and half of each marched on a side of the road. While marching, everyone was responsible for keeping pace and maintaining an equal distance between the marine in front of them. Because of the placement at the back of the formation, I practically had to run all the way, and the dust from those marching in front of me was unbearable.

The next part of the second phase was infantry training, and the best part was throwing a live grenade. Like the rifle range, the DIs weren't present. We finally made it past the second phase and returned to the Recruit Depot in San Diego and were on to the third phase. Still regretting not qualifying at the rifle range, I thought that perhaps I could redeem myself by qualifying in the water-survival course. It was important that marines, by definition, knew how to function on land and water or both. My only swimming adventure beforehand had been at the Jackie Robinson YMCA in San Diego. At that time, the YMCA didn't have a swimming pool, so we'd practiced at the house of Archie Moore, the famous boxer. His swimming pool was shaped like a boxing glove, and one could see it from the freeway.

During the first phase of the water-survival training, the instructors tested everyone's ability to float. Those who could float had an opportunity to earn a first-class-water-survival qualification. I never tried floating before and may not be able to do so today. I tried to float, went straight to the bottom of the swimming pool, and was placed in the "unable to float," or swimming remediation group. Most of the individuals who couldn't float were African Americans. They called us rocks because we sank to the bottom of the swimming pool. We spent about a week trying to swim for a distance to earn a third-class water-survival qualification. To qualify for third class, I had to swim two laps across the pool (yeah, right). During the qual-ification, I was able to swim one lap but was unsuccessful swimming the second lap. *Dirt pit like dropping out of the first run, here I come,* I thought. Bends and thrusts forever. "One," "Loyalty, sir," "Two," "Discipline, sir."

At the end of third phase, it was time to take my final physical fitness test (PFT). My goal was to achieve a first-class score. Then for a first-class score, a recruit must complete eighty sit-ups in two minutes, complete twenty pull-ups, and run three miles in less than twenty-one minutes. However, during the final PFT, I wasn't able to attain a first-class score. I came close and earned a second-class score, but my greatest accomplishment was completing the three miles in less than twenty-one minutes. Perhaps the motivation intervention by the Dis, and sliming like a fish after dropping out during that first run was effective. I'll state that in most situations during my enlistment in the Marine Corps, I was able to earn a first-class PFT score and, in some instances, was able to run three miles in less than eighteen minutes, one time near the seventeen-minute mark, and I smoked cigarettes. The experience in boot camp explains my affinity for physical fitness today. However, at that time, I still needed to learn about the other side of the equation, which was proper nutrition.

Before we graduated, an informant house mouse said that the DIs were thinking about sending me to the motivation platoon, a place where they send recruits and put them through rigorous training to enhance motivation. These individuals slime through mud and other situations to help increase motivation. Perhaps all my shuck-ups during boot camp was leading to the decision to send me to the motivation platoon. It's probably a good thing that it didn't happen, because I might be writing a different story now. I should say, though, that I appeared to be motivated less than other recruits. However, I was still trying to figure things out about me and life-an important evaluation for traversing fool's hill and discovering the why. Besides, we were in the third phase, and sending me to motivation was a moot point. In my opinion, motivation develops internally and not by sliming through mud. I now know.

However, I wasn't the only one still adjusting to military life, and some individuals didn't get it. We were in the third phase and about a month away from graduation. At night, all the recruits stood on footlockers in white skivvies (white underwear). We held out our hands in rotation for inspection, and as the DI passed, the recruit said, "The private has no problems, sir." Well, one individual decided to wear his polka-dot underwear, and as the DI passed, he happened upon the individual who wore the polka-dot skivvies. Before the recruit could say, "The private has no problems, sir," the DI hit him square in the stomach. Yes, the same DI who had grabbed my collar. I later concluded that that the DI was probably prone to domestic violence or someone who liked to punch defenseless individuals. After the punch, the DI shouted, "Everyone, get down and give me twenty-five, for we still have an undisciplined puke with girly skivvies."

Damn. I thought we were done with this madness. However, at the time, I hoped the DI didn't see the smile on my face as I laughed internally because the recruit had the gall to wear polka-dot skivvies. What was he thinking? Today I still chuckle when thinking of the event.

Another time, as we stood on those footlockers, the DI happened upon one individual who said that the private had a problem. The DI shouted, "Speak, recruit." He turned around, pulled down his skivvies, and on his upper ass was a gigantic boil bigger than my fist. The DI shouted, "Holy Joe Schmuckatelli!" They carted him off to the medical platoon, and he didn't graduate with us. Too bad, because he was the fastest in the platoon at running the obstacle course and almost won a race when competing against other platoons, despite a dislocated shoulder.

It was finally my day to graduate, and I felt accomplished. Everyone marched to graduation proud and in unison. On the way, we passed new recruits who experienced what we had approximately three months before. As they tried to march, the drill instructor for the recruits commanded, "Left, right, left, right," and then said, "Okay, herd, stop!" Some of the new recruits might have thought that we were a well-oiled machine as we marched by. Similar to my thoughts when I was a new recruit and saw a platoon in third phase strut by. As we passed the new recruits, I wondered if there was perhaps, someone who would eventually venture to the dirt pit as many times as I did.

During graduation, I knew my mother was present as well as my sisters. The ceremony started with a movie that displayed some of the training we'd endured in boot camp. I was proud, especially thinking back to when I was knocked off the pitcher's mound in Little League, dropped out of high school, lost the love of my life, and failed the opportunity to be a patrol boy. Not to mention the other challenges I faced. During the movie, tears came to my eyes. Boot camp finally ended, and I shook hands with the DIs, except the one who had grabbed my collar. I said goodbye to the individual with whom I smoked weed with prior to AFES and wished him farewell, and I have never seen him again.

After the graduation ceremony and after I had shaken hands with departing recruits, several marines mentioned that I looked best in my uniform. I was on my way out of the gate and on my way home for ten days' leave. I was thirty pounds lighter, and I'd developed muscle tone in my arms, and my chest was larger. From a physical standpoint, the dirt and exercise pit weren't all that bad, and I laughed. I transitioned from a hood rat to a recruit and then a marine. I thought I was just someone from the hood who'd accomplished an important goal. I got my chance to fulfill a childhood dream to be an "army man," as I called it. However, the issues I faced would further challenge my life in the United States Marine Corps.

Chapter 7

THE REAL MARINE CORPS

T he real Marine Corps created new challenges for me. I was still a seventeen-year-old trying to figure out life without a role model to follow other than the Marine Corps. I didn't think about what I needed to accomplish to be successful at anything, nor did I have the wherewithal or knowledge for a successful life.

After boot camp and my ten days' leave, I reported to ammunition-storage training at the Army base, Redstone Arsenal in Alabama. Imagine that, someone who couldn't manage to take a movie projector to the office, failed at an attempt to become a patrol boy, took money from his mama's purse, was a failure at the rifle range, didn't pass the swimming survival test, and a number of other issues, was sent to handle explosives. Perhaps the GTC score and the inclination to obtain a guarantee before volunteering to enlist in the military helped.

As part of my MOS, I was in training to care, store, and, in some cases, destroy ammunition. While in Alabama, I was happy that I enlisted in the marines, which gave me the opportunity to see the world. Nonetheless, I remember the flight and landing in Alabama and observing all the cotton fields, some of which were near the airport runway. Seeing the cotton fields was somewhat discouraging. When thinking about attending training in Alabama, I remember the conversations between my father and my uncles about the challenges black men faced in the southern United States, especially during the 1960s. These discussions included lynching black men, segregation, separate drinking fountains, and of course, the challenges Dr. Martin Luther King, Jr., faced during the civil rights movement, which for me didn't seem that long ago. In addition to Dr. Martin Luther King Jr, my influences from the past were the Black Panthers, Medgar Evers, Muhammad Ali, Malcom X, Motown, and others, and I thought that my attitude would be a problem for me while in Alabama. Shucks, the first book I read was Soul on Ice by Eldridge Cleaver. Afraid of facing challenges while in Alabama, I thought about staying in the barracks most of the time. I was a few months away from my eighteenth birthday.

At Redstone Arsenal ammunition training school, I was in a class with about twenty marines right out of boot camp and a few who reenlisted. It was important that I passed the class to avoid retaking it or getting orders for infantry training. I was amazed at the difference between boot camp and the real Marine Corps. No more "Yes, sir." No more marching, for the most part, and for me, most importantly, no more dirt or exercise pit. Everyone was more relaxed.

While at Redstone Arsenal, of course, I gravitated toward individuals who had challenges with conforming to the system, like those I hung out with while living in Ohio. One individual, Duke, was cool and knew all the slang words. He was from New York and had the accent. He walked like a person from New York as well. Duke was a good dancer and a womanizer. The other person was Jones, who was from Los Angeles, California. He was a player as well. At that time, females weren't on my radar; my only experiences had been with the girl next door with the pickled-beets breath, the lost love of my life in sixth grade (by my own hands), and the girl next door in Ohio.

Looking back, I now call Duke, Jones, and me the Three Musketeers. The three of us, among others, spent ample time in the enlisted men's club after hours. Ladies' night was fun. I was shy and didn't know what to do with a female. I attempted to pretend as if I were a player like Duke and Jones; however, my lack of savvy eventually "came out in the wash," a saying my mother often conveyed. Eventually, we became bored and took partying to the streets of Huntsville, Alabama. Another individual, Russ, attempted to associate with us; however, Duke didn't like him. One day I suck-er-punched Russ in the face because the other two Musketeers didn't like him. Here I displayed a follower mentality, and my action was an attempt to better relate with Duke and Jones, like my days as a youth moving to a new neighborhood or attending a new school.

Eventually, Russ and I became somewhat good friends after training school. Both of us had orders to the same duty station after ammunition training school. Looking back, Russ was a good guy, and my actions during training school were unfounded. Russ should've kicked my ass; he was stocky enough to accomplish it.

During the Three Musketeer escapades, I learned that Alabama was nothing like I'd feared, except for one occasion. One day, the Three Musketeers went to buy something from a small convenience store near the military base. A police person (omitting "officer" for a reason) entered and asked if "the niggers" were giving the clerk any problems. Of course, I heard the comment. Other than that, I didn't experience any racial problems while in Alabama. Nonetheless, challenges shaking my past and adjusting to military life became evident.

One night, the Three Musketeers were partying, and we bor-rowed Corporal Jenkins's car; he was in the same class as the rest of us at the ammunition school. We wanted to find a juke joint in the country because most of the nightclubs in the city had closed. Duke had a driver's license, and we cruised around town asking if someone knew where there was a juke joint. I asked an individual standing on the corner if he could help us find a juke joint, and he said, "Sure." He jumped in the car and proceeded to gave us direc-tions to a location in the country. We gave him some of our wine, which was a condition for leading us to the juke joint. The individ-ual asked us to drive down a long dark country dirt road. We drove around for a while, and it became apparent the individual was more interested in the wine rather than leading us to the joint. All of a sudden, we heard a thump, and the car stopped moving. Duke exited the vehicle to assess the damage. We'd hit a dirt mound and were stuck. We tried rocking the car to no avail; however, the individual giving us directions was sipping on the wine and began to walk away. Duke was cursing, and he grabbed him and punched him in the face.

Next, Jones joined. By my hands, the individual was beaten with a huge tree limb I had grabbed. He lay unconscious in a fetal position, and the beating didn't stop. Finally, we walked to the main road and hitchhiked back to the base.

In the morning, we told Corporal Jenkins where his car was and expected him to retrieve it. However, Corporal Jenkins told Sergeant Mills (both African Americans) what had happened. Sergeant Mills commanded that we retrieve the car at all costs. "And don't come back without it." I came to my senses about what had taken place the night before, and I was scared that when we found the location, the beaten individual would be dead. Phillip, a Caucasian individual who had a red hot rod, helped us find the car. I was relieved to find that the beaten individual was gone, and so was the wine bottle he'd consumed before the beating took place. There were bloodstains on the ground. Believe me, the memory disturbs me today. We retrieved the car and had to reimburse Corporal Jenkins for the damages over the course of a few paydays. At this time, it appeared that fool's hill wasn't in sight, and I wasn't thinking about making the ascent as my grandmother believed I would. The event described here was in preparation for my journey and discovering the why.

Eventually, I was successful completing ammunitions training in Alabama and had orders to report to Camp Pendleton in California. I was proud; in addition to boot camp, I'd finally accomplished something. While I was at Redstone Arsenal, I passed the course for the six-thousand-pound-capacity forklift. I was so proud, and I wished my parents could see my accomplishment. In fact, I was so proud that while driving the forklift, I leaned to the side, like when I drove a car in the hood or attempted to drive one. On one occasion on that forklift, I hit an outlet on a utility pole, and the sparks began to fly.

After graduating from Redstone Arsenal, on my way to California, I decided to stop by my neighborhood in Ohio and visit some of the old gang members. Duke joined me. We made amends with Corporal Jenkins, and he drove us part of the way. We partied one night with Corporal Jenkins and afterward Duke, and I hitchhiked to my old neighborhood in Ohio. I wanted to see my brother, but I discovered he was in jail. He had returned to Ohio while he was still a minor and continued the error of his ways. Today he is a deacon for a church.

The first night while in Ohio, I didn't visit my stepfather. I found some of my old gang members and hung out with them instead. A mistake. Eventually, we went to the store and bought some wine. One of the individuals took us to a place where we could buy some windowpane acid, a hallucinogen. We were partying, and Duke and I took a hit of the acid. For me, the acid was a bad trip. I had on a long brown coat like the one I'd used to steal albums when I was younger and lived in Ohio. That brown coat had a belt that became detached while we were partying. A person told me it was a snake, and I began freaking out. We were on about the sixth floor, and an individual threw the belt out the window and asked me to check and see what happened to it. I looked out the window, and proceeded to climb out and stand on the window ledge. One individual asked me to jump. Stoned, not realizing that I was on the sixth floor ledge, I almost jumped. The drug began to wear off, and finally I realized where I was standing and quickly averted the jump. Another brush with death. Meanwhile, those inside were laughing at me, and one said, "The dumb mothershucker almost jumped." We were supposedly friends. He was the same individual I ran down the alley with while being shot at and the same individual with whom I stole the minibikes. Last, I heard, he was a deacon in a church.

At any rate, still somewhat high from the windowpane acid, Duke and I managed to make it to my stepfather's house. We made it to my old hangout in the basement and tried to sleep. Almost instantly, I felt as if I was in a deep pit, and the drug wore off completely. We slept, got up the next morning, and left without almost any conversation with my stepfather. Duke caught the bus home to New York, and I took the Greyhound bus to California.

The Three Musketeers all had orders to report to Camp Pendleton in California, which was approximately forty miles from my home in San Diego. Upon arriving, Duke, Jones, and I hung out for a while. Jones finally went absent without official leave (AWOL) and went back to Alabama. While in training school at Redstone Arsenal, he got someone pregnant and she gave birth, so he had a child in Alabama. The last time I saw Jones, he was hanging out in front of a Greyhound bus station in California. Before enlisting in the marines, he claimed to be a hustler; however, I do believe, from his appearance at the bus station, his life took a drastic turn for the worse. In passing, I don't believe he recognized me.

Someone told me that Duke was strung out on drugs. I also heard, while he was walking guard duty one night, he decided to steal rifles from the armory and sold them to an undercover agent, perhaps to support his addiction. Duke was sentenced to prison, and while he was in there, I heard he killed someone, which extended his sentence. Later Duke sent me a letter and it appeared to be from a prison.

And then there was me. I had problems adjusting to military life. After boot camp, typically, it took about six months for someone to earn that first stripe or rank. Some can earn that first stripe before leaving boot camp. It took eighteen months for me to earn that first stripe. For the first eighteen months, I worked in a warehouse instead of a munitions storage facility. This was during the end of the Vietnam War. I worked in the receiving department and processed incoming shipments that had items from the war. Some of the armor that marines wore had blood, hair, and dried skin. Some of the dental instruments still had teeth attached to the tools. The stench was unbearable. In addition, almost every night, I heard an ambulance as it carted someone away because of a drug overdose. Some marines returning from Vietnam brought demons back with them. I was barely eighteen years old, and it was an interesting experience for me.

At Camp Pendleton, there was some racial unrest. A white staff sergeant had a dislike for me. He often said that if I were in Vietnam, he would have made sure I was on the front lines until I met my demise. I thought, *Yes, and if I were in Vietnam, you might wake up one morning with a fragmentation grenade under your pillow with the pin already pulled.* An ammunition specialist sometimes had access to munitions while on field maneuvers and I do believe the same applied to those in Vietnam. I asked why he had a dislike for me. He said it was because of my calm demeanor, which was mostly my outside appearance but not the case internally. The latter is a learned behavior that I use today, calmness as opposed to chaos in most uncomfortable situations. Anyway, the staff sergeant lived up to his promise, though: while performing field maneuvers, I would be on the front line next to other infantrymen. I guess my mother was partly right; the reason she was opposed to me volunteering to enlist in the military was individuals such as this sergeant.

Remember, I had a guarantee before volunteering to serve in the military. That guarantee was for occupational specialties that supported the infantry. However; while we were performing amphibious operations for maneuvers, the staff sergeant ordered that I disembark from the side of a ship and climb down a net like the other infantryman. This was different from other field maneuvers in which I disembarked the ship from Mike boats and hit the beach in the same manner as other supply personnel. Anyway, while I was climbing down the net, the ship was teetering and this was an unfamiliar situation, especially for someone who wasn't accustomed to exiting a ship in this manner. It was somewhat scary for me because the net was slamming against the ship. Other marines who I assume were in the infantry were on the net as well which made matters worse. There was yelling and chaos, and I thought I was going to fall into the water or fall into the Mike boat. Certainly, my fear of heights didn't help. Eventually, that staff sergeant had orders for another duty station and that was the end of that.

Nevertheless, on another occasion, there was another staff sergeant who had a dislike for me as well as other African Americans in our unit. One day, he mouthed off from a window while we, the African American males, were playing basketball near the barracks, a favorite pastime for us. The next morning, he found his motorcycle, which he'd parked near a window by the barracks, on its side. The bike was damaged and leaking fuel. After that day, I never saw that staff sergeant again.

At Camp Pendleton, I was exposed to the "dap." "Dap" is a handshake or form of greeting that as far as I know, was developed in the African American communities. I wondered what the dap meant.

Someone finally explained how the dap was developed and mostly used by black soldiers in Vietnam. Each hand gesture had a meaning.

As far as I know, DAP stood for "Dignity And Pride." Before entering or leaving the mess hall, most of the African American marines checked in and out with one another using the dap. If meeting or passing another male African American marine on the base or in town, checking in using the dap was commonplace. Today, if greeting another African American, some use what one might call the N-word nod. A slight gesture of nodding that is similar to the dap when greeting another African American.

In addition, while on base and an African American marine met another African American, the individual threw the Black Power sign (clenched fist over one's head), and then placed his fist over the heart beating it twice. The expectation was that all African American marines performed the ritual if they wanted to be accepted. The actions denoted unity principally important for those who served in Vietnam, especially if an individual experienced challenges like I faced from a staff sergeant who didn't like my demeanor or other attributes about me, for whatever reason. Today, I see individuals using variations of the dap, mostly on television or those playing sports. Those variations include bumping elbows, hip bumping, and elongated handshakes like the dap. However, most don't know the dap's history or have an understanding of the significance, mostly important to African American soldiers during the Vietnam era. My experience in the military resembled the days in the hood surrounding the civil rights era and wanting to be a Black Panther or an individual fighting for civil rights or equality. In the hood I saw individuals wearing uniforms, like the Black Panthers, which I thought was cool. Back then, I thought they were the semblance of a black army man, and I wanted to be one later in life.

One of the challenges of military life for me was getting a haircut. The grooming regulation affirmed that a marine's hair must graduate zero inches from the ears to three inches on top, which reminded me of the soup-bowl cut I wore as a child while in Ohio. Often in the Marine Corps, I grew my hair as long as I wanted. That time was an era of rebellion, which exacerbated my nonconformist demeanor. I finally squared myself away concerning the hair issue and then decided to pierce my ear. I put an ice cube on it for a period, put a potato behind it, heated a needle, and then pierced my earlobe. However, I pierced the wrong ear. At that time, piercing the right ear was taboo for males. Oops. I then pierced the left ear. I reported to formations with a Band-Aid on my left ear that had a piece of straw to keep the hole open. That was a no-no. Today, that ear still has the hole from my military days.

During that time, I was sometimes late to formation, especially after partying all night. One payday, some of us drove to Tijuana, Mexico (TJ). Being from San Diego, I had ventured to TJ many times before my enlistment. During one escapade, while in the Marine Corps, I wanted to go there to party; however, the others wanted to pay for sex. We found that special house, and I couldn't imagine paying someone twenty dollars for sex. I paid the fee and went to a room. She said I was no good for her, and she could only satisfy me orally. "You no good, you no good," she kept stating. Perhaps my 13 EEE shoe size was why she kept making those comments. Anyway, I left the room and donated the twenty dollars. I pretended that I went through with the act, pulling up my pants and adjusting my belt.

Afterward, we started terrorizing the town and getting drunk. Soon after, what seemed like twenty police cars arrived. They handcuffed us and threw us in the car. It seemed like there were ten policemen in the car with us. Having frequented TJ, I knew that money talked. Everyone paid them twenty dollars. They took us to the border, about where we'd left the car, and opened the car doors. They gestured that we should get out, and I think they cursed us out in Spanish. One thing I understood was, "Don't come back." We returned to Camp Pendleton and, about an hour later, had to report to formation, wobbling from alcohol consumption and from the events of the night before. In my estimation, we were performing like marines should. Consuming alcohol in my youth and now the Marine Corps was commonplace.

During my enlistment at Camp Pendleton, I had run-ins with the law. On one occasion, I was in town walking past a driveway near a fast-food restaurant. A car almost hit me, and the individual started giving me lip. Wrong choice. I reached in the car and started beating the individual. A female was in the car, screaming. I thought nothing about the incident, and the police didn't show up. After I had walked around town for a while, a barrage of police cars surrounded me. They asked me to get on the ground. The beaten individual was in the back of the car. They took me to jail. At that time, I thought, imagine that, I almost got hit by a car, the guy mouthed me off, and I went to jail. Justice was served I believed. The individual didn't press charges; however, the car that almost hit me and was a deadly weapon in my estimation.

While I was stationed at Camp Pendleton, a Hispanic marine and I worked in the same unit. He drove from the base to San Diego every day and asked if I wanted to carpool and share the cost. I accepted the offer because I didn't want to sleep in the barracks, participate in field days, and clean the bathrooms. Therefore, carpooling presented an opportunity for me to live off base.

In the meantime, I sometimes associated with an African American marine who had spent time in Vietnam. I asked him if he knew where I could buy a handgun. He said he did and asked if I had a ride. I asked the Hispanic gentleman if I could borrow his car. "Certainly," he replied. Off the base, we went to buy the handgun. I wanted to buy a gun because someone had broken into my locker and stolen my clothes. I had an idea who he was, and with the gun, I would approach him and retrieve my clothes. Anyway, off we went to purchase the handgun. On the way, we stopped by the liquor store and then scored a controlled substance. We went to about three houses, which I later found were places for him to buy drugs with my money. I also found later that he was a junkie.

We stopped to indulge in the controlled substance. I was driving the individual's car I'd borrowed, controlled substance in the trunk, open beer containers in the car, one in my hand. I ran a stop sign in front of the police. The red lights came on. I tried to hide the beer, but to no avail. They smelled the controlled substance and searched the car and found it in the trunk. The police handcuffed both of us, took us to jail, and impounded the individual's car.

Here we go, back to jail. I clearly remember the processing and remember them checking every orifice. In jail, I remember the lousy food, well below the quality of the food when I was in juvenile hall. The next day, I was released. They tried to charge us with possession; however, the car wasn't registered to me, and the controlled substance was in the trunk. When asked who owned the controlled substance, of course, the junkie and I blamed each other. Eventually, they dropped the possession charges and gave me tickets for running a stop sign and the open container in the car.

Nonetheless, after I was released from jail in the morning, I wasn't in formation again, and a gunnery sergeant whom I hated made a public announcement that I was in jail. Upon returning to the base, I found out, and man, was I furious! I walked around the base looking for the gunnery sergeant. My intent was to kick his ass, seriously. It was probably a good thing that I couldn't find him, because I probably would be imprisoned today.

Concerning the Hispanic marine whose car I borrowed and had impounded, I had the nerve to ask him if he still wanted to carpool. You see, he paid the impound fees for his car. From that point on, I never saw the marine again. Regarding the individual who took my money to buy drugs, one night, I modified a barbell and wrapped it with red and white tape, like the colors used for my Levi's jacket when I briefly ran with the gang in Ohio. I was on my way to give the individual a blanket party while he was sleeping. I was going to beat his brains out. While I was on the way, something told me to turn around and go back to my barracks. Overall, for the junkie, the individual who broke into my locker, and me, it was probably a good thing I wasn't able to buy the handgun.

One day, I was escorted to the judge advocate's building, and I wondered why. While there, I was arrested for not paying the traffic tickets that I'd received for running the stop sign and the open container in the car. I stayed in jail, and my mother drove to Oceanside to pay the bail after court, an embarrassing event, as I think of it constantly. I paid my mother back with interest. Was my grandmother right about fool's hill?

At Camp Pendleton, I continued doing stupid things. One day, one of my poker-playing buddies asked if I knew how to cut hair. "Yes, of course," I replied. All he needed was someone to trim the hair on his neckline. I did a good job. The word got out that I knew how to cut hair. An individual had an inspection in the morning and didn't have time to get a haircut in town. He needed more than just a trim, and I was confident that I could help him. When finished, his head looked like a dog that had the mange. I didn't know how he fared in the inspection. I gave him his money back, and the individual never spoke to me again. He eventually went to the barber who repaired my damage.

I continued to find ways to push the envelope while in the military. Anyway, I was once on KP duty and assigned to wash dishes in the scullery. I was in charge and did a good job keeping the dishes clean and making sure that scullery was spotless at the end of the day. A platoon sergeant heard about it and said that the only time I did a good job was when someone put me in charge of something. In the interim, I discovered that the lock on the back window in the mess hall was broken. On occasions, I raided the food storage lockers and the freezers late at night when I was hungry. Most of the time, I took the food back to the barracks and we feasted, especially on the weekends. I was well-liked by my peers because I found ways to get food whenever. It reminds me of when I was in elementary school; to treat my friends, I had taken money from my mother's purse to buy snacks.

In the military, I never told anyone where I obtained the food but most could probably figure it out. Others living in the barracks didn't have the nerve to enter the mess hall after hours and take-I mean, steal-food. On one incident, I took some food so we could watch football and feast in the barracks over the weekend. I stole several canned hams, and everyone was eating sandwiches with, mayo and mustard. We drank beer in the barracks as well, which wasn't allowed. Then came early Monday morning, when the duty officer made his round. There were empty ham cans scattered about the lounging area in addition to other stuff we had accumulated while watching games. No one snitched, and for the duty officer, the empty cans remained a mystery. After about six months, someone finally fixed the window, and the feasts ended.

A noteworthy experience while at Camp Pendleton during my early years was the opportunity to work at tent city on a temporary detail. Tent city was a remote location for Vietnam refugees. I had fun especially with the children. Interestingly, the Vietnamese children rated an individual by the calluses on a male's hand. Immediately when meeting someone, they examined the calluses on an individual's hand, mostly the one on the right. If the calluses were large, they rated you number ten. If you didn't have calluses, your rating was number one. The higher the rating, the greater your worth, denoting a hard worker. I was awarded a Humanitarian Service Medal for my work with the Vietnamese refugees in the tent city, an early accomplishment. Today, I have pictures with some of the children, and I still have the money they gave me, which is worthless because of the defunct South Vietnamese government.

After working at tent city, I was finally transferred to a remote location on the base. Most of the individuals in the unit were shit birds, or individuals who had challenges in other units. There was a reason I was sent there. One day, I jumped on a forklift and thought I could drive one (the forklift was smaller than the larger one I'd driven at Redstone Arsenal in Alabama). I put a big hole in the wall. Everyone was laughing. I didn't have a forklift license for that particular model at that time, and luckily, I had the skill to fix the wall thanks to the handiness that I'd acquired prior to the military. After the repairs, no one could determine that the wall had been damaged. One individual complimented me on my skill. Nonetheless, someone snitched. Soon after, I had orders to a desolate area on the base.

One day, I was playing basketball for physical training and heard a pop near my big toe. The next day, I went to sick call, and the corpsman couldn't believe how big my foot was from the swelling. Back then, medical staff didn't take X-rays; however, for two months, I could barely walk. Today I suffer from an ailment in that foot and can barely walk sometimes. However, the Veterans Administration claimed the damage in my foot didn't happen while I was in the military, but my records proved them wrong. All I can mention at this point is that I "donated" the damage to my foot to serving in the United States Marine Corps.

After transferring to the remote location, most of the time, I kept to myself. I played basketball almost every day and was slowed by the foot injury, but I continued to play. Two individuals approached me one day and asked why I didn't attend college to play basketball. "It wasn't my calling," I replied.

Eventually JP, another marine befriended me, and we hung out often. He was shorter in stature and was an avid weed smoker. I believe he and I became friends because I was much taller and could serve as protection if adverse situations arose. JP and I had the same MOS. One night, he and I were lurking around a lone path that was poorly lit, and a Caucasian marine was walking from the bus stop, heading to the barracks. Suddenly, I jumped him and started beating him. I made him give me his wallet, and he did. He started crying and asked us not to kill him. Keep in mind that, we were on the base. I grabbed the wallet, and we took off running. In the wallet was six dollars. If caught, I could've faced serious consequences for six dollars and more so for the act. Looking back, again, it is a regrettable experience in my life.

JP and I had orders to a remote duty station at Camp Pendleton. The duty station was the best place to work on the base considering our MOS. I finally had an opportunity to work in my field as an ammunitions specialist. The unit was close-knit and the group mostly consisted of Caucasian marines, like the previous location where I had been transferred. The single marines lived in quarters versus barracks or squad bays. Two or three individuals lived in rooms. I had arrived. JP and I were the only African Americans in the unit. At that time, in the Marine Corps, individuals of the Caucasian race typically occupied an ammunitions specialist unit. In the early 1970s, the Marine Corps goal was to integrate the occupation specialty. I speculate that JP, the other African Americans in my class at Redstone Arsenal, and I were the pioneers in the government's attempt to accomplish the integration goal.

However, my antics weren't a good representation of someone who could handle explosives, a tremendous responsibility. JP and I were new to the job at the remote location. Both of us were assigned different rooms. After about three weeks, individuals just out of boot camp were assigned to our unit. A couple of them were African Americans. One night, someone lit a marijuana joint, and everyone was getting high. Suddenly, the military police showed and confiscated the weed. The situation was a big ordeal, lights flashing, drug-sniffing dogs running, and turmoil. The next week, someone snitched saying that the weed belonged to JP and me. Believe me: it wasn't mine.

I received a message to report to the commander's office, and they said that I was going to have an Article 15, which was a hearing for violating military law. A few days later, I was transported to the main base, which was miles away from my duty location. It was time for my Article 15 with an officer, which the marines called office hours. Of all the disorderly conduct while in the military, this was my first office hours. I entered the room in military style-uniform pressed and starched, which it always was. The officer proceeded with the evidence and my punishment. He said, based on the evidence, that I would be fined, earn extra duty, and be restricted to the barracks.

The officer asked if I had any comments. I said, "Not guilty." My comments were that the marijuana wasn't mine and was in a common area. "The room wasn't mine, and if your decision is final, I request a court-martial in accordance with Article 15 of the Uniform Code of Military Justice." I was at attention and didn't establish eye contact with the officer.

He looked at the paperwork for a minute while I was locked at attention. There was silence, and to paraphrase, he said, "Get out of here, mothershucker! Charges dropped, and I had better not see you again." I did my about-face and marched out of his office in elation. The ride back to my duty station was a relief. Soon after, I had orders to transfer to another duty station. I thought it had something to do with a potential dope-smoking marine handling explosives. However, I went to the dentist in the same location. The dentist, an African American was in the navy, part of the corpsmen (navy medical personnel). The smell of marijuana on his hands was pungent. As

I think back, he did a good job, however I am fortunate I didn't leave the dentist office resembling a walrus and or a similar creature, long in the tooth if you know what I mean.

At my new duty station, one day, I received a message to report to the admin office. The clerk said that I had orders to transfer to Okinawa, Japan. In other words, the Rock. I'd heard stories about the Rock, and I wasn't enthused about going. The tour of duty was for thirteen months. In a few days, I had another message to report to the admin office, and the clerk said that they'd made a mistake-my orders were for the Marine Corps Air Station, Kaneohe Bay, Hawaii, on the island of Oahu. The tour of duty was for two years. I cracked a big smile. *Me, Hawaii, yay!*

At that time, I'd always wanted a boom box with a cassette player. An individual who bunked upstairs had a nice one with a television. One day, while visiting a friend upstairs, I noticed where he put his wall locker keys. Periodically, while preparing for my move to Hawaii and in the barracks alone, I found the keys and opened the locker and the boom box was in there. Then came the day for me to go on leave before transferring to Hawaii. In the barracks, all alone, I struck. I put the boom box in my duffel bag and was off for ten days' leave before reporting to Hawaii. I felt redeemed for someone breaking into my wall locker and stealing my clothes during my first week of being stationed at Camp Pendleton. Today, I deem it an invalid justification. Back then, I would steal the eyelets in someone's shoes if they weren't tied down. When I transferred to Hawaii, I'd been in the marines for about three years and was only an E-3.

JP and I arrived in Hawaii about the same time. I took out my boom box, and he asked me where I'd obtained it. I said that I'd bought it while on leave. We took that boom box everywhere, especially to the softball games when the females played. Finally, I traded the boom box for a set of speakers.

While I was in Hawaii, a first sergeant immediately promoted me to an E-4. He said, "I don't care what happened while you were in the States. This is a new start." I was now a noncommissioned officer. I believed Hawaii was a new start.

Hawaii I imagined, a better place than the Rock, Okinawa, Japan. The weather was always warm, and it was a beautiful place. I thought Hawaii was a party place. The legal drinking age was eighteen, and the package store (place to buy liquor on base) was a stone's throw from my barracks. After drinking, occasionally I got into fights after ladies' night at the enlisted men's club. I was at ladies' night to party, not because I was a ladies' man. At that time, I was too shy to meet females, let alone have a girlfriend. I thought the Polynesian females on the island were beautiful, though.

At that point in my life, I had little experience having sex with females. However, when I was younger, I'd discovered XXX-rated books hidden by a parent in the house. Reading those XXX-rated books was an experience. When I was younger, a parent visited the adult bookstore, and I was allowed to walk around inside. In addition, many of those books I found in the house I read from cover to cover. Back then I believed those books were what sex was supposed to be between a man and a woman. Instead of a discussion with my parents about sexual relationships with a female, XXX-rated books were my introduction. No talks about the birds and the bees from a male perspective. Later in life, when rearing my own children, I explained the birds and the bees to my son, but I could've done a better job. I do believe he understood what I said. I regret not doing the same with my daughters, but I thought my wife at that time was responsible for that. My children fared well regardless.

Early in my life, there were a few black females on television-Diahann Carroll, Teresa Graves, Bern Nadette Stanis, Nichelle Nichols, and Ja'Net Dubois-the foxiest. I loved them all and they were on my favorite shows. Otherwise, my reference points were the XXX-rated books and Caucasian females on television. However, I might say that my mother and aunts were some of the most beautiful African American females one could encounter. I even had a crush on one aunt. Besides the discussion here, I might add that my sisters were and are beautiful Nubian females, especially when I look at pictures from the past. In looking back, I might add, parents, it doesn't matter what you hide in the house-children will find it! I did, including cigarettes, money, handguns, and XXX-rated books.

Back in Hawaii, concerning females. On one occasion in Hawaii, several of us went to a nightclub in town on a payday. I was feeling good, and everyone wanted to leave. I didn't know how I was going to make it back to the base and asked that everyone go ahead and I would see them later. I caught the eye of a local Caucasian female, and we had a few dances. I asked her for a ride to the base, and she said that I could stay at her place. I was bold enough then to say, "All right." She drove me to her place, started undressing, and then got into bed. I joined her and thought, *Oh, shit, what am I going to do now?*

Immediately she began crying and said, "Don't beat me. Don't beat me." I was dumbfounded and scared shitless, and I calmed her down. All I thought about was one of those movies like *To Kill a Mocking Bird.* I slept on the couch, and next thing I knew, it was early morning. She gave me a ride to the base. It was still dark, and I decided to lie against a chain-link fence and take a breather before going to the barracks. Next, all I heard was "Left, right, left, right," and marines were marching in formation all around me as I lay against the fence. I was fortunate to have guard duty at that time and didn't have to report to formation. I ran upstairs, shaved, changed clothes, and reported to the guard shack. That day, our unit had a day for a picnic, and I was assigned to answer phones in the commanding officer's office. I slept most of the time, and on my mind was that female asking me not to beat her, which produced disturbing thoughts.

In another situation in Hawaii, I was riding my bike on a partly constructed freeway that led to the main gate at the Marine Corps Air Station. A plainclothes military detective approached me after reentering the base and asked some questions. He ordered that I meet him at his office because he wanted to take my picture for a rape case-lineup. Allegedly, a black male raped a white female, and the detective needed my picture as part of the lineup. I complied, but note here that that detective was rude and acted in a threatening manner. He took my pictures, and that was the last time I saw that asshole, but these were the first and second incidents concerning Caucasian females. I'll describe others later in this book.

Anyway, the duty station in Hawaii was a decision point for me. I had little time left in the Marine Corps and wasn't sure about my future and was undecided about what came next regarding my career and life. It reminded me of the time my mother threatened to throw me out of the house. I felt the same pressure at that time. I could opt to discharge or reenlist in the Marine Corps.

I decided to clean up my act and make a new start. Although I smoked about a quarter pack of cigarettes per day, I began a structured physical fitness regime and was always in shape. My uniform was always pressed, and I was squared away. Most of the time, I was on time to formation. I was trying to change the error of my ways and integrate to military life. Most of the challenges I faced were off base and not while on duty, except for one more.

One day, I was observing a softball game and didn't have an alliance or a familiarization with either teams playing. Nonetheless, I rooted for one team, and they won. Next, a fan of the opposing team, a marine, approached me in an aggressive manner and said, "You had a big mouth during the game, and what about your big mouth now?" I was in a semi-inclined position, resting on my elbows while on the bleachers. All of a sudden, he punched me in the face. I was confused as to his actions and struggled to get up and defend myself. I had a six-pack of Löwenbräu beer purchased from the package store. When I was finally on my feet, individuals separated us. I was pissed. I struggled to get at the individual who'd hit me unexpectedly. I had a few unopened beer bottles within arm's reach. I grabbed one of the bottles of beer and hit the individual over the head with the full beer bottle. I was amazed because the bottle didn't break. He fell to the ground with blood rushing out of his head. I jumped in my car and headed to the gate and was able to make it home without intervention from the military police. This was a Friday afternoon, and I had the weekend to think about what took place.

On Wednesday morning of the next week, the MPs didn't arrest me, but they questioned me and then drove me to the unit of the marine who'd attacked me. An officer in a closed room asked me what had happened. I gave the officer the facts and said that those at the game could be witnesses. He showed me pictures of the individual who'd attacked me before he had been admitted to the hospital. From the looks of it, it appeared that blood gushed from his head. The pictures were grotesque. He also showed me pictures as he lay in the hospital. I said that none of this would've happened if the individual hadn't attacked me and that he was probably drunk. His comments were, "I could pursue this and throw your ass in the brig. Get out of here, and I'd better not see your face again. You're free to go. Dismissed!" I did an about-face and smiled as I walked out of the door. The event reminded me of the time when I was in office hours for the marijuana charges.

It was a long walk back to my section of the base. I never saw the officer, the individual, and that side of the base again. However, I was involved in two more fights before leaving the base, and I'll say that the individuals I fought with weren't the victors. Fortunately, none of the individuals were from the unit the marine who'd received the blow to the head. So much for trying to make improvements in my life. It seemed like trouble followed me, and I wondered why. My efforts to traverse fool's hill weren't looking good.

While stationed in Hawaii, I visited home in San Diego several times on leave, but I was getting island fever. It was time to go back to the States. On one occasion, while on leave in San Diego, I borrowed my mother's car and decided to have a good time. One too many drinks, and I was charged with driving under the influence, which was later reduced to reckless driving. On another visit, I wrecked my mother's car. This time, I wasn't creating havoc, and my nephew and niece were in the car. For both events, I made restitution, including attorney fees, fines, and the cost to repair my mom's car.

Back in Hawaii, after I'd seen the same places repeatedly, it was starting to affect my psyche. Truthfully, I was bored. With the thought that I might not reenlist, I enrolled in a locksmith school. At that time, rules were lax regarding the locksmithing tools one could buy. I finally finished the course with the hopes of opening a locksmith shop one day. After finishing the course, I bought some locksmithing supplies, including books that contained combinations to locks. I bought another tool in which I could learn how to open soda machines. I was learning how to pick locks. Also, I made keys and had a small key-making machine. Eventually, I completed the advanced locksmith course as well. At that time, I was dating a local girl and told her brother about my tools. One day, we discussed going on a rampage and opening soft drink machines. I was supposed to meet him one night, but that never came to fruition.

However, before leaving the island, I enlisted for four more years. At that time, I was concerned about my future. After all, the marines provided three hots and a cot (a place to eat and sleep). Before reenlisting, I decided to obtain my high school diploma. I had to weigh the factors of giving up on partying or sitting in classes and earning my high school diploma. I thought, my father didn't have a high school diploma, and at that time, it appeared that he was doing well. After all, I made it this far without a high school diploma. I debated the importance of earning one.

I decided to go for it and gave up the nightlife to earn my high school diploma. I attended classes, where I was the only African American, a situation that I became accustomed to while embarking on my future education endeavors. The classes were challenging; but I didn't mind attending because I had a crush on the instructor. I came to find that she was married and had three children. During the classes, I was quiet and never asked for help. If faced with a problem, I eventually figured it out myself. I finally graduated, and it was one of the exceptional accomplishments in my life. Although I graduated three years after the original date for my high school graduation, I was happy. Party time. My diploma displays that I graduated from a high school in Honolulu, Hawaii.

Hawaii was where I married someone twelve years my senior. She'd lived in California previously. After we had dated for a while, I found that she was involved in a serious domestic violence case concerning a self-defense issue that was disturbing for me. Nonetheless, I took the risk. However, looking back, marriage was something I should've waited to pursue. Marriage life presented a different challenge. I wondered how I could pursue life with the added responsibility. Because of my experience with life, relationships, and marriage, while consulting with my son about marriage, I recommended that he wait until he was thirty years old. Find yourself before marriage was my message.

My time was up in Hawaii, and it was time to return to the States. Again, the Marine Corps attempted to send me to Okinawa, the Rock. I whined and called my monitor in Washington, DC. My monitor changed my orders to the Marine Corps Recruit Depot in San Diego. Drill instructor (DI), yeah, right. An assignment to the drill field was for those who maintained a good service record for a period. At that time, I earned a medal for good conduct, which meant I'd stayed out of trouble for at least three years. Drill instructors represent the personification of the Marine Corps. I accepted, and in hindsight, returning home was probably not a good idea. The next phase represents a drastic change in my life and perhaps one of the most valuable concerning my ascent or descent of fool's hill. Off, I went.

Chapter 8

THE DECLINE AND A
NEW BEGINNING

I was now back in San Diego, challenged with DI school. The six-week school was an abbreviated version of the twelve weeks of boot camp. I didn't know what to expect after graduation. Some of my family missed the boot camp graduation but attended the one for DI school. I was proud to complete DI school and was assigned to the Marine Corps Recruit Depot in San Diego. I had an opportunity to visit the exercise pit, which I spent so much time in as a recruit in boot camp, and memories resurfaced. I also chuckled when thinking about Porky and the challenge he faced at the dining facility.

If successful at completing the two years on the drill field as a DI, one could earn a promotion, but my career in the military took a turn in the opposite direction. My marriage began to take a turn for the worse as well. The partying didn't help. While retuning home wasn't a good idea, the issues might've persisted regardless of my location.

While I was on the drill field and since the time I completed boot camp, things changed. Hazing, to the degree I'd experienced while in boot camp, wasn't accepted. Since my days in boot camp, recruits had experienced serious injuries because of hazing. Some were newsworthy events. Another difference was that recruits now wore tennis shoes and shorts for physical training. In my day, we wore boots and fatigues. I had an M14 rifle, and recruits now use M16s.

After DI school, I was assigned my first platoon but spent insurmountable time partying in San Diego, my home. Several times, I was late reporting for duty. Then I wasn't one who could scream at recruits, and besides I was still shy. Perhaps the DI demeanor deviated from that happy-go-lucky child that I mentioned in the beginning of this book. I recall one incident when I called the recruits to the classroom and taught them a class. I had my DI face on and posed in my command stature. The recruits were sitting on the floor by the DI hooch (office), all in alignment. All had their first haircuts, and for most, I could see their scalps, which brought back memories.

For a period during instruction, there was silence, and one of the shaved-headed recruits farted aloud. The act reminded me of the days when my brother and I tried to determine who could fart the loudest. I began laughing at the memories. Drill instructors don't laugh or crack a smile, and there went my Drill Instructor Sergeant Cubit persona. More importantly I was probably one of the most compassionate DIs, and I believed the recruits could decipher that.

Since I was the junior DI, it was my responsibility to conduct the first-phase marching test; for me, it was a tremendous undertaking. Yes, the same test when I was in boot camp and couldn't resist scratching my nose. To prepare for the test, I practiced with my sword at night at home. To practice for the test with the platoon, I marched the recruits everywhere. In the beginning, I commanded turns on the wrong foot. Most knew I was a rookie. However, whenever marching, recruits follow the DI's every command. One incident, I was marching the platoon and another platoon was approaching our direct path which would've caused a collision. I was calling cadence and became confused. I called for a column left on the wrong foot and almost marched the platoon into a wall. Instead of commanding the platoon to halt then conduct an about-face, I hollered, "Everyone, just stop and turn around!" Eventually, I became proficient at calling cadence while marching the recruits.

Typically, a DI team consists of three marines. Each takes a turn teaching subjects and pulling duty to watch over the recruits at night. One day, while pulling my duty, I walked the barracks as the recruits cleaned the squad bay. The cleaning wasn't to my satisfaction; therefore, like what happened during my time in boot camp, I ordered one recruit to get a bucket of dirt. As the recruit collected the bucket of dirt, an officer walked by and asked what he was doing. The recruit proceeded upstairs with the bucket of dirt. I ordered him to place the bucket in the middle of the head (military name for bathroom), and I kicked it. Dirt went flying. In my military voice, I commanded, "Clean it up, you maggots." Imagine that, applying more dirt in an effort to reinforce cleanliness, the adverse of what one wanted. That afternoon, I was reprimanded for hazing and the dirt-in-the-bathroom act.

A few days later, after I'd spent the night partying, it was time to take the recruits on a run. Usually, I was in good shape physically, but that day, I couldn't keep up. No slime or fishlike punishment like when I was a recruit and dropped out of a run. Quitting in the presence of recruits was sacrilegious. I usually made that run without an issue, but not that day. Again, I was called into the office. The partying continued for me, and at that time, I had been married for approximately eighteen months, and the marriage was just about over.

One day, I was out partying and missed my duty assignment for the day. A day became two, and two days became three. Actually, I was AWOL. I returned and explained my situation and was relieved of duty. I believe the Marine Corps couldn't risk what appeared to be an unstable DI on the field, especially because of the bad press for hazing and other incidents that took place in the past. At this time in my life, I was despondent. I didn't believe I had a grasp on things. Perhaps all the issues of the past were catching up with me. *Why was I in this place?* I wondered. At that time, there was a recommendation that I should attend rehabilitation for drug or alcohol consumption or both. Internally I felt like an amoeba, a single-cell organism without boundaries and no structure, or the blob creature in a 1950s movie that consumed everything it came in contact with. The blob had no form and, in comparison to today's cinematography, appeared to be as nonrealistic as my why.

I was assigned to test proctoring while awaiting orders to transfer from the drill field, and the partying continued. One night before I was transferred, I was out drinking with my brother and driving my first car, a black Pontiac Firebird that had been shipped from Hawaii. While driving through familiar streets, I approached a hill that I used to ride my bike up as a kid. I floored the accelerator, and the car became airborne. I slammed into a parked car. The impact could've killed both of us. Immediately, I put the car in reverse and drove off, tailpipe hanging, sparks flying, and rear bumper partly detached. The drive home was some distance, and I don't remember most of the drive. Another brush with death averted. I ditched the car, called my insurance, and claimed the car had been stolen. Believe me, no one could find the car. From the insurance proceeds, I bought a brand-new customized van that was popular during that time.

I had orders to Camp Pendleton, a tank battalion that was forty miles from San Diego. After duty hours, I drove to San Diego. During this time, I took a part-time job to pay my debts and drove a taxicab at night and on the weekends. My brother drove a taxicab as well. We were two characters sometimes meeting at stores to buy beer.

Many memorable events happened driving that taxicab. On one New Year's Eve, I decided to drive the cab that night. I was in Chula Vista, California, outside the boundary of National City, the area I was assigned. A request for taxi came over the radio for a pickup at a residence. I was in an affluent area, and an older Caucasian male asked me to take him to the Mexican border, specifically TJ which I did. I said that I couldn't drive the taxicab across the border, and he said, "OK, park the cab and leave the meter running."

Once across the border, we caught a taxi, and the individual asked the driver if he knew any place that we could buy sex from a female, however we used a different word for sex. The taxicab driver took us to a part of town where the ladies of the night frequented. There I was, in the same place where I was that night in the Marine Corps when others with me had paid for sex, but now it was a different situation. He asked If I wanted to have sex with another female at his expense. I didn't say no, but hell no, remembering what had taken place that night when I'd been in the Marine Corps.

I sat at a bar and had a couple of beers while he did his thing. Afterward, we spent the rest of the night partying in TJ while the taxicab was sitting in the parking lot with the meter running. It was time to go home, and we caught a taxicab to the border. When we'd entered the taxicab and I'd proceeded to take the individual home, I could hear the dispatcher calling my cab number because I was over the twelve-hour limit driving. I took the individual home. His fare was about a hundred dollars, and when I dropped him off, he gave me a one-hundred-dollar tip. I was happy. I believe I was the high-booking fare for all the taxicabs that night, and I had some fun as well.

In another situation, an individual jumped in the taxicab and said, "Follow that car." The car entered the freeway and was moving really fast. The individual in the cab said, "Faster, follow them." I drove all over the city chasing this car, and the individual said that his wife and another man were in the car, and at that point, I slowed down and pretended that the car had lost me. I didn't want to be caught up in a marital dispute. I took the individual back to his car, and he grumbled and slammed the door and paid his fare but no tip for me.

I could write a book about the interesting times driving that taxicab. Some experiences were scary, especially when I thought the individual in the cab was making a drug run. The fares that I imagined were illegal aliens trying to get past some checkpoints were interesting as well.

After an eventful night of partying, I missed the morning formation again. I was apprehensive about reporting to the base for fear of what would happen. I didn't report for about two weeks. Sometimes I slept in the well-equipped van, that had a sofa bed, sink, and refrigerator. Besides my current challenges, I had a good time in that van. Some called the van a p __ y wagon. The interior had baby-blue carpet, like the colors of my favorite football team. Sometimes I drove the taxicab for extra money. At times, I was lowered to eating soup out of a can and pawning some of my goods. I wrote checks and didn't have money in the bank. This was a challenging time for me. I eventually returned to duty on my own and earned a reduction in rank from an E-5, a status that was difficult for me to attain, to an E-4. I was still a noncommissioned officer, but a poor representation of a leader of men.

One night, I was staying at my then-girlfriend's house and overslept. I made a decision that drastically affected my career in the military. I was AWOL again, this time for even longer than the last. The fear of returning and facing the consequences overwhelmed the need to return. I was scared because of what I thought might happen. At that time, I didn't have the interpersonal skills to face the officers and explain my position. The inability to face what I did wrong and the stress of it all prolonged my AWOL status, and one day led to another, to another, to another.

At that time, I was still seeing my then-girlfriend and had made a decision to get my life together. I said to her that I wouldn't see her again and was returning to the base. A few days later, my then-girlfriend called me and said that she was pregnant. The call changed my life forever.

I reconciled with my girlfriend and returned to the base. I didn't want my child growing up without a father. I assured her everything would be fine. I returned to the base, and they placed me in a holding cell. None of the MPs checked me before detaining me, and I had an empty bottle of alcohol. I used the empty bottle to serve as an excuse for my absence. The next day, I handed an empty bottle of alcohol to the MPs. From that point on, my next stop was the hospital, which was the first step to starting alcohol and drug rehab. As the MPs escorted me in handcuffs, a marine recognized me and said, "Drill Instructor Sergeant Cubit, remember me from boot camp? I was one of your recruits." Talk about an embarrassing point in my life as they carted me off in handcuffs. I hoped that the marine thought I was in handcuffs for fighting or something other than the real reason.

After about six weeks in rehab, I was released for duty. I was somewhat a different person afterward, and the event started my life on a different path. However, I couldn't stop having a good time in San Diego. In the back of my mind, I knew I had a responsibility of raising a child. At that time, I wanted to stay in San Diego and decided that my time in the military was over. After another night of partying, I was AWOL again, this time for longer than the last. I finally made a conscious decision to return to the base, and upon my arrival, they escorted my ass straight to the brig.

The brig was a completely new experience, of course. I was assigned a judge advocate like a defense lawyer and learned I was going to be court-martialed. The combined time I was AWOL, including the first and second time, was over thirty days; therefore, a court-martial was in order. I intend to appeal the action someday, because the thirty days hadn't been consecutive and I'd returned on my own volition. Nonetheless, I was in the brig, awaiting my fate. While I was in the brig, visiting the judge advocate's office was an experience that brought to light the seriousness of the challenge I faced. I was in the company of hardened criminals. In the holding cell, I remember sitting across from individuals with leg irons and handcuffs attached to a waist belt. Supposedly, the group raped and killed someone. An escort accompanied some, and one individual appeared to be in a straitjacket. After sitting there practically all day, I met with the judge advocate, and he explained the challenge I faced. Finally, the military police returned me to the brig.

The brig was a challenge and a place someone could learn about the mechanics of being a criminal. With the right connections, anything was possible. I learned how to mask the smoking. I saw individuals picking the handcuff locks and handing them to the guards. Anything was available.

While in the brig, I kept to myself most of the time. One of the inmates asked why I was locked-up and then he said that I didn't appear to be someone who'd do something wrong and be in the brig. I didn't want to say the real reason, AWOL, so I said assault and battery. Everyone else in the brig probably knew the real reason though. I wanted to appear as though I was hard core. A reason for not telling the truth was because the hard-core detainees weren't fond of me, and some mentioned that I was a pretty-boy. Although I was stand-offish, I knew what it took to defend myself and always looked for ways to use ordinary items as a weapon.

The brig for some was a holding cell for individuals awaiting transport to federal penitentiaries. The greatest challenges were the times in the yard during the evening. I played basketball or ran around the court for exercise. However, tension grew between the hard-core and me. Plus, I served as a model inmate and had an opportunity to participate in KP and other activities outside the brig. Working in KP seemed to lessen some of the tension between the hard-core and me, especially if I could put an extra scoop of food on their plate.

Finally, it was my day for the court-martial. My mother was there for moral support, and during the entire time I was in the brig, she'd written letters and intervened on my behalf. She'd also made restitution for the bad checks, and I paid her back with interest. My mother visited several times and gave me messages from, my then-pregnant girlfriend.

Anyway, during the court-martial, the prosecutor grilled me, but afterwards, he said personally that he wished me well and was doing his job. I earned a reduction in rank and now was demoted from and E-4 to an E-3. I asked for an early discharge from the military, which was denied. Today, I'm fortunate that the discharge didn't happen.

After my stint in the brig, I attempted to retrieve my van; however, because of nonpayment while I was in rehab and the brig, the van had been repossessed. I was now without wheels, but I managed to find ways to get from place to place. Sometimes I carpooled or caught the Greyhound bus. At that time, I was shy and didn't want to ride the city bus to the Greyhound bus station, so I walked from National City along Harbor Drive to the bus station downtown. Life in the military was different now. The marines I'd given orders to were now giving me orders. How humiliating! At that time, I was at the bottom of fool's hill instead of an ascent, and it appeared that I was starting to dig a tunnel underneath.

After release from the brig, I tried to figure things out. My girlfriend was getting ready to give birth, and I had a short time left in the military. I still struggled with deciding what I wanted to accomplish for the future. Based on the many challenges I'd faced, I knew the military wasn't a career for me. I wanted to do something that represented me, but I hadn't found that place. Looking back, other than the military, at that time, I didn't have the tools to fashion a career path or have the mechanisms or provide a sustaining life for a family.

During all the challenges, my son was born. This was another life-changing event. I had a son now, and I needed to be responsible. I remember catching a bus to the hospital, and at that point, I knew I had to do things differently. I needed to find ways to provide a viable life for my family, but I didn't know how. However, I still had the demons of the past to deal with. Things needed to change, and I vowed that my son wouldn't grow up without a father. I wanted something different from what I faced as a child.

A few months before I was discharged, my brother-in-law kept calling and wanted me to look at a business opportunity. I was too busy trying to figure out what I wanted to do after the military. I still drove the taxicab part-time, and perhaps I thought that was a career for me. I knew I could go to school using the GI Bill, but based on my experiences in the past, I knew going back to school wasn't for me. In the meantime, my brother-in-law insisted that I look at a business opportunity. I gave in, and what I discovered would be the beginning of another life-changing event. The birth of my son and the business opportunity were instrumental to changes in my life.

Chapter 9

DURING THE WAR-WITHIN

A fter reviewing the marketing plan for the business opportunity that my brother-in-law recommended, I was apprehensive at first. I then started meeting African Americans who
were involved and decided that the business opportunity might be
a way for me to support my family. My brother-in-law, my sponsor,
asked that I have a meeting at my place and invite my friends and relatives. Some of my friends and relatives attended the meeting, which
was a success. From that meeting, several individuals purchased
products, and some became distributors.

I started working diligently at the business opportunity, and I
was amazed with the personal growth I acquired. During the leadership training, I learned about goal setting, integrity, honesty, faith,
and doing the right thing, all of which enhanced my personal growth.
Most could see a change in me. For example, sometime before my
discharge from the Marine Corps, I'd found my way into a part of
a warehouse where personal items had been stored. Yes, I hadn't
completely freed myself from the error of my ways. Well, I'd helped
myself to a few items, of which one in particular was a military sword
that I prized. However, after taking part in the leadership training
that enhanced personal growth, I decided to return the items regardless of the risk. I arranged for a meeting with the officer in charge and
returned the items. Nothing happened; however, when it came time
for a promotion, he said that I didn't make the grade, and I replied,
"Thank you, sir." While leaving his office, I said to myself that I only

had a few weeks left. *Besides, I'm going to make a million dollars in my newfound business opportunity.* I had a smirk on my face.

I continued attending meetings for my newfound business and thought back to when I was a teenager selling brushes door-to-door. I believed this business opportunity was different and better than selling those darn brushes. I had the vehicle to now become rich. I attended seminars in some of the best hotels in Southern California. I began purchasing products for my newfound venture. In the meantime, knowing that I was about to be discharged, and because I'd completed the locksmith courses while in Hawaii, I decided to start another business.

I bought an inventory of locksmith supplies, including keys, a new key-making machine, locks, and a host of other materials. I had some cards made for my locksmith business. I thought I could continue driving the taxicab, working in my locksmith business, distributing cleaning supplies, and maybe going to school-what could go wrong? *I'm on my way to success,* thought the twenty-five-year-old entrepreneur.

A few days before my discharge, a career planner from headquarters contacted me and asked to speak with me. I traveled to headquarters. He had my service record, and his goal was to encourage me to stay in the military. I thought, with my service record, excelling in the military wasn't possible. My comment was, "Are you serious?" "We can draft the papers today, and you can reenlist for as little as three years." I asked him to let me think about it, and I wanted to hum the *Jeopardy!* game show music. My next comment was, "I'm outta here!" I found it ironic that the career planner asked me to reenlist because my discharge papers display that I'm ineligible, forever, unsuitable for the military.

The day finally arrived. I woke up, quietly dressed myself, said no goodbyes, took my discharge papers, and off I went. After discharge, I continued to work on building the distribution business, and in the meantime, I looked for a full-time job because I had a child to support and needed health-care benefits. I attempted to look for work at several locksmith places, and at that time, some of the shops had training for Vietnam veterans but there were no openings. I also attempted to apply for federal jobs, to no avail. Federal jobs were and are hard to come by in the beautiful San Diego area. During that time, occasionally, a family member stopped by and asked me to make a key. Some wanted me to repair or rekey a lock or remove a broken key. To grow the locksmith business, in addition to the business cards, I distributed flyers but didn't get a response.

The income from driving a taxicab wasn't enough to sustain us; therefore, we had to move in with relatives. Times were tough. More importantly, because of the personal growth I achieved through the leadership courses in the business during my final years in the Marine Corps, my goal was to do things right. I was no longer bound by my environment and the past. At that time, I thought about comments some had made that I wouldn't make it past my sixteenth birthday. I also thought about the comment my grandmother made constantly, that I would be all right once I got over fool's hill. One day, I asked her what she meant, and was there an age when an individual makes it over fool's hill? She said that it depended on the individual and his or her life experiences, and that sometimes it was around the ages of thirty and forty. At this stage in my life, it appeared that I was still attempting to climb fool's hill and ascend over the top.

I decided to go to college using my GI Bill. I knew I could earn money for attending college. I wondered how I would handle raising a family, attending college classes, driving a taxicab, and managing my other ventures. One day, I met a young Caucasian man, and we talked about locksmithing. He expressed an interest saying that he had completed the same course I had. The individual had a challenging start to life, like my situation as a young person. To help him get started in his business, I eventually sold him all my locksmith supplies at a discount and was out of business. I was still attempting to build the product distribution business, though.

I enrolled full-time in a local junior college, and my GI Bill stipend was approximately five hundred dollars per month, tax-free. I hated sitting in the classroom and didn't speak if called upon to answer a question. I wanted to devote more time to my business venture and believed the opportunity would provide my family with the lifestyle we needed. I eventually applied for a student loan, and combined with the money I received from the GI Bill and driving the taxicab, we were able to make ends meet.

While in the two-year college, I enrolled in child development and economics classes in addition to other core courses. I was a full-time student. At that time, I hadn't declared a major and was stressed about the thought of returning to school. The first semester, I earned two Ds and two Fs. Going back to school was a challenge. First, I wasn't motivated and decided that college wasn't for me and dropped out. At that time, I wasn't exactly sure what I wanted to accomplish in life or career-wise other than building a product distribution business. That was all I had to cling to.

After leaving college, I vowed never to return to school and swore that making a million dollars distributing home-cleaning supplies was my destiny. I had what I thought was the last check from the GI Bill and the remaining check from the student loan. The days of my past were no longer on my mind but were still part of me subconsciously.

At that time, my girlfriend left San Diego and decided to move to Long Beach and live with her parents. Beforehand, I'd asked her to marry me, and she'd said yes. We were going to be married in my hometown, San Diego. I called a reverend, who was the pastor of the church I'd attended as a child-well, almost. My mother made sure we were dressed to attend church; however, I ditched and took the offering money to buy candy. I was too shy to sit in church, and I hung out in a drainage ditch near the church and Southcrest Park in my Sunday clothes and threw rocks at pollywogs instead.

Well, we waited at the church for the pastor to marry us, one hour became two, and then two hours became three. From a phone booth, we called the pastor's number several times, to no avail. I was somewhat upset. The pastor had agreed to marry us at no cost; however, I had a donation for the church, which I thought was penitence for ditching church when I was a child and taking the offering to buy candy.

A few days later, I told my father what had happened, and he informed me that the reverend had a heart attack and passed away the same day we were supposed to be married, perhaps while in transit.

The newspaper obituary confirmed this. Well, that definitely delayed our marriage plans. Talk about cold feet, which should be frozen feet at this point. Perhaps it was an omen, and I believe one should listen when God sends small subtleties, because an individual may find himself or herself in the belly of a big fish like Jonah, which I'll explain later. Soon after, my girlfriend moved to Long Beach. During that time, I lived in several shabby motels. On one occasion, one place was infested with fleas. I still aspired to make a million dollars distributing home-cleaning products. Finally, I stayed with my father and continued driving a taxicab.

Occasionally, I drove to Long Beach in my junker to see my girlfriend and my son. At that time, I began attending church and was baptized. While I was sitting in my taxicab, waiting for a fare, on the radio was a pastor from the Calvary Chapel system. I listened to the pastor every day and became a student of his teachings. I had a Bible in my backpack, and when it was time for him to broadcast, I parked my taxicab, ate my lunch, and followed his teaching sermon verse by verse with my Bible in hand. I was hooked, and on one occasion, when visiting my child and girlfriend, I went to his church, which was a converted supermarket. I became a student of the Bible and the teachings of Christ.

At that time, my son lived with his mother and grandparents, and several children resided in the house. One Sunday while visiting, I took my son to church with me, and after the service, the attendant asked if she could talk to me. She said that my son was disruptive and, to put it bluntly, unruly. If he was to return, his behavior needed to change. I took my son to the car, prayed, and at that young age, I had a talk with him. He must've been less than three years old and could barely talk. However, based on the look in his eyes, I knew he understood me, and from that point forward, I had no problems leaving my son in the church with the other children. Situations like these were stressful. Living in San Diego away from my child and girlfriend. Driving a taxicab. A child on the way. I knew I had to do something to be with my girlfriend, son, and soon-to-come daughter. I had to do something to get control of the situation

I continued to follow the teachings of the Bible and one day asked God what was in store for my life. I was in tears. Keep in mind that I wasn't perfect and was still having a good time, but a change was occurring. I was still shy. For example, I remember asking my girlfriend or brother to return items to a store because I was too shy or didn't have the skill or confidence to effectively communicate while doing this. About that time, my first daughter was born, and I drove to Long Beach after her birth. I knew then I had to do something, and the goal to make a million dollars building a business distributing cleaning products was put on hold.

On the way back to San Diego, I noticed a magazine storage area, a place where the navy stored ammunition. I thought, *What a cool place to work!* It would be like what I'd done in the Marine Corps. After submitting applications for federal jobs in San Diego with no luck, I didn't put too much stock in obtaining a job at that navy base I saw when visiting my girlfriend. I submitted an application anyway. About a month later, I received a letter at my girlfriend's parents' house from the navy base. They asked if I was interested in a job and, if so, to call to confirm a physical. Back then, the internet was almost nonexistent for job searching and hiring. I drove to pick up the letter and called to schedule the physical. A few weeks later, the navy (Department of Defense) offered me a job as a warehouse person for ammunitions at $8.14 per hour. I believed I had arrived. Thank you, USMC and the military, for the experience that helped me qualify and obtain the job.

I was now working in the Los Angeles area and missed San Diego. Almost every weekend, I drove back to visit. At that time, I lived with an aunt in Compton, and one Sunday, I took my wife to the church I was attending. She and her family were of another faith, and after attending church with me, she had the knowledge to make informed decisions about her faith. I still thought that I was going to earn a million dollars distributing home-cleaning products.

One night, my girlfriend and I believed it was time to tie the knot. We had two children, and I wanted to settle down. Besides, I didn't want my children growing up without a father. We went to a place to get married in Long Beach, and it was an establishment where gay people went to tie the knot, which was illegal at that time. Later we went to a public agency to obtain the marriage license. Today I question if the person who married us was legally ordained to do so. Anyway, at that time, I still had some growing up to accomplish, but I was starting to climb up fool's hill, maybe.

After the marriage ceremony, we stayed in several flea-bitten hotels. Some rooms had food seeping through the shower drain, and the stench was almost unbearable. Sometimes, after church we drove to San Diego to visit and drove back the same night. I missed living in San Diego.

During one visit to San Diego, I attempted to tune up my junker and dropped a tool down the spark plug hole and couldn't retrieve it. Like a backyard mechanic, I started the car, and that was the end of the car's engine. If that car could talk, what stories it could tell! For example, one night, I decided to take a drive to TJ and then to Ensenada. I purchased a beer and was driving late at night in unfamiliar desolate areas of Mexico. I was driving in some of those small streets, and shanties were on every side. Around 2:00 a.m., my alternator light came on. I decided to turn around, and I had about a two-hour drive home. I finally reached home and parked the car in the garage. The next morning, I needed to go to the store, and the car wouldn't start. I called my brother, who was an expert mechanic. He ran some tests and said that the alternator wasn't operational and needed replacing. He also said that apparently, the car was running off the battery, and finally, the car battery couldn't operate the electrical systems. He noticed the car was muddy and asked, "Where the hell did you go?" I said that I didn't remember. Nonetheless, another narrow escape from what could've been a dire situation. Well, I leave to the reader my placement on fool's hill at this juncture.

That car helped improve my mechanical skills, which I appreciated later. In fact, my brother-in-law, my brother, and I had the same make and model of car, a Mercury Capri. Concerning my mechanical skills, I remember the steering giving me problems once. I was heading home and about to merge on the freeway, and as I was making a turn on the on-ramp to a busy 405 freeway during rush hour, I heard a noise like something was stripping. I was approaching the fast-moving traffic, and the gears stripped from a part on the steering column. I lost the ability to control the car's direction. I was fortunate that it happened before I'd merged onto the 405 freeway. Another possible brush with death averted. My brother-in-law helped me retrieve the car. I went to the junkyard, found the part, and replaced it. I was leery, and I later carried an extra part just in case.

I have many good memories about that car, and some I'll not mention here, but now we were without wheels and caught the bus back to Long Beach. The next morning, I woke at 4:00 a.m. and rode the bus to work. I was upset because the early departure time took away my morning runs. When I had wheels, I rose early in the morning and ran four to five miles before going to work. On the weekend, I jogged ten miles almost daily and developed that routine after discharge from the military while smoking about a quarter pack of cigarettes per day.

Being without wheels and riding the bus were a strain on the family, so I returned to school to earn money from the GI Bill. I rode the bus but didn't want to deal with the crowds and wanted to walk but couldn't. I arrived at the base early in the morning and sometimes jogged in my civilian clothes in the dark. After work, I hit the gym on the base and then rode the bus home, although I feared doing this. I came home, ate dinner, then rode the bus to school. Often, I walked home after school because I didn't want to deal with riding the bus. My routine was to catch the bus at 4:00 a.m. and then return home about 6:00 p.m. then I went to school at 7:00 p.m. and walked home after school, arriving around 10:45 p.m.

One of my first classes was typing, and I appreciate what I learned. I obtained an old electric typewriter from my mother and practiced typing every chance I had, including after work and on the weekends. I believe my wife and children were annoyed with the constant pounding of the typewriter at the dinner table in those flea-bitten motels. After all that work practicing typing, I only earned a C in the class.

Finally, with the extra money from the GI Bill, excess money from student loans, overtime, money from my wife's employment, and income tax, we were able to purchase a decent car and then move into a two-bedroom apartment. Earning a college degree wasn't a goal in life. I still said I was going to earn a million dollars distributing home-cleaning products. After we moved into our apartment, I decided to step up my distributing activities and did a pretty good job. However, in time, production declined.

I was going to school for about a year and still didn't have an education goal. I wasn't motivated to attend classes, but I made a commitment to earn at least an associate's degree in advertising and display. I believed the associate of arts degree in advertising and display would complement my product distribution business. Eventually, I declared a college major to satisfy the requirements for going to school and earning a stipend through the GI Bill. At this point, I became bored with college, dropped out of school again, and was persistent about making a million dollars. I wasn't giving up on that. I consulted with my sister, which I often did, and she attempted to encourage me to continue with college. Earning a degree wasn't my ultimate focus though. I can understand why she encouraged me to continue with my education. You see, she was a single parent who had a difficult start as well. She earned an associate's degree from San Diego City College and a bachelor's degree from San Diego State, and attempted to encourage me to continue going to school. "Nope," I replied. "I'm going to make a million dollars in the business [as we called it]. You'll see. You'll see."

At my job, I was what one could say a company man but a temporary worker. I was punctual, devoted, a good worker, and was forced to take a break. However; there was an individual who was allegedly having an affair with a married supervisor. I later found that the supervisor who was having an alleged affair was attracted to me. Although married, the supervisor was jealous and thus had a dislike for me. Like the challenge I'd faced in the brig, I was labeled a pretty boy, and some were jealous. The supervisor occasionally stopped by the section where I was working, put his hands on his hips to represent a commanding position, and watched me sweep the floor, to emphasize superiority. It appeared that the supervisor wanted me to know that he was the head N-word in charge. I prayed for the supervisor and asked God to assist me in resolving the situation.

Concerning the supervisor and the person he was allegedly, having an affair with, I was a victim of their circumstance. The situation was challenging, and that gave me a reason to continue building the product distribution business. In addition, I thought the individual that the supervisor was allegedly having an affair with was unattractive; however, the supervisor appeared to be enamored with her.

One day, after I'd arrived at work and punched my time card, my supervisor told me to report to the admin office. I received a notice that because of budget limitations, I was going to be laid off. I later found that the supervisor who disliked me had something to do with the company's decision. When I departed the job, the last person I saw was the supervisor who had a problem with me. He was in his superiority complex command stance and had a shit-eating grin on his face. At that point, I swore I would never be involved in a similar employment situation again. I vowed that what I experienced in the brig, the pretty-boy dilemma, and what was currently happening at the navy base would never happen again. Was I wrong!

Looking back, I do believe God answered my prayers about alleviating the situation with the supervisor; however, at that time, I was upset and didn't know what the future had to offer. My wife was pregnant, and I was perplexed about what to do next. I decided to return to college; however, I was not sure what I wanted to do with my life, and my quest was unknown. More importantly, fool's hill was in my rearview mirror, but I was still trying to figure things out concerning life. Little did I know the events described here would have a positive impact on the rest of my life and lead to my why.

During that time, I received unemployment compensation, and the funds for going to school were sustaining. While attending school, I decided to dress professionally, and that underscored the end of my elementary school Pig-Pen days. Prior to that, when in public, I always looked my best, but now I believed a professional demeanor would enhance my career. One day, an individual in one of my classes approached me and asked if he could take my picture for his portfolio. He was a freelance photographer. Of course, I declined because I was shy and didn't want anyone taking my picture. However, later in life, that stance changed, and I found myself feeling differently about having my picture taken. I was without a job and now I had the opportunity to spend more time with my children, especially my daughter. As previously mentioned, she was born when I was living in San Diego. She wasn't use to me and cried every time I tried to pick her up. One weekend, my wife was away for a while, which presented a challenge for my firstborn daughter and me. I was committed to resolving the situation; I wanted to develop a relationship with my daughter. When my wife left, my daughter cried. I picked her up and held her in my arms until she stopped crying and fell asleep. After that event, she never cried in my presence again.

In my unemployed state, I had the opportunity to teach my son that death is real. While he lived with his grandparents, a favorite pastime of his was watching violent cartoons. Sometimes the cartoon character experienced a violent act, such as dynamite exploding in its presence or a rock falling on the character's head. Most of time, the character stood up and walked away, and I concluded that my son might think that death wasn't real. Therefore, I talked with my son to communicate that if what happened to that cartoon character happened to him, he wouldn't get up and walk away.

At that time, individuals who watched cop shows also surrounded my son. In those shows, while a law enforcement officer arrested an individual, he or she pointed a gun at them and commanded, "Hold it." My son had a transformer toy that converted into a pistol, and where we lived wasn't in a decent area. One day, an individual was passing by the window, and my son took his transformer gun and held it out of a window and said, "Hold it." I wondered what would happen next. The individual scampered, and I caught up to him and explained the situation. I counseled my son about what was real and the consequences of his actions, and it appeared that he understood. However, from that point on, my son never had a toy gun again, and I restricted the time he spent watching violent television shows.

Anyway, while I was unemployed, my wife worked during the day, and I stayed with the two children. I fed them, dressed them, and battled with my son during his potty training. I prepared lunch and dinner, which was the beginning of my opportunity to cook good food. Time with my children was exceptional, and I will take the experience to the grave. I remember reading an article about individuals in a senior citizen's home. Someone asked seniors in the home, if they had an opportunity to repeat anything in their life, what would that be? Some mentioned that spending more time with their children would be cherished moments. Today, I agree, and because time moves fast, all parents should cherish every moment spent with their children. Again, the time in my unemployment state was beneficial and allowed me to connect with my children. It's a time in my life I'll never forget.

Nonetheless my unemployment situation was stressful, and I had to do something. I began reading entrepreneur magazines, and in the advertisement section of one, I read an article from a company that explained how I could make money while at home. I purchased the training materials from the company, studied the coursework, and earned a certificate that displayed my name above an *account executive* title. An important title, I thought. And I still have that certificate. For that organization, I was an independent contractor, and as an account executive, I contacted companies that had overdue receivable assets, typically debt owed to a company. The organization I worked with provided information about the type of companies to contact. If the company gave me information about the debt owed to them, I gave it to the organization from which I'd obtained the course materials. The organization then attempted to collect the receivables. If successful, I received a portion of the amount collected. After about ten nervous cold calls, my account executive position ended. However, I continued working on building the home-cleaning product distribution business.

One day, I tuned into a show on television and the topic was real estate and investments. I became interested in investments and real estate and shifted my focus in college from advertising and display. I began attending investment seminars, especially those about real estate. Most of the real-estate seminars had a "get-rich-quick" theme. However, real estate was the most interesting investment topic, and I was hooked. I began listening to investment shows on the radio and reading books about the topic. In junior college, I took courses and studied to be an investment counselor. Imagine that, an individual receiving unemployment insurance opting to be an investment counselor. But I had dreams and aspirations, and wasn't giving up. I wanted to be a wealth guru. Additionally, in the back of my mind, I wanted to prove individuals wrong, to show them that I continued to thrive and that my life didn't end at my sixteenth birthday. I also wanted to set an example to those who faced similar challenges while growing up in not-so-favorable conditions.

Anyway, one day, based on the information I learned from one of the get-rich-quick real estate seminars, I decided to make an offer on a house that was for sale by the owner, commonly called a FSBO, or *fizz bow*, for pronunciation. I scoured the neighborhoods and scanned the newspaper and finally found a FSBO. The house was in a decent neighborhood, and the seller wasn't in distress. Nonetheless, I prepared an offer to purchase the house based on what I learned in the courses. After the owner-seller had read my offer, I thought he was going to crucify me. He was disgusted and said, "Who would be stupid enough to accept this ridiculous offer?" I still have that offer in my files, and after I read it years later, I wanted to crucify myself. I kept the offer as a reminder and vowed to make a million dollars in real estate. The home-cleaning product distribution business became an afterthought.

In the meantime, the navy base called, and they asked if I wanted to come back to work. Of course, I said yes. I had only a few weeks of unemployment compensation left. *Thank you, God.* However, the checks from attending college at night were steady. I returned to the navy base job, and the supervisor who'd watched in his command position when I'd left had a different demeanor. I heard that his wife had found about his shenanigans and had put a stop to it. Upon my return to my job, he was apologetic, and I never had a challenge with the individual again. Thank you, God, for the entire experience and answering my prayer.

At the navy base, I assumed my old job, and nothing had changed. I was back to the routine of warehousing explosives and wanted to do something different. As part of the training for the home-cleaning products distribution business, I read a book about goal-setting and changing one's life, and I wasn't satisfied with a wage-grade job and warehousing explosives for the rest of my life. I wanted to be a success or to make a difference. However, I didn't know how to accomplish the goal. At my job, I earned career status, and I was no longer a temporary employee. I also earned a promotion, and I was assigned to the ammunitions renovation section.

Renovation was an interesting job, and I worked on an assembly line repairing and restoring ammunition. Based on my experience in the military, I was familiar with some of the munitions-for example, the projectiles for the sixteen-inch guns. These projectiles weighed about 2,500 pounds and fired from guns on navy ships. While in the military and stationed in Hawaii, I had the opportunity to assist the explosive ordnance disposal (EOD) team. On one occasion on an island off the coast of Oahu, I took part in destroying some of the unexploded sixteen-inch projectiles called duds. JP and I assisted EOD in exploding the duds. On the small island near Oahu, we stayed in a shanty that didn't have running water, so we had to improvise. To wash our clothes or to clean ourselves, we walked a few miles to the ocean. The scenery was beautiful, and only the the military was authorized to access the small island. We carried a container of Joy dishwashing liquid because it was the only cleaning solution that foamed in salt water. One time, we were on our way to the beach when we heard small explosions. We happened upon the area, and two individuals were using a small amount of explosives to dislodge rusty bolts from machine guns that were attached to an airplane that was shot down during the Pearl Harbor bombing by the Japanese. I thought that was an exceptional experience.

Unrelated to working with those sixteen-inch projectiles, which I'll explain next, I need to communicate another event here concerning working with munitions in Hawaii on that small island. On one occasion, JP, the EOD team, and I conducted a range sweep to destroy any unexploded napalm igniters. Exploding a napalm bomb required an igniter. The igniters detonated by motion. Once it inserted into the bomb, dropped from an aircraft, and hit the target, the igniter would explode the napalm. Sometimes the igniters didn't ignite and dislodged from the explosives.

To conduct the range sweep and find the igniters, we used the infantry. Once an individual in the infantry found an igniter, they signaled for one of us-JP, the EOD team, or myself-to examine the munition and then explode it in place. This was one of the few occasions where the ammunitions specialist was allowed to set a charge and destroy an unexploded device. While we were conducting the range sweep, one of the infantry individuals found an unexploded igniter, picked it up, and brought it to me and asked, "Is this one?" I asked the individual to calmly put the device on the ground and walk away. I thought, *I'm so happy that my military entry scores were high enough to prevent me from being an infantryman.* After the infantry person put the device down, we were able to set a small charge and destroy it in place. From that point on, I increased my distance from the individuals conducting the range sweep. I didn't want to mimic individuals on the EOD crew, for most of them had one finger missing. I enjoyed my military experience in Hawaii.

All right, back to my experience working with the sixteen-inch projectiles while in the military. On one outing on that small island, we hiked in the wilderness with EOD and found a sixteen-inch projectile dud. We assisted EOD in placing TNT and setting the blasting caps in order to demolish the dud. EOD made sure the time fuse length was correct. The blast was set for twenty minutes, and EOD synchronized their watches. I wanted to run, but a cardinal rule when setting a charge was to walk and never run. In about fifteen minutes, the EOD person in charge commanded that everyone get down and take cover. A few minutes later, there was a loud *kaboom!* What was challenging to hear was the shrapnel slashing through the vegetation near us. Next was the baseplate of the projectile, which actually flew over our heads, and I could hear *swoosh* and a whistling sound.

Now at my existing job at the navy base, I was renovating the same sixteen-inch projectiles like those we'd exploded in Hawaii some eight years earlier. The job at the navy base was somewhat risky, and I earned hazard pay.

To fire a sixteen-inch projectile from a naval ship took three one-hundred-pound bag charges or three hundred pounds of black powder. While working on the one-hundred-pound black powder bag charges, we sometimes wore cotton underwear, hairnets, and straps on our wrists to decrease static electricity and prevent an explosive mishap.

However, the hazard working in renovation wasn't from the explosives but from the individuals working there. Some had a couple of drinks, mostly beer, at lunchtime and lost the dexterity in their hands. Often, individuals dropped projectiles for the five-inch 54-caliber guns that were smaller than those for the sixteen-inch guns. Those projectiles weighed about seventy pounds. Sometimes when they were dropped, individuals took off running, and I laughed. With fifty thousand pounds of explosives in the building, running away would only serve as exercise before being consumed by the explosive chain of events.

From the renovation job, I was temporality assigned to the small-arms destruction unit. In that unit, employees worked near an incinerator that burned the ammunition until it was destroyed. Working near the incinerator, an individual was exposed to fumes that could cause lead poisoning; therefore, we wore a respirator and protective clothing. Eventually, my supervisor asked if I wanted to transfer to an ordnance repairperson trainee position and learn how to assemble and test surface-to-air missiles. Of course, I said yes, and I was transferred.

Working in that ordnance repairperson trainee position was interesting, and before I started, only one person of color worked in that unit. The missile repair section was an elite unit, and most of the employees were Caucasian, a good-old-boy network. At the time, I was one among three African Americans transferred to that unit. Soon after, the supervisor retired. At the same time, I noticed the difference between those working in the munitions warehouse occupations and the missile operations unit. Most in the warehouse section were people of color, and those in missile operations were Caucasian. At that time, the goal was to diversify the missile operations unit, which was a good thing, especially for me. The integration of the missile repair division reminded me of my ammunition specialist position while I was in the military. In those units were few people of color. JP, me, and the African American corporal and sergeant in the classes in Alabama were a few of the firsts. Now in the missile repair division, I was experiencing a similar situation. However, I believed the job repairing missiles was retribution for my inability to work with electronics, computers, or radar when I volunteered to serve in the military.

In the meantime, I continued attending school and working on an associate's degree. While at my job, I studied in my car during lunch, during breaks, and on the weekends after working overtime. However, I missed the time spent with my children, and on the weekends, I often took my son fishing on the navy base. I wasn't satisfied with my level of achievement concerning my career. I wanted something more in life, and now with the personal growth obtained from reading books and experience acquired through the product distribution business, I believed that earning a million dollars was feasible. All the time I focused on real estate as a means of enhancing my life, and I believed that investing would provide a way to accomplish my goals.

Soon my third child was born, and I was concerned about the additional responsibility. At that time, I was also committed to giving my children a better life, better than I'd experience as a child. I remember my grandmother viewing my interaction with my children. She called me Daddy Ronnie and said that what she saw was unbelievable. During the first family reunion in the mountains, after I'd counseled one grandchild about throwing a plastic bottle, my girlfriend at that time approached me and said what she saw during the intervention was amazing. So much for an individual not supposed to make it past his sixteenth birthday. I wondered about my placement on fool's hill.

Investing in real estate was my focus, and I knew that I needed to increase my credit score, especially if I wanted to purchase a house. However, the "nothing-down" real estate gurus said that I could purchase real estate with no money down and with bad credit. After unsuccessful attempts with the latter, I conducted research and discovered ways to increase my credit score. It took me about a year, but I was successful. Now, I believed my credit score was satisfactory which would allow us to buy some property, and I applied for a VA loan for land in Perris, California. The idea was to buy the land and then place a triple-wide mobile on it. At that time, my goal was next to impossible, especially by way of a VA loan. Nevertheless, I used the excess money from one of my student loans to put a deposit on an offer for a piece of land. After making an offer and waiting about three months, the loan was denied.

One day, a friend mentioned that he had looked at houses on his way back from Las Vegas and was amazed at the low prices. The location was in the High Desert in San Bernardino County. The main cities were Hesperia, Apple Valley, and Victorville. At that time, the homes in the High Desert were about sixty-eight thousand dollars. My friend explained that the homes were on large parcels of land. He also said that during the winter, sometimes there could be freezing temperatures, snow, and the freeways were sometimes closed. *Snow in Southern California?* I wondered. At that time, I was still devastated from the recent rejections trying to purchase two homes; however, I vowed to visit the place. Before visiting, I dreamed that the High Desert was rural. I envisioned a place where my children could attend school without the challenges of living in the inner city.

What increased my desire to relocate at that time we were living in the Long Beach. To paint a picture, often I sat in college classrooms and most times I was the only African American there. However, the community was changing. In addition, I wasn't pleased with the schools my son attended or with his friends who visited the house. I didn't want my children growing up in an area where drive-by shootings took place. I wanted to give my children a chance to succeed without the challenges of growing up in a tough neighborhood. I wanted to give my family a chance to live in a safe area regardless of the cost. Therefore, relocating to the High Desert appeared to be a good idea. I also wanted to purchase a house and build a real estate empire.

After church for the next two Sundays, we visited the High Desert, and it appeared to be a bedroom community for the Los Angeles area. We discovered that the main street had one stoplight, and there were few businesses in the area. Hesperia, our chosen city to live, had one high school, but there were plans to build more schools. Fortunately, there was one junior college where I could continue going to school. The small shopping mall only had a few stores. While driving back to Long Beach, I was excited about relocating to the High Desert.

After more visits to the High Desert, a few searches, and working with a real estate agent, we placed an offer on a house, and it was accepted. My experience with real estate helped us when we assembled our offer to present to the seller. One request was the closing cost, and the seller paid the entire amount. Good thing, because we didn't have money to pay the cost. The owner allowed us to move in and rent the property until everything was finalized. We were now homeowners, and I thought about what it took for us to purchase the property, including repairing our credit. My wife at that time said, "Wow, you didn't give up." However, at that time, she was employed, and other things fell in place, which helped make the purchase happen.

As I sit here writing, I do believe the move to the High Desert was a good idea as far as the quality of life. Beforehand there were many questions for me asking if I made the right move. I lived in the High Desert for over fifteen years, and my daughter still lives there. Today, I still have an affinity for the High Desert; however, it took an effort to relocate. But I believed we were on our way to build that real estate empire.

Chapter 10

THE MODEL (HMMM)

Moving to the High Desert resolved two problems but created another. We resolved the problem about a safe place to raise our children. The other resolution was that, we had a house to live in, a yard, and soon, a dog. However, a challenge was making it to my job, which was approximately ninety miles away. At first, the trade-offs seemed to balance. Nonetheless, I should note here, back then, we were one of the few families of color in the area. The occasional racist groups in the area was interesting but I believed they disappeared.

Mostly, we felt safe in our new neighborhood, and we were happy that we could leave our garage door open without fear of things going missing. My children left their bikes on the driveway overnight. I breathed a sigh of relief because my children could play outside safely. They could run and play on that half-acre property to their hearts' content.

Now we owned our home, and it was time to explore, and since I was health-conscious, why not grow vegetables and raise some chickens free of hormones? I wanted to be in control of what we ate; therefore, the first goal was to grow a large vegetable garden. I admired my neighbor because his garden flourished. He could grow anything. I decided to plant corn and other vegetables. I bought some seeds, planted them, and nothing grew but stems about the size of my thumb. I bet folks chuckled. Later on, my neighbor gave me some tips, but I was so immersed with the drive to and from work that when the microplants in the garden died, so did my garden aspirations at that time. Later in life, I developed the skill to grow anything I wanted, including a well-manicured yard, with rosebushes and other plants including a garden that was admired by neighbors.

Next was raising the chickens. I built a coop, and we saw an advertisement in the newspaper: "Chickens for Sale." We took a long drive in the country and came to a farm where the chickens were sold. After arriving, I identified the chickens we wanted to buy and said, "I want that one and the other one over there. Give me that one as well." Then the person selling the chickens educated me about the difference between a hen and a rooster. She also warned me about purchasing too many roosters and not enough hens. She also said that only the hens lay eggs. I then asked the female selling the chickens to pick some for us, and off we went, chickens cackling in the back of the station wagon.

We arrived home, and the goal was to feed the chickens corn and scratch, free of hormones. Well, that worked, but we couldn't understand why the hens didn't lay eggs. One day, we looked behind the stoop where the hens roosted, and there were upward of thirty eggs hidden from view. We collected the eggs and rented an incubator to hatch the eggs. We planned to eat some of the eggs and use the rest to raise more chickens. In the meantime, we decided to eat the chickens we bought, and it was my job to cut off the heads. I grabbed one of the chickens and couldn't chop its head off. I began losing my taste for homegrown, hormone-free chicken. However, my wife at that time had some experience with dispatching chickens, and she was successful.

Well, it came time to eat the chickens, and we were at the table. I looked down at the freshly baked poultry, and then a thought about eating Herbie, a pet, came to mind. I believe my children thought the same as well. What made matters worse was that my children took pictures petting the chicken, and I have that photo today. I venture to say that was the end of the attempt to dine on hormone-free chicken meat. I don't believe I could've slain another chicken for a meal.

By the way, the eggs hatched, and my children had fun playing with the chicks. The chicks contracted what I believe was a virus, and although we bought an antibiotic, they all died, as well as the adult chickens. So much for eating natural chicken meat. Now I had an appreciation for purchasing organic, all-natural, hormone-free poultry from the store. Every time I go to the store to purchase poultry, I think about the experience and Herbie the chicken.

Another challenge living in the High Desert was the distance to everything. Often, we drove to San Bernardino to shop or to dine at a decent restaurant. Additionally, getting to and from work was a 180-mile round-trip, and add another fifteen miles if I went to school. But we were homeowners, and that thought counterbalanced the challenges of driving to and from work and school.

During that time, the same friend who told me about the High Desert asked if I wanted to attend a real estate seminar. A prominent, nationally known real estate sales company sponsored the seminar. At the seminar, the company sold materials so one could study for the exam to obtain a real estate license. I bought the course and went for it. I studied the content and was excited about the new venture. I was determined about obtaining my real estate license in California. I was sure the license would open new doors for me in addition to completing an associate's degree in real estate. Nevertheless, the idea of investing in real estate and purchasing property consumed my life.

Because I was about to complete an associate's degree in real estate, taking additional state-required courses wasn't necessary to obtain my license. However, while I was completing the coursework for the degree, some said that obtaining the California real estate license was difficult, but I was tenacious about passing the test. Especially since some said that passing the test was difficult. It was another challenge I imposed upon myself.

Then came the time to take the real estate exam for California. I believed I was on my way to success. However, during the test, I was lost, and passing was more difficult than I'd thought it would be. I was halfway through the test and had a few minutes left. From that point on, I circled any answer with the hope that some were correct. I waited for the results and expected to be successful. I recalled my thoughts in my youth about Logan Realty, which was across the street from Jerrys Market and wanting to tell Lavonnette about my hopes and desires to be successful in real estate. Now I was at that juncture, but, of course, without Lavonnette.

Well, I received the results from the real estate exam, and it wasn't the outcome I'd expected but I should've seen it coming: of course, I wasn't successful. Nonetheless, I began studying again for the exam, and this time, I was sure to pass. Months later, I applied to take the test again. While I took the test this time, finding the correct answers seemed easier. I finished taking the test and was one of the first individuals out of the room. I received the results in the mail, and the letter stated, "Congratulations for passing the California real estate exam." I was excited and thought I was on my way to making a million dollars in real estate. Passing the California real estate exam would eventually have an impact on my career, both positively and negatively.

Meanwhile, I was still dealing with relocating to the High Desert. Although my family was safe and we owned a home, I needed to find a way to get to work at the navy base and to school at night. First, I attempted to drive, but doing so took a toll on me and my family.

I estimated the time it took me to drive to and from my job equaled about three months of commuting. I spent approximately ninety days a year sitting in my car. I also spent most of my time on the weekend repairing my car or studying for school, and I mean every weekend. So much for the quality of life. However, my family had a home and a safe place to live.

Those mechanical skills working on those junkers, well, they came in handy, for I was constantly repairing my car. Eventually, I bought an economical car and blew the engine. I attempted to rebuild the engine and then drove the car to and from work and to school several times, and it smoked intensely from the exhaust. I mean smoking more than a smoldering bonfire! While driving down and up the I-15 and on the I-10 or I-60 freeways, I felt sorry for those behind me. I could see some waving their hands to clear the smoke spewed from my vehicle. Eventually, after about three trips, the car blew a piston.

Then I drove the larger vehicle, that was a gas-guzzler, and I devised a plan. Since my classes were on Monday and Wednesday nights, I drove to work on Monday, went to class, slept in my car, awoke in the morning, did my workout, lifted weights at the YMCA, and took a shower. I went to work and then drove home Tuesday night. I drove to work on Wednesday morning and did the same routine as I did on Monday, and then drove home on Thursday night. Always, I drove home on the weekends. Still, this was a challenge, but eventually, I earned my associate's degree in real estate. Driving to and from work was challenging, and I had to find a way to resolve the dilemma.

One day, I was at work, and some of my coworkers commented about a rash on my face. I looked in the mirror, and I wasn't concerned. By noon, the lesions were all over my body. Alarmed, some of my coworkers asked me to leave the building. One reason was that they were concerned for my health and another was that they didn't want me to spread some kind of epidemic throughout the building. I attempted to drive home, but the gas-guzzler car didn't make it. I knew what was wrong with the vehicle and called my wife. I asked her to purchase a part from an automobile parts company and then drive approximately fifty miles to my location, which she did. With spots all over my body, I put the part in the car and drove home. I went to the doctor, and he said that I had chicken pox. Imagine that, in my thirties and contracting chicken pox. While home recovering, I made sure to cook food for my children, and I was always around them. My goal was for them to catch the chicken pox early. I wanted them to get it out of the way instead of contracting the ailment later in life. The challenge of driving what seemed like ungodly miles to work and the added challenge of contracting chicken pox made me wonder if I'd made the right decision relocating to the High Desert.

After recovery, I was back to the long haul to and from work and school. While I slept in my car, sometimes the police hassled me. For example, on one occasion, I slept in my car in an old neighborhood in Long Beach near where I used to live. Male and female police officers woke me and searched my car for no reason, other than me sleeping. The female office searched everywhere and had my underwear and clothing on top of the car, which was a nice-looking automobile. Of course, they didn't find anything but my books from school, and after the exhaustive search, they told me to vacate the area. About a month later in the same area at a different location, a police officer knocked on my window while I was sleeping in a super-market parking lot. He asked me why I was sleeping in my car, and I explained the situation. He said, "Okay, go back to sleep, and next time, find another area." Finally, I had enough of sleeping in my car, chicken pox, driving, and working on cars all the time. I had to find a way to resolve the dilemma. I began applying for government jobs where I lived, but to no avail.

I decided it was time to fix the economical car, the one with the blown piston, and leave the gas-guzzler at home. Perhaps I could make the drive until I found a job near my home. One day, I saw an advertisement for Japanese engines, cheap. Fortunately, some were the same design as the one I'd attempted to rebuild. To purchase the engine, I had to give them the one with the busted piston. I had never replaced a car engine before, so I bought a repair manual. I then rented a cherry picker (like a hydraulic crane) and attached the harness to the engine. With the manual in hand, I read the instructions, detached all the bolts, and then removed the engine. I put the engine in the trunk of the gas-guzzler. I drove about fifty miles to where I needed to purchase the Japanese engine. After blowing the engine, I had already taken the head off to assess the damage. When swapping the engines, the individual taking mine spoke Spanish, and I couldn't understand him. I believe he asked me what the shuck happened to that thing, meaning the engine I was swapping. He was shaking his head when looking at the engine.

I drove home, took the used engine, and installed it with the car repair manual in hand. *Voilà!* I was back in business, driving to and from work every day and sometimes to school. No more car exhaust! However, the air conditioner in the car didn't work. In the summer in the Cajon Pass, the temperature was over one hundred degrees when driving home. Nevertheless, that Datsun B210 became my workhorse. For example, after purchasing our house, I decided to install a chain-link fence around our property. I'd never done anything like that before, and I bought a book about how to install the fence. However, most of the stores to purchase items to install the fence were in San Bernardino. Therefore, I drove to San Bernardino in that Datsun (approximately thirty-five miles away), purchased the items, tied the gates to the top of the car, and off I went. As I traveled up through the Cajon Pass from San Bernardino to the house, the car looked like a vehicle from a *Mad Max* movie. I made it up the hill with the gates tied to the top and eventually installed a fence around the property. This is one of the many experiences about adapting to life in our new house. Nonetheless, I continued to make that ninety-mile drive one way to work and school in that Datsun with the engine I replaced.

The drive to work was taking its toll, and I had to devise a plan to remedy the situation. I wanted to earn a decent income and didn't believe that assembling and building missiles and housing explosives was the end of my career. After about two and a half years of driving approximately two hundred miles a day, finally, I made a decision. I increased my effort in applying for jobs near my home, and some were outside the federal government.

One day, while reading the newspaper, I saw a job advertisement for positions in a newly built glass factory in the area. The glass factory was less than a mile from my house. I applied for a laborer position and was hired. Still, my goal was to make a million dollars investing and selling real estate. However, above all, my goal was to make life better for the family. I also wanted to prove that an individual from the hood could improve his or her life regardless of the circumstances. Easier said than done.

I took annual leave from my federal job and attended orientation at the new glass factory. Finally, I left the secure government job and took the full-time position at the glass factory. Working at the glass factory was a challenge. Transitioning from a government job to one in private industry requires some consideration.

While working at the glass factory, I was on rotating shifts, which created another issue. In addition, I worked on an assembly line, which was boring and nonsensical work for me. When working near the glass-producing machines, we wore outerwear that prevented workers from getting cut by the glass. However, the fine glass fibers managed to find ways to invade all parts of my body. I mean everywhere, and sometimes showers didn't help. I spent an enormous amount of time in the shower to remove those glass fibers out of the crack of my ass as if I had hemorrhoids.

Eventually, I realized that assembly line work combined with evading glass crystals in the crack of my butt and the shift work wasn't what I wanted to do for the rest of my life. The time at the factory took a toll on my schooling, and I'd just started taking classes to earn another associate's degree. However, I had a job that was local and didn't require me to drive two hundred miles to and from work. Nonetheless, I believed the job didn't allow me to utilize my knowledge, skills, and abilities, and one day, I decided the glass factory wasn't for me. I woke up one morning and simply didn't return. After several calls from the employer, the company finally gave up. In the back of my mind, my ultimate goal was to invest in real estate and earn a million dollars. Later, I found that having a real estate license wasn't necessary to becoming a successful real estate investor. However, I still had something to prove to the naysayers, those who said that I wouldn't make it past my sixteenth birthday.

In the midst of everything, I began applying for sales positions in real estate companies and eventually landed a referral agent independent contractor position with a prominent real estate company. *I have a real estate license. Why not use it?* I thought. However, the referral agent independent contractor position was like the receivable accounts executive position for which I attempted to collect receivable assets years ago. That didn't last long. Finally, I saw an advertisement in the paper for full- and part-time real estate agents. An African American female real estate broker managed the office. She allowed me to work out of the office as an independent contractor, not an employee, a different situation than I was used to. Keep in mind, at that time, I had a family, a house, and other financial obligations, and I took the risk. The real estate broker gave me some tips about how to get started, but I thought I could use technology to aid in accomplishing my goal to make a million dollars in real estate.

When attending those get-rich-quick real estate seminars, I had information about how to search for distressed property. I thought I could find distressed properties and then list them for sale. I'd just bought a computer and subscribed to an online service that allowed me to search property titles. The technology was new at that time. Back then, my computer had a forty-megabyte hard drive, which was large at that time. To connect online, I used a telephone modem, and accessing the information took some time. I just knew I had the answers to finding properties to list for sale.

After attempts to find listings using my computer, one of the experienced real estate agents said that a good way to obtain listings was to conduct cold calls. At that time, I hadn't overcome shyness. As previously mentioned, for example, if I needed to return something to a store, I put my wife up to the task, and if my children had been old enough, I would have put them up to the task as well. If I wanted to be a successful real estate agent, I now had to conduct calls or find other ways to develop a client base. To do so, I had to develop a sales-person persona, which was a challenge for me. I was realizing that a real estate salesperson was just that, and there were no shortcuts. I remembered back in the day when I attempted to sell the cleaning brushes door-to-door. *Here we go again, fava beans or black eyed peas if you remember.*

Another real estate agent mentioned that I could use direct mail and send out flyers, and I liked that approach. I used my computer to download owner information for one property tract. I printed mailing labels from my computer, bought some stamps, and mailed postcards that had the property information, my address, and my phone number. The postcard had a blurb about how I could help the owner realize a profit from selling their property and I could list it for them. The results from the direct-mail approach was surprising, and I received several calls. The same agent who gave me the tip about the direct-mail approach said that I must ask the owners who called if I could conduct a listing presentation. She said that during the list-ing presentation, I needed to convince the owner that I was the best agent to sell their property. She also gave me tips on how to conduct the listing presentation.

From my computer, in addition to a microfiche file in the office and a property profile from a title company, I gathered information about the property. I also obtained information about comparable sales in the area. From the combined and other information, I prepared a portfolio for the owner and was ready for my first listing presentation. I drove to the property and was at the front door. The situation reminded me of the time I'd attempted to sell cleaning brushes. I wondered about the property owners and if they would eat parts of me with fava beans or black-eyed peas. Nonetheless I did a good job. After about my third presentation with a homeowner, I was able to relax. What helped was conducting those presentations when attempting to sell products for the home-cleaning products business. However, I was still uncomfortable speaking in public and couldn't effectively communicate verbally in some situations.

One day, I was canvassing the newspaper and looking for FSBOs. I located one and had some money for the down payment. Using some creative financing (nothing illegal), I purchased the property. However, I learned that the house was overfinanced and the loans were more than the value. The real estate broker who allowed me to work from the office was upset because she thought I'd purchased the property using resources from the office. If so, I owed them a commission. I explained that I'd used my own resources to purchase the property and showed her the newspaper advertisement. Purchasing that FSBO was some recompense for that first ridiculous offer I'd submitted to an owner years ago.

Ultimately, I discovered that real estate sales were just that-sales. Constant contact with people was something that was still a challenge for me. Property listings didn't fall out of the sky. However, from the direct mail, I was able to list one property. Another challenge at that time was, I didn't effectively manage my finances, which is definitely a must when pursuing a sales career. I learned that an individual venturing into real estate sales must have at least six months of income saved or an additional source of income, which I didn't have. At that time, commissions from real estate sales took about three to six months, and if an individual didn't have the funds to support him or herself, and a family, for a period of time, unfortunate situations could happen. Something I didn't take into consideration. No opportunities to get rich quick here.

I continued working in the real estate office and hated the weekend work. Especially if there was a walk-in, because I was responsible for working face-to-face with a potential client. Most of the walk-ins just wanted information about a property, and at that time, our country was in a recession, and ditto for real estate sales. My funds were almost depleted, and I did everything within my power to make the situation I faced work, but things around me were collapsing. At that time, I wondered if moving to the High Desert was a good idea. What would things be like if I were still driving the 180-mile round-trips to the navy base? What about my family? What about my mother, who now lived in the house we purchased? At that time, I thought back to the time I was in elementary school, riding the cart down the ramp with the movie projector but wanting to be a patrol boy. Had I made the right decisions?

It was time to go back to the drawing board and figure things out because I couldn't turn around and go back. Sales wasn't for me at that time, and I was definitely not tailored for a job in a people profession or one that involved contact with others. Perhaps a job as an engineer, computer programmer, accountant, or gardener would suit me better. In those jobs, I could work in isolation. Maybe a job that allowed me to work in a vacuum. Later in life I learned that I might've benefited from taking a career or personality assessment. The data from the assessment might've provided information about which careers to pursue based on my personality. Looking back, I was someone who definitely would have benefited from career counseling as well, but I don't believe I would've been receptive to the advice. Perhaps I needed to see a psychiatrist, as my mother often said. In addition, little did I know that what I faced here was part of my fool's hill challenge? Was I still on fool's hill at this point? To continue my journey, I needed the challenge I faced here.

During my real estate sales debacle, I continued applying for government jobs locally. I returned to school and somewhat supported my family with funds from the VA for going to school and the excess from student loans. However, during the process, we did purchase another property, and I still believed I could be successful.

Eventually, I applied for a home-improvement loan from the Federal Housing Administration, and the goal was to add a 535 square-foot addition to the house. I thought I could do most of the work myself and save some money. Remember: before enlisting in the Marine Corps, I'd gained some experience building houses. During my real estate ventures, I also completed a building construction course and earned a certificate. Nonetheless, I was thinking that the addition added value to the property and I could refinance it and then use the excess funds to recover financially and then purchase another property to build a real estate empire. Well guess what? The materials to build the addition far exceeded the loan amount. But the loan was based on an agreement to build the addition, and so I began.

The house was already a three-bedroom and two-bath home. My daughters slept in one room, and my son had a room of his own. Because in my youth, I'd share a room with my brother, I wanted my children to have rooms of their own. My first challenge: the City of Hesperia required plans for the addition, and I drafted some on my computer. I think the city inspectors wanted to laugh when I showed them the plans. Eventually, I hired an architect to draw the blueprints. From my building construction course, I learned how to read blueprints, and I went back to the city planning department and explained what I wanted to do, and they approved the plans. The addition to the house, when finished, would consist of a bedroom, office, bathroom, and den. Almost half a house for the fifteen thousand dollars borrowed. I should've converted that patio to a room and been done with it-definitely a learning experience.

Because we owned our home, we could hire subcontractors to complete part of the addition to the home. Here I learned not to pay a subcontractor until the work was completed. I paid a subcontractor to pour the foundation, and after I paid him, it took weeks before he completed the job. I had to threaten him physically before he completed the job, a back-in-the-day maneuver. "I'll kick your ass if you don't pour the slab," I said. I was pissed! Before the foundation was poured, I paid a neighbor across the street to rough the underground sewer lines for the bathroom. However, after the concrete for the foundation solidified, I discovered that the sewer line wasn't in compliance with the building code. Actually, the neighbor, he screwed it up. I rented a small jackhammer and took out some of the concrete, adjusted some fittings, and the sewer lines passed the next inspection. I framed the entire 525-square-foot addition in about a week, and the first phase passed the city's inspection.

Next was the challenge of cutting back the eaves to attach the roof joists from the newly framed structure to the house. I used my just-purchased circular saw, which I still have today. At one point, I was sawing the ends of the eaves and thought I was cutting into a knot in the wood. I forced the saw blade, and soon I smelled gas and stopped cutting. With that new skill saw, I'd partially cut a gas line. My wife at that time called the fire department as gas spewed from the line. I finally managed to turn off the gas, and the fire department arrived and put a lock on the gas meter. Another brush with death averted. Because of the lock on the gas meter, we didn't have hot water, couldn't cook anything, and couldn't operate anything associated with gas.

That Monday morning, I contacted the city building department, and they explained what I needed to do in order for them to turn the gas back on. To fix the gas line, I unscrewed it from the source. Where the pipe was cut, I paid someone to thread both ends. I bought a coupling, went home, screwed both pipes into the system, screwed the newly threaded ends into the coupling, and there was my fix. At the gas meter, I inserted a gauge and then used a foot-operated tire pump to put air into the system until the gas lines reached the required pressure. However, I had a leak. Using soapy water in a plastic spray bottle, I found the leak, unscrewed the pipe, put some extra pipe dope on the threads, and reconnected everything. I then pressurized the system for a period and was successful. However, the city said that the system must maintain the pressure for forty-eight hours after the first inspection. After the first inspection, I knew my fix was adequate. I removed the lock so we could at least have hot water.

Before the inspection, I depleted the gas from the system. Then I pressurized the system with air using my foot-operated tire pump and passed the inspection.

Eventually, I completed the framing, added the wire for the stucco, and then called the city inspector. The exterior passed after I added a few more staples to the stucco mesh. Next, a subcontractor applied the stucco, and then I installed the windows and doors and then finished the roof, which didn't match the existing roofline. However, the exterior was complete, and the view from the outside appeared as if the entire project was finished.

Subsequently, it was time to add the water lines for the bathroom plumbing. I purchased a small torch, some solder, and proceeded to sweat the joints (like welding) and add the water lines. The City came to inspect, and my plumbing passed. Great. Winter was approaching, and neither the plumbing nor the interior was insulated. One morning, I awoke to a flooded structure because during the night, the water lines had frozen. Because the plumbing had already passed the City's inspection, I was able to repair the water lines and continue. That same day, I insulated the pipes and, soon after, hired someone to insulate the interior. At this point, the structure was about 75 percent complete.

Then I thought about the days I'd spent repairing my car on the weekends because I was driving approximately two hundred miles five days a week to the federal job from which I'd resigned. I recalled replacing the Japanese engine in that Datsun B210. Adding improvements to the house was a similar event, a book of instructions in one hand and tools in the other. Then I wondered if I'd made the right decision to relocate to the High Desert. Darn, was I exhausted, not only from the addition to the house.

Eventually, because of the lack of planning, debt from all sources began to mount. I was still trying to make things right, but the situation was spiraling out of control. One day, a neighbor stopped by, and I explained my situation and said that I wanted to buy some real estate. However, I had bad credit. He gave me the name of someone who could help. I contacted the person and drove approximately a hundred miles to meet him. He offered a way for me to establish a new identity that included a California driver's license and a social security card. He also explained that if I wanted to buy another house, I could do so after establishing credit under an assumed identify.

The cost to establish the new identity was expensive, but I was desperate. After paying the fee, I had a new identity in no time. Keep in mind my real identity still existed. The individuals coached me through the process of obtaining credit cards and identified which banks to contact. They reinforced that I must remember, when applying for anything, to sign my assumed name and not my real name. I went to one bank to apply for a credit card and signed my real name. The loan person was confused and about the signature, and I said that I often signed papers for a family member and forgot. Nevertheless the loan for the credit card and an associated account was approved. The process worked, and it was time for me to purchase property using the alternate identity.

Everything was in place, and I was about to sign loan documents under the assumed identity when I had second thoughts. It was time to sign the loan papers, and I didn't show up. Thirty years later I can't recall who were the individuals involved or where they were located. For any illegal activity, mentioned here, I believe that the statute of limitations applies. At that time though, I felt guilty, and eventually, the person under my assumed name disappeared. I burned everything associated with the pseudoidentity and never revisited it again. At that time, my conscience got the best of me. The greater fear was the idea of getting caught and going to jail and the impact, of everything on my family. This was definitely a mistake for me in relationship to my climb over fool's hill. I figured that the price of being caught was too steep for me to pay. I'd rather lose everything than go to jail for fraud.

A few weeks later, I received a call from a marine base in the area. They asked if I was interested in a position as a packer, five grades lower than my previous government job. Of course, I accepted, and for now, that was the end of my real estate sales career. The goal was to take the job, catch up on my debt, and eventually invest in real estate.

The real estate office manager was upset because I was leaving, but I had to support my family. The experience in sales was challenging and rewarding, and I did appreciate the opportunity provided by the office manager. From the time I resigned from the last federal job to the offer from the marine base was about six months. Much happened during that time, and recovering from what took place was challenging.

I admit, that during the time I was making that approximately two-hundred-mile trek to the navy base, I wrote my congressperson, and explained my situation. I communicated that I was a veteran from the Vietnam era and how I attempted to make the transition to the High Desert. I explained that I applied for jobs at the marine base. The response I received from the congressperson was encouraging. Yet the response from the marine base to Congressman Lewis was more encouraging. I don't know if know if the inquiry from the congressperson influenced the marine base; however, I was thrilled. I had a steady job. But the challenges associated with my ventures were devastating on every aspect of my life.

At that time, I thought about the trade-off and if driving almost two hundred miles a day to work was worth it. However, we were still trying to recover from my real estate endeavors and pursuit of success. More about this in book 2 concerning family and work-life balance.

Importantly, I had a job nearby, and the drive was thirty miles each way on an open highway, which was far different from the nearly two-hundred-mile drive to and from the navy base and driving on crowded freeways that served the Los Angeles metropolitan areas. In addition, the new job paid less than the navy base job. However, I figured that the quality of life for me was better because the drive to the new position wasn't as stressful, thank God. Besides, I figured that I wouldn't be fixing cars on the weekend like the time I spent repairing automobiles while driving to the navy base. With more time at home now, I decided to complete the coursework for another associate's degree, this time in management, something I'd started previously. At this time, I gained some confidence and was now developing the skill to communicate verbally. I do believe my education and the challenges I faced helped improve my confidence in most areas of my life.

Now I thought I was on my way to success with two associate's degrees. In the meantime, I continued to learn what I could about real estate. To earn extra income in addition to the overtime, I had a paper route for a few months, but the early mornings, seven days a week, and the wear-and-tear on my vehicle weren't profitable. I took a part-time job cleaning offices, which was okay. I was able to work in seclusion, and everything was easy. However, I longed to be in the real estate game.

In time, I asked the real estate broker who presided over the office that I'd left (when accepting the offer for the government job) if I could work part-time. And she was hesitant at first but eventually allowed me to return. I quit the part-time custodian job, and upon my return to the real estate office, I learned that a property I'd listed during the first time I'd worked in the office had been sold. Therefore, the company owed me a commission. I was happy, and after the previously owed office fees were subtracted, the remaining funds helped and were a motivator for me to continue with real estate sales.

As a part-time real estate agent with some experience, I worked in the office at night and fielded incoming calls, which were few. I didn't care and was happy to be back in the real estate game. While in the office at night, I conducted cold calls to convince property owners to sell and list their property with me, but the calls were still a challenge for me. I developed a script and managed to contact a few property owners at night. I was still trying but didn't manage to list or sell any property.

I wondered if I could recover from the challenges of leaving the federal job at the navy base. Again, I questioned if moving to the High Desert and leaving my comfortable well-paying federal job were the right decisions. I was happy because the federal government rehired me, this time at a Marine Corps Logistics Base. Including the time I had been laid off, the federal government had hired me twice and rehired me once for a total of three times. Considering the ventures, the school-loan payments, and the dilemma with the house, it finally led to bankruptcy. We lost both houses and were now renting again.

On my new job at the Marine Corps Logistics Base, eventually I earned a promotion, and the pay increase helped. I continued to look for investments in real estate. I then started applying for entry-level real-estate-related jobs in the federal government, and most were local. I must've applied for twenty entry-level real-estate-related jobs and was willing to work in desolate areas. I believed I was qualified, after all. I had two associate's degrees and one in real estate. I had a certificate in building construction and in real estate appraisal, to name a few. I also had sales experience with two companies and not so much as an interview.

One day, the real estate broker called me into the office and said that the current situation wasn't working. The months working part-time didn't produce any revenue for me or the office. Therefore, she terminated the independent-contractor relationship, and I felt as if I were fired. However, I still had my government job.

Then I learned that I could obtain a bachelor's degree in business and management in two years and I eventually returned to college. At first, I was hesitant because I hated writing. I remembered my community college days and the remedial college writing classes. I remembered my instructor returning my papers, and I couldn't see my words on my paper because of all the red ink from the instructor's corrections. I was an extensive case, and she recommended that I ask a tutor to assist me with writing.

Eventually, I enrolled in a university, and guess what? The instructor in my first class when I pursued my bachelor's degree said the same thing: "You need a writing tutor." At that time, I remember writing something for my sister, and she thought someone from a foreign country who learned English as a second language had written the paper. Then I went on a quest to improve my writing. My employer offered correspondence courses for writing (no internet at that time). I paid for courses as well, which helped. I continued to look for ways to improve my writing. I completed several writing courses using my funds and during my own time. When I attended college my instructor offered words of encouragement and said that a way to improve was to keep writing, suggesting that I shouldn't give up on my education because of the challenge. Today, I enjoy writing for myself and don't do so well when editing or writing for others. I have a writing process that works for me. Eventually, later in life, I taught writing courses at two colleges or universities. Recently, I wrote a policy letter for my employer, and the admin person said that it was one of the most well-prepared and well-written document that he'd seen leave the office.

Anyway, I continued pursuing my bachelor's degree, and because I'd previously earned two associate's degrees and had ninety undergraduate college credits, completing my bachelor's should've been easy. I thought all I needed was 120 credits. However, because I changed majors so many times, only sixty credits transferred to the university. Now my goal was to obtain a bachelor's degree, a better job, then invest in real estate. I was determined to earn that million dollars through real estate investments, and I wasn't giving up.

The college classes I took while I earned my bachelor's degree were a challenge. I was quiet in class and I didn't mingle with others. At break time, I sat in my car while other students in the class mingled. I was the only African American in the class, and the situation reminded me of the time completing my high school diploma and associate's degree at Long Beach City College. It was the same for Victor Valley College, only a few African Americans in my classes. During a semester break, an African American student joined our cohort, as it was called, after a few weeks he disappeared.

In one class, the assignment was a debate. In a textbook were case studies that presented opposing views. Each student was assigned a role: one presented arguments in support of the issues, and the other student presented arguments against it. The goal was to convince the class that the viewpoint you were arguing was the best strategy. I was the student who supported the issues in the case study. To prepare to present my case, I studied diligently I wasn't going to lose the debate. During a class, I was nervous as hell, but I presented my side of the argument, and the other student presented hers. Easily, the class agreed with my argument. I was proud of myself. This was an accomplishment and a confidence builder. I, the shy person, was ecstatic during the forty-mile drive home that night.

I completed all the classes for my degree, but to graduate, completing a final research project was necessary. I researched a topic of my choosing and then presented my research results to an audience in an auditorium. For the final project, I chose to research and analyzed the rate of return for investing in low-income housing versus the rate of return for investing in non-low-income housing projects in the High Desert. Beforehand, I was devastated knowing that I had to conduct a presentation in front of an audience. I practiced but I couldn't overcome my fear of speaking and wrote my entire presentation on three-by-five cards. I bought a new suit and tie for the event.

Then the time came to present, and I was successful reading my final project. Afterward, my instructor approached me and said that I'd passed. He also said that I spoke well and didn't need the cards. I said jokingly, "Thanks for the encouragement." He said, "Really," and told me that I should investigate speaking more. This was interesting because he was the same instructor who said that I should look for ways to improve my writing.

Now it was graduation day. My sister, mother, children, and wife were present. My sister reminded me that five years ago, she'd recommended that I earn my bachelor's degree. At that time, I told my sister that a degree wasn't necessary because I was going to earn a million dollars distributing home-cleaning products. On that graduation day, I bet her thoughts were, "How far has that gotten you?" Anyway, I remember the day before graduation and at the commencement verbally thanking my wife for her support. The time was emotional for me. Someone who had dropped out of high school and then earned a bachelor's degree. I thought about the challenges I'd faced in my youth and now, I'd completed a bachelor's degree. Who would have thought? During graduation, I needed to use the restroom. I was walking down the hallway, and behind me, someone yelled, "Cubit!" I looked behind me, and there was Smitty, an individual whom I'd worked with at the navy base. He was in some disbelief about me completing my bachelor's degree, but he congratulated me for the accomplishment.

At graduation, I made sure my children were present with the hope that they'd learn to never give up. After all, statistics about African American males who had troubled lives indicated that I should be in prison or six feet under. I thought about those who'd said that I wouldn't make it past my sixteenth birthday. I also thought about my grandmother's comments about fool's hill. Where was my placement now? Additionally, I was proud to be at graduation with my family, especially my children. I thought back to the day when my son was born and I made a vow to change my life. The road had been challenging, though, and in finding my "why" (as in the Mark Twain quote in the beginning of this book), I believed I still had peaks and valleys to navigate, especially in relation to fool's hill.

Now I had three college degrees, including a bachelor's, and I was thrilled. After graduation, I took my family to eat hamburgers at a place in Riverside, California. At that time, the enormous hamburgers were called dream burgers, and the name was fitting for someone who just accomplished an important goal that at one time had been a dream. These were the largest hamburgers in the world, about fourteen inches across. I wanted the event to be a lasting memory for my children with the intent of communicating that achieving a goal should be something memorable, like the times they'd earned good grades and placed their report cards on the refrigerator for all to see. Most of all, I wanted to set an example for my children. Well, the strategy must've worked, because my eldest daughter earned her bachelor's degree while raising a family, and my son earned a degree in the technology field.

After graduating, I recalled the last few years when my credit score was low. I thought about losing two houses prior to graduating and driving sixty miles to work and approximately the same distance to school, but now I had three college degrees, and that offset the challenges associated with achievements. I continued to apply for federal real estate-related jobs, and wasn't successful at obtaining one. Not even an interview.

After the bankruptcy, about five years passed, and I looked for ways to earn a better living. Actually, I was bored, and I believed that life had more to offer than just packing boxes at my current job.

I still had goals, and I wanted to do more with my life. I renewed my goals periodically, a learned practice from the training for distributing the home-cleaning products business and a practice I still perform today. I still placed pictures of goals on the refrigerator, and then, before running or working out in the morning, I read a chapter of the Bible and said my affirmations-all with the intention of reaffirming my goals and enhancing life for my family and me. However, I still hadn't recovered from relocating from the job at the navy base to the High Desert.

Years ago, my sister had looked at photos and said that I was photographable. She also said that I should investigate becoming a male model. Who, me? I couldn't do that. In addition, since the military, I'd kept myself in good physical condition. Some might question my mental condition at this time in my life, though. A little pun here, well maybe not. Then one day, my sister called unexpectedly and briefly mentioned that she was looking at some pictures from a family event and reiterated that I was camera-friendly. I thought back to years ago, when I'd been laid off from my federal job and a friend in a class I'd attended was a freelance photographer and wanted to take my picture for his portfolio. I thought I should investigate the opportunity now; after all, what did I have to lose?

I did some research about becoming a model. Then I asked my wife to take some pictures (head shots), and the photographs were sent to several agencies. I was excited when I received calls from agents who asked me for interviews. Some said that they could create a portfolio for me for a fee. My sister warned me about these. Several weeks passed, and another agent called and wanted to talk to me. I took a day off and drove about ninety miles to Hollywood to a nice office. The agent didn't ask for any money and said that their fees would come from my placements. He also said that he pictured me in a magazine posing with a cigarette in my hand.

I talked to my sister, who did some acting and modeling. Let me state that later in life, she transformed from that skinny girl with braids and glasses, trying to kill me because of the "spydarrr" taunts, to an attractive female. Not only did my sister experience a metamorphosis, but our relationship transformed as well. Concerning the modeling, my sister said that the agent seemed legit. The agent called and said that he was hosting a picnic and wanted me to attend. I feared that I had to be present and talk to people, so I asked my sister to accompany me, which she did.

I thought the picnic was amazing. All the food was delicious. What was interesting were the others in attendance-aspiring actors and models. Some of them brought portfolios that displayed pictures of characters they'd portrayed or photographs of modeling they'd performed. Most of the pictures in the portfolios didn't resemble the individuals in person. The difference from the individual and their portfolios was exceptional, and those in attendance resembled a person one might pass on the street. One individual was goofy and in his portfolio for acting, a character he portrayed was a lumberjack. Another female was a hand model, and she wore gloves.

After the picnic, I met with the agent, and he mentioned that I needed to be available when called. The agent also said that he remembered my portfolio and that I was dressed in a nice suit that appeared to be expensive-my graduation suit. He said that based on the suit I was wearing and the distance from Hollywood, he was concerned. He also said that I needed to demonstrate that I was hungry for a modeling career. I was desperate, and I wanted to fully recover from moving to the High Desert. I also wanted to prove the naysayers wrong about not living beyond my sixteenth birthday. *Wait until they see me in that magazine with a cigarette in my hand. I'll show them,* I thought. A quiet voice in the back of my head said that I should never give up on my dreams; however, at that time, I wasn't sure about finding my "why," but I was willing to try anything.

One day while at work at the marine base in the warehouse, over the public address system, was a message to call home. I called my wife at that time, and she mentioned that the modeling agency had called and wanted to talk to me. At that time, cell phones were nonexistent. I went to the local phone booth, used my long-distance account number, and returned the agent's call. The agent asked me to audition for a photo shoot that day, a few hours from the time he'd called me. I told him I was at work and couldn't make it. The agent said that I needed to be hungry for the business and had to leave now for the audition to make it in time. I declined. I called the agent after work, but he never returned my call, and that was the end of my modeling career, at that time anyway. *Perhaps if I were still living in Long Beach, things would be different,* I thought. "Was the move to the High Desert the right decision?" I asked myself. Nevertheless, I aspired to become a real estate investor.

With a bachelor's degree, now I believed I had the tools to advance my career. At my job at the Marine Corps Logistics Base, in a warehouse, working as a packer, I'd volunteered to be the safety coordinator, and this was my first opportunity to speak in meetings. I was still shy and sometimes muttered through my comments. I wanted to improve my public speaking, and before meetings, I practiced and prepared. Eventually, employees complimented me for my comments during the safety presentations. One day, I received a letter from my employer asking if I wanted to participate in the equal employment opportunity advisory committee. My supervisor thought it was a good idea, so I volunteered. At the first meeting, everyone voted that I become the chairperson.

In the interim, at the Marine Corps Logistics Base, I applied for entry-level training positions at the repair division. Most of the jobs were for those who were mechanically inclined. Well, remember my days repairing cars on the weekend, changing car engines, and tuning up cars? Did I have entry-level mechanical experience? In addition, at my last job at the navy base I had been a journeyman missile repairer so I was well qualified for the training position. One day at the Marine Corps Logistics Base, I was handed a letter that asked if I was interested in an entry-level ordnance equipment mechanic helper position in the Repair Division. Of course, I said yes. I then asked what the job entailed. The individual in human resources said that I would be repairing and servicing tanks and other military equipment. If successful after training, I could become a pneudraulics systems mechanic. "Cool," I said, and then I asked what duties they perform. He said that a pneudraulics systems mechanic is someone who repaired and maintained systems operated by either air or hydraulics or both. "Cool," I said again. I couldn't wait to get started.

The training position was a downgrade from my warehouse packer job, but I was able to retain my pay. There was also room for advancement, more than in my current position as a packer working in a warehouse. However, the job paid more because of overtime work. I was hesitant, but I accepted the position. In the pneudraulics shop, another African American male worked there, and the situation reminded me of the time I'd been a missile repairperson at the navy base in addition to my military experience as an ammunitions specialist. Like what had taken place at the navy base and the military, I believe the Marine Corps Logistics Base wanted to diversify the shop at the repair division. Besides, in my packer position, I was a hard worker, proficient at my job, educated, and overall, a good employee. Not to mention, as a warehouse packer, I earned a promotion within the first six months, which usually took a year, unlike the eighteen months it took me to earn my first promotion in the Marine Corps when it usually took someone six months. At that time, I transferred to the training position in the repair division at the Marine Corps Logistics Base.

The pneudraulics shop in the repair division for which I was now employed was a preferred place to work. We were a semi-close-knit group, and sometimes we had fun while working. A Hispanic individual who worked in the shop tried to be the shop comedian; however, based on my experiences as the class clown, I believed there could only be one-me. Besides, I had many comical role models in my life. There was banter between us daily, and sometimes he bested me, and sometimes I bested him. One day, we started a conversation about skiing, and I chimed in. The Hispanic person said, "What do you know? Black people don't ski." I responded, another stereotypical comment, and then I said that I skied regularly. I proceeded to mimic someone skiing, moving my arms and shifting my body from side to side. I had never touched a ski in my life. In the presence of everyone, he asked me what a binder was. I said that it was the device that binds one foot to the ski, the thing one puts his or her foot in. He looked at me, and I guess I gave the correct answer, which was a commonsense one. He then asked, "Where did you learn to ski?" Off the top of my head, I quickly said, "Montana." Everyone roared with laughter. I won the session that day, and he quickly walked away in short, choppy steps with his head down, shifting it from side to side and mumbling over and over, "Ain't no black people in Montana, and black people don't ski."

One day, I took the family to the tram near Palm Springs, and we rode it to the top of the mountain. At the top, it snowed heavily. We were playing in the snow, and fortunately, in the distance, a person was skiing, and he wore clothes like mine. I took pictures and brought them to work. I showed everyone the pictures of me and the one individual skiing who resembled me. Then I said to the Hispanic person, "You owe me an apology. You see? Black people do ski." He was speechless. From that day forward, my name was Montana. When some called me Montana, they did so with a country and western twang in their voice. By the way, I still have the pictures.

The repair division experimented with implementing total quality management (TQM), and they selected the pneudraulics shop for a special project. The goal was to implement self-directed teams. The TQM coordinator asked for volunteers, and somehow, I was selected to be the team facilitator. As the facilitator for the team, I was trained, and at the government's expense I was able to visit companies in the private industry that were successful at implementing self-directed teams. Then I knew sometimes I had to speak in groups and give presentations; therefore, I needed to improve. I joined Toastmasters and, after giving my first speech, nothing but compliments, but attending the meetings for me was like pulling my teeth without Novocain.

Once a week, the shop had a team-building meeting, and I was the facilitator. To tell the truth, at first, I didn't have a clue what I was doing. Eventually, the shop decided to implement the self-directed team with one section of the shop. We were somewhat successful at implementing because we were a cohesive group; however, effecting a true self-directed team in the federal government at that time was almost impossible, but we did a good job. As the team's facilitator, I gained valuable experience.

Beforehand, I'd earned a permanent position as a pneudraulics systems mechanic and I was no longer a trainee-helper. I continued facilitating the team in addition to completing my work assignments. The team was somewhat successful, more so than other units that attempted to implement TQM, but we weren't perfect. Because of our efforts, the repair division spent funds to place a large placard that almost resembled a billboard in front of the shop. Then the Marine Corps Logistics Base published a newsletter, and on the front cover, the pneudraulics shop was featured. The newsletter had a two-page article highlighting the shop's successes working as a team. With that article was a picture of the entire shop, and behind us was the placard. For the article, the individuals generating the newsletter wanted to interview me, but I declined because I believed our success was a team effort. However, the newsletter publisher managed to mention my name in the article.

At this time, I still wanted to improve my employment position and decided to up the ante as far as my career was concerned. Well, I decided to earn a master's degree. I thought a graduate degree increased my chances of obtaining a higher-paying job. I was grateful for my current position but I felt as if something was missing. I wondered if I was destined to repair vehicles the rest of my life. Besides, I hated the constant smell of hydraulic fluid that permeated my pores, which reminded me of the fine glass particles in the crack of my ass while I'd worked at the glass factory. In addition, I kind of sucked at repairing pneudraulics. Still, in the back of my mind, I wanted to prove the naysayers wrong about their predictions for my life.

For the master's, I enrolled in the same school from which I'd earned my bachelor's degree in business and management. The focus for the master's degree was business administration. Once a week, I drove that sixty-mile trek from my work to class and then home about another thirty miles. After class, I spent time in the university library, sometimes arriving home late at night. At that time, the university library had a system called interlibrary loan. I could request publications from affiliate libraries and I waited about a week to pick them up. Sometimes the university mailed the publication to me. The internet wasn't available yet.

I also spent most weekends in the library at the California State University in San Bernardino. I drove about thirty-five miles to the library and stayed there until about 9:00 p.m. on Saturdays. I took my lunch and everything I needed for the day. I repeated the same for Sunday; however, the hours were different. I remember those days conducting research prior to the internet. To find a publication, I used the library cards in drawers. I used the microfiche machine to find scholarly sources. I also remember using a tape machine that helped me locate sources. Not to forget the librarians, a vital source at that time, and I constantly asked them for help. Then arrived the internet, and that changed the way I studied to complete my master's degree. Research was easier, and I could find resources from my computer at home.

Concerning my job at the pneudraulics shop, the work wasn't fulfilling, and I wanted something more. I submitted applications for federal government jobs, mostly for those in a professional series as opposed to those related to mechanics. Because of my real estate background, I applied for federal jobs with the Department of Housing and Urban Development and the Bureau of Land Management. I qualified for some positions, but the effort resulted in few interviews.

After applications to federal agencies for real-estate-specialist positions failed to produce results, I applied for jobs outside the federal government. Most of the jobs were in the real estate sector. I believed that my education would help, and I remembered society's push to educate me when I was a child. I remember a slogan on television and radio that said, "To get a good job, get a good education." Because my efforts failed to produce results, I thought perhaps I was excluded from acquiring a good job or that the playing field wasn't level for me.

One day, my supervisor approached me and said that he was going to promote me temporality to two grades higher, and of course, I accepted. About three months later, he said that there was a permanent position in the shop for my same grade and series. No longer would I be temporary in that position; all I had to do was apply. In the meantime, at my current place of employment, I applied for a trainee position for a human resource specialist and wasn't selected. The staffing specialist explained that I needed one-year experience at the next lower grade to qualify for the trainee position. I asked if three college degrees helped me qualify for a trainee position. He promised to review my application again, and I never heard from the individual. After numerous applications for real-estate-related positions in the federal government and after the many rejections, I determined that civil service probably wasn't a place for me to enhance my career. My supervisor approached me and asked why he didn't see my application for the permanent position. He said that I might've missed the opportunity. A week later, he found out why. I resigned on my birthday, which was symbolic of a new birth for my career and for me. What was I going to do now?

Chapter 11

MORE GROWTH CHALLENGES AND CHANGE

I thought I had it all planned. Previously, my goal had been to complete college and then find a better job. Now, the goal was to find a job. I was certain that I would have another job soon; after all, I was well-educated and had some experience. Because I was well-qualified, I wasn't looking for a handout, just an opportunity to be employed and enhance the organization's mission using my knowledge skills and abilities. However, I was learning that education and some experience wasn't sufficient to obtain a job or advance a career, especially while working for the federal government.

While working at the marine base, I'd met another African American gentleman who was thinking about becoming a schoolteacher. At that time, he'd worked in a tire shop but had aspirations to do something different with his life and career. Both of us were looking for opportunities to enhance our careers beyond our existing employment situations. Before leaving my federal job, I recalled he'd mentioned that someone with a college degree could earn an income from substitute teaching. I already had a degree, and upon investigation of substitute teaching, I learned that for most school districts I needed to pass the California Basic Standards Test (CBEST). After leaving the job at the marine base, I decided to explore whether substitute teaching was something I could do. The individual who'd told me about the substitute-teaching opportunity eventually left his federal job and became a full-time teacher. He's probably a school principal by now.

As previously mentioned, for a short period, I took an early-morning paper route. After leaving the marine base, I decided to take another early-morning paper route, which I did because I was desperate. This time, I took a route with a local newspaper. This route was in a prime location. The customers paid on time, and excluding expenses (gas, wear-and-tear on vehicle, etc.), my net was about five hundred dollars a month. In the meantime, I studied and took the CBEST. The test was as challenging as the California real estate exam. For the CBEST, I earned a passing score for the reading section, I barely passed the writing, but I didn't pass the math section by just a few points. I then took a CBEST preparation class, and the instructor said that passing was more about test-taking skills than the content in the test. I was amazed at that class, and the second time I took the test using the methodologies taught in the class, I passed. I was on my way to becoming a substitute teacher.

Before venturing into substitute-teaching, I enrolled in a new substitute teacher orientation sponsored by one of the local school districts. The title for the class was "Surviving Your Substitute Teaching Experience." The word "survive" gave me the impression that I was in for a challenging experience. As part of the orientation, the presenter said that substitutes should stand their ground and not back down. Be fair, stick to the rules, keep them busy, and complete the lesson plans. The presenter also said that a substitute should never allow the class to get out of control; otherwise, the teacher would never be able to restore order upon his or her return. *Oh, shuck,* I thought.

I applied at three local school districts. All of them hired me. I had to pass a background check, which I did. Now I had two sources of income, one from delivering newspapers and the other from substitute teaching. In the meantime, I continued to apply for federal real-estate-related jobs.

I remember my first substitute-teaching experience. I was terrified by the thought of entering a classroom with snotty-nosed students waiting to hear what came out of my mouth. I remembered one word in the title of the orientation I attended, and that word was "survive."

During that time, teachers and students in all the districts were mostly Caucasian. For substitute teaching, I decided to dress professionally because I believed all students should see and experience an African American male in another role besides a comedian, basketball player, or rapper. Anyway, I believed I had an advantage for substitute teaching, and I was thinking, *Well, I went to drill-instructor school, was on the drill field, and was a marine.* Maybe I should use that military persona, for that was my only reference point for teaching and training anyone. Early one morning, I received a call for my first substitute-teaching assignment.

My first class was fourth graders, and I was scared shitless. They never knew it, though. I had little experience talking in front of people, including fourth graders, and I thought they would eat me alive. I put a mean look on my face, like when I'd lived in the hood, and I went for it. I was drill-instructor, substitute teacher Mr. Cubit. I asked students to call me Mr. C because of the constant questions about the pronunciation of my last name. During my first class, the teacher came back early and she was shocked. Her students were busy working quietly and politely. My first day substitute teaching was a success.

Well, good thing I had the military experience, because it worked, at least for substitute teaching. I also speculate that students behaved in class because in their eyes, I was a tall African American male, talked like a military person, had a mean look on my face, and never smiled. That was tough. In some substitute-teaching assignments, when I asked students to complete a task, they marched as if they were in the military. Several gave me a salute. In time, I was able to relax the military demeanor; however, for survival, I maintained the stern approach, and the students knew their expectations. I do believe some appreciated the structure, and some of the reserved or quiet students appreciated the order in the classroom when the teacher was away. In time, I was most effective communicating with students on their level, which was mutually beneficial.

Several times, I received substitute-teaching assignments for junior high students, which required a different approach, and I wasn't quite as successful. I echo the last for high school freshmen. However, I could better relate to sophomores, juniors, and seniors. For substitute teaching, I only accepted assignments for fourth, fifth, and sixth graders and sophomores, juniors, and seniors. I identified best with sixth graders, my screw-up years. Seniors were my best substituting opportunities as well, especially late in the school year.

I refused substitute-teaching assignments for the primary grades because the students ate me alive, and some situations reminded me of scenes from the movie *Kindergarten Cop*. On one occasion I was assigned a kindergarten class, and one student was afraid of me. He hid under the table, and my military demeanor didn't work. I called a teacher from an adjacent room, and she was able to remedy the situation and saved me. I thought she was amazing. She knew how to speak in that kindergarten teacher's voice, which encouraged the student to crawl from under the table. She knew all the techniques. In a junior high class, a student I disciplined called me gay and ran out the classroom. He had a visit to the principal's office the next school day.

I was a successful substitute teacher, and didn't mind a school district calling me in the morning. Sometimes two districts called. The substitute teaching was steady. Teachers sometimes called me at home to ask if I was available, but the districts put a stop to that. Several teachers mentioned that they appreciated returning to their class and finding that everything was orderly. Some said that the time it took to settle the class down after their absences was minimal. Several teachers said that they usually left more class work than students could finish and upon returning, all the work was completed.

I became a regular at schools, and some assignments extended to a week or more. For the longer assignments, I wasn't as successful. During the weeklong assignments, students discovered my softer side and idiosyncrasies opposed to the structured demeanor and vice versa. I did my best work substitute teaching for the one-day assignments-in and out and then on to another class the next day.

For one weeklong assignment, a student went home and said that I was yelling and screaming at the class and she didn't want to attend school until the regular teacher returned. The parent called the school and asked to observe my class. When teaching while the parent sat in the room, I didn't deviate from my everyday substitute-teaching strategies. During lunchtime, the parent approached me and apologized. Next, she started crying, and I thought she was going to put her head on my shoulder. *What the shuck do I do now? I hope the principal doesn't see this.* Accused of yelling at the class and now the parent crying and her head almost on my shoulder. Finally, in her tears, she told me about all the problems she faced at home and how much the issues affected her daughter. That was a challenging moment for me. What the shuck man.

On an extended substitute-teaching assignment, one African American student mimicked my walk and said that long hair went out in the seventies. He had one of those soup-bowl cuts, in style then. He kept acting out in the class, earning a free trip to the office more than once. The next day, he didn't return, and I was happy, because he disrupted the class and my tactics didn't work. The days he was absent, I thought about the times I'd misbehaved in class, and I figured that perhaps my teacher had been relieved when I was sick. One of my elementary teachers said that I'd better behave in school because I might become a teacher someday, which made some in the class laugh, including me.

There was an African American female student, one of few at any of the schools in the three districts, who ran across the playground to greet me every time she saw me. "Mr. C, Mr. C, how you doing today?" She followed me around and asked childlike questions. I believe she was happy to see someone who resembled her. Sometimes she extended her hand, but touching students in any fashion was a no-no for me.

An advantage of substitute teaching was that sometimes I had assignments at my children's school. Now and then, unannounced, I visited their classes and politely sat in the back and observed. I did this prior to my substitute teaching days as well. Don't misunderstand me-a reason for the unannounced visits was to be involved in my children's education. I was a concerned parent. The teachers and principals understood my intentions, I believe. At that time I believe my children hated the unannounced visits at their schools, however after my daughter had children of her own, I found it humorous when she mentioned that she was considering an unannounced visit at her children's school as well.

In the meantime, I continued to apply for jobs in and outside the government, with few opportunities developing. I continued working on my master's, and the excess from the student loans helped alleviate any challenging financial conditions I had. Essentially, I had three sources of income to make. These included excess from the student loans, a paper route, and substitute teaching. I believed that real estate investments would help resolve the financial challenges someday. I realized that leaving my job at the marine base hadn't been a good idea, for well-paying jobs in the High Desert were few. I had faith, though, and I wondered about my position on fool's hill because of leaving my secure government job.

While I was juggling substitute teaching and the paper route, the supervisor for the newspaper mentioned that the district sales manager in the Barstow office was out on medical leave, and they needed someone to fill in until the company figured things out. I thought, *Well, I delivered routes for two companies and should inquire about the position.* The next day, I was going to ask, and before I could get my words out, the manager asked if I would consider taking the district sales manager position. I did well with my route, and he thought I would do well as the interim district sales manager. He spoke to the regional manager, and they offered me the position. My title was district sales manager. The job was thirty miles away in Barstow close to the marine base. I thought it was going to be a piece of cake. I was concerned about the *"sales"* function in the manager's title, though. *Sales,* I thought. Immediately, I began to reminisce about selling those darn brushes when I was a teenager and my real estate sales experience.

I finally arrived at my new position and found the office in disarray. There were numerous phone calls about poor service and missed deliveries. Most of the newspaper carriers were unhappy about errors in their pay. I had to manage missed deliveries. I was also responsible for ensuring that funds from all the routes were collected. Several routes didn't have carriers and I had to deliver the papers myself pay or someone to do it. Although I had worked at the marine base in the area, I wasn't familiar with the streets in Barstow. Some of the customers lived in the middle of the desert, and the only way to identify the property was a rock or a Joshua tree. The directions for the route actually showed, "Turn left at the third Joshua tree" or "Turn right at the fifth boulder."

As the district sales manager, I supervised a support person, and all she could do was field the phone calls and respond to complaints. My hours were from about 2:00 a.m. until the job was done. Usually, my day ended at about 7:00 p.m. I then drove thirty miles home. On top of all this, I was working on completing my master's degree and trying to keep up with the demands of schooling and family. I remember getting up at 2:00 a.m., working all day, and then driving from the office straight to school about sixty miles and then back home another thirty miles. Sometimes I didn't get home until 11:00 p.m.

Meanwhile, I received a lump-sum disbursement from my previous employer, the federal job. We caught up on some of our debts, and in conjunction with a student-loan disbursement, using my knowledge of real estate, we bought a house with our bad credit (two foreclosures, a repossessed car, and bankruptcy). My wife begged me to buy a new car, but I was set on making a fortune in real estate. Later, I discovered that buying a new car would've alleviated many challenges we later faced.

The house we purchased was much larger, but on the far end of town. To purchase the property, we assumed an FHA loan, and I thought we were on our way to real estate investing success. Concerning loans on the property, I was in third place, and the property was overmortgaged, like the last house we'd bought. Here I learned that financing is an important aspect of successful real estate investing. At that time, an individual could buy a property with a minimum down payment. However, the monthly payment tended to be extreme. In our case, the payment was higher than our budget could withstand. Here I realized that I could buy property for nothing down, but I didn't take into account the amount of the monthly payment. Looking back, financing real estate investments was the challenge for me. In addition, the loans on the property were more than the value (loan-to-value ratio). And forget about refinancing. However, if an individual desired to live in the house forever, then the value might not be as important. Live and learn.

After purchasing the property, again, I pursued a home improvement loan and decided to turn the patio into an office. This was a much smaller than the 535-square-foot addition at the other house. This time, I was fortunate to have a helper, my son. This home-improvement project didn't take long, and eventually, I had a fully functional office at the back of the property. Working with my son was an advantage for two reasons. One was the time spent with him, and I noticed that my son was interested in computers. Secondly, after helping me with some of the home improvements, including the 535-square-foot addition, he acquired knowledge as well. From watching me work with computers and working with me on the additions to houses, my son often, at an early age, communicated his desire to draw houses using a computer. Today, he is proficient at both and has traveled throughout the world performing computerized architect functions.

In addition to the home-improvement, I was busy attending to the district manager's sales position and almost dropped out of the master's program. I was distressed because the district sales manager position wasn't in my plans. However, the opportunity to earn an income had arisen, and I'd taken the bait. The income as a district sales manager was steady, I had an opportunity to increase my management skills, and the bonuses were helpful. In about ninety days, I received a call, and the individual said that the district manager was returning to the job I occupied. The company offered me a similar job in San Bernardino. But I was through with the newspaper industry. I wanted to focus on completing my master's degree.

We settled into our house, and I was back to substitute teaching. All the districts welcomed me back. I continued working on my master's degree and applied for real-estate-related jobs. I stopped applying for federal jobs and felt that approximately fifty applications were enough.

I received a call from a mortgage company, and they asked me to sit for an interview for a loan-processor trainee position. The company was one that I'd submitted an application to weeks earlier. Of course, I said yes because I needed to earn an income to support my family. The loan company was about thirty-five miles from my house, and that involved a seventy-mile round-trip. After the interview, the next day, they offered me the job. Finally, something involving real estate. My automobile was almost ready for the junkyard, but I took the job anyway, and I was just about finished with my master's degree. I arrived on the first day, and I noticed the female-to-male ratio. Approximately 95 percent of the employees were females. Another African American male worked for the company, and he was a full-time loan processor.

I found that loan processors pushed paperwork all day, and the work had little to do with working with property. I went to work every day in a dress shirt and tie. In addition, at that company, I felt the pressure of harassment. Almost every day, someone propositioned me. I didn't believe what was happening. I told everyone I was married, but some didn't seem to care, and one individual asked if I was *happily* married. After about three weeks of the challenges there, I began dreading going to work. I feared walking around the establishment. I was experiencing what I guess some females undergo when they're harassed. I was still somewhat shy, and I felt uncomfortable. On top of that, my car gave me problems, and I was late a few times. My wife at that time had been right about purchasing another vehicle. Combined with the car problems and the working conditions, I opted to leave the job. Well, it was back to substitute teaching. I was determined to work in real estate, though, and I wasn't giving up.

I was desperate for a job, and I saw an advertisement in the newspaper for a home-delivery manager for a local newspaper company. I thought, *Well, this company is local, and if hired, I don't have to drive miles to work.* I applied for the home-delivery-manager position, and I was hired. I found that the job was in Barstow, the same place as the temporary district sales manager position. *Oh, shuck,* I'd thought.

In my home delivery manager position, I now had an assistant and I supervised an office support person. At first, things ran smoothly, and the paper was an afternoon delivery. The only morning paper was Sunday. The regional manager mentioned that the paper would become a morning delivery. As the home-delivery manager, I was supposed to be responsible for the administrative functions of the job and managing newspaper delivery. Wrong. After switching to a morning delivery, the newspaper experienced similar problems as the previous newspaper I worked for. Most of the newspaper carriers quit, and I was delivering newspapers again. My assistant helped, and I delivered the balance. The situation became dire, and the regional manager, who lived approximately fifty miles away, delivered newspapers as well.

My car was almost ready for the junkyard, and I don't know how it survived. Again, my drive to and from the job was a seventy-mile round-trip. Then I drove over fifty miles while delivering two or more routes. I remember one route I delivered took me about six hours. Here I was in my clunker, throwing newspapers in desolate desert areas, shirt, and tie on. Again, some of the homes didn't have addresses. Eventually, my car wasn't able to endure delivering the routes, and some customers went without newspapers.

Now I was in a situation worse than the previous newspaper delivery manager's position. On top of everything, the company had little respect for the delivery staff in comparison to other departments in the organization. I remember early one Sunday morning, I received a page on my pager and called my supervisor who said a carrier had quit. I had to deliver a route on my only day off. After I arrived at the delivery dock, some of the company executives were present. We were in a scramble preparing the morning delivery, and I knew the customers were going to get their papers. On top of that, I needed to stuff the advertisements and put the papers in my vehicle
. All the executives did was watch, and one snickered. One mentioned that it was my job and loading papers was beyond him. I felt like leaving all the papers on the dock and going home.

I continued working for the company, and I was a highly paid newspaper carrier who often wore a tie to work. I did little of the job for which I'd been hired. Again, I was behind working on my master's degree and believed there was no end to the madness. I was confused about my career as well. At my age, I wondered, why the struggles? I was educated, a veteran, and I had some experiences. I was a newspaper carrier twice, a district manager, and a home-delivery manager. All the managerial positions were nothing more than glorified newspaper carriers. I finally decided that the newspaper industry wasn't a career for me. After several months, I opted to leave the organization and return to substitute teaching. The newspaper offered me a higher salary; however, I was through with all the madness. I vowed to never work in the newspaper industry again. My only experience with a newspaper after that would be reading one.

I returned to substitute teaching and focused on completing my master's degree. In one class, I missed taking the final exam and had too many absences. If I failed the class, shit would hit the fan my student loans and the Pell Grants, and taking the class again would definitely be a challenge. I explained to the instructor what had happened, and at first, he was hesitant to help me. He said that the university didn't pay him for working with students after the class ended. Finally, though, he relented. I took a makeup final test from home, which was mostly essay. The instructor faxed me the test, and I had two hours to fax my answers back. I faxed it back in approximately two hours and fifteen minutes. We spoke on the phone, and he said, "I'm not going to give you a grade for the test. However, you earned a passing grade for the class. Nonetheless, here is your charge." The instructor went on to explain, "I ask that you recall what happened here, and you must remember to help someone who may be in a similar predicament. You owe it to society." A pay it forward situation. Of course, I promised to honor my charge and was able to pass the class and continue completing my master's degree.

At that time, I became interested in equal employment opportunities for the workplace. Thinking back, when working at the marine base, I'd had an opportunity to serve as chairperson of the equal employment opportunity advisory committee. Now I could enhance that experience. In my master's program, I had the opportunity to structure assignments in areas of interest. I completed a paper and was responsible for presenting the information to the class. Imagine that, me, Mr. Shy, presenting a paper to the class. I was apprehensive but had a passion about what I was presenting. My topic was about the dynamics of affirmative action (AA). When presenting the paper, I posed a question to the class: state your understanding of affirmative action. A Caucasian manager thought AA was a quota system. Another answered, "AA means when you have a white applicant and a black applicant, give the job to the black guy." I quote. I presented my research results, and the class thanked me for the enlightenment, especially the two managers who didn't have any clue about AA. From that point on, I directed my studies toward managing diversity as a tool to enhance productivity and, sometimes while in class, explaining the difference between AA and why managing diversity was necessary.

Meanwhile, I continued to study real estate courses and began working on my broker's license. I figured, as a real estate broker, I didn't have to sell property; I only had to manage an office. Besides, for California, I had all the qualifications to be a real estate broker. I just needed to pass the test.

We lost our third house and were now living in a rental. I applied for a real estate appraiser's job at a county agency and was called for an interview. The office was near where I worked as a loan processor. I went for the interview and showed them my portfolio. The county agency called me for a follow-up interview, and I agreed to a date and time. On my way to the second interview, a rail tanker carrying hazardous materials overturned near the highway, and the Cajon Pass was closed. I couldn't make it to the second interview. I attempted a detour in that clunker but had to turn around and go home. I called the county agency, and they rescheduled me for another interview.

I was successful at my second interview and was hired. I completed a three-month internship as a real estate appraiser trainee. I liked the training and thought I had arrived. As previously mentioned, I took several courses in real estate appraisal and liked the work. While employed by the county agency, I applied for jobs in the federal government in real estate and figured I could add appraising to my résumé. Several federal agencies interviewed me, but not one job offer. I wondered what the problem was. I was a Vietnam-era veteran. I had permanent status and three college degrees, including one in real estate. I was completing my fourth college degree and had completed several real estate courses on my own. I had experience as a sales agent, a short tenure as loan processor, and appraising experience.

I completed the real estate appraisal training and was then assigned to the Palm Springs, California, area. I had about a ninety-six-mile drive each way to work and sought a transfer to the city of Riverside, to no avail. Here we go again, the long drive to and from work in another clunker. The drive reminded me of when I was employed at the navy base and had to drive ninety-six miles one way to work. When traveling to and from work, I remember stopping at a truck stop several times to allow my clunker to cool down. Several times, I had my car towed home. I thought about relocating to the Palm Springs area, but two of my children were in high school then.

I was happy about my new job in the Palm Springs, California, area. I finally finished my MBA. One day, I was talking with one of the supervisors in my department. She was on the panel when I interviewed for the appraiser trainee position and recommended me for hire because she attended the graduation where I earned my master's and saw me walk across the stage. "What a coincidence," I thought. I said that my doctorate was next. I also said that long ago, someone told me that completing my master's wasn't possible and certainly a doctorate was out of reach. I also said that a doctorate would be challenging, but I would take it on and hopefully earn a PhD in something related to real estate. Actually, I didn't believe I could complete a doctorate-I was only trying to impress her.

I continued working at the county and making the long drives and dealing with my clunker. I thought about carpooling with another individual, but that wasn't possible. Making the rendezvous for the carpool would be almost impossible. The remedy for making those long drives every day appeared to be nonexistent.

I enjoyed appraising affluent property in Palms Springs and the surrounding areas. I was amazed at some of the houses that individuals owned. Sometimes when I appraised one of those mansions, it was necessary for me to enter the property. Often, I talked to the owner. Some were doctors and medical specialists, some were lawyers, and most were entertainers. At one memorable home, the owner mentioned he was an orthopedic surgeon. I thought, *Wow, healing people's feet earned the individual an affluent life.* None of the affluent homeowners mentioned that he or she was an appraiser for the county. Having an affinity for real estate investments, I wondered if I would own similar properties someday.

In about two months, my car took a turn for the worse, and after I arrived at work, a female senior appraiser mentioned that she had a spare room in the back of her property. She said that I could stay there during the week and go home on the weekends. After assisting her in the field several times, and considering her advances, I thought not. One day, she and I went on an assignment to appraise property. During lunch in a restaurant, she asked if I could look into her ear because she was having some pain. She led on to propositioning me to having an affair. I was taken aback and found a way to downplay what was happening. I do believe she understood I wasn't interested. After all, I was married. I believed she understood, and I returned to the office and talked to an individual who went through the apprenticeship class with me about what had happened. He said that I should honor her advances and go for it-perhaps free room and board. It didn't matter. A few days later, my clunker was inoperable, and that was the end of that job. I didn't have the ability to drive ninety-six miles to and from work for almost two hundred miles.

Because of all the challenges I'd faced, I left that job. I struggled with leaving that job because I had worked so hard to obtain the real estate credentials and experience. When I resigned, the female who'd made advances asked if she had something to do with me leaving that job. My comment was, "Not at all." Substitute-teaching here I come.

It was now summer, and substitute teaching was slow. During the summer, because many of the districts were year-round, most substitute-teaching assignments were reserved for full-time teachers.

I needed a job badly, so I took a full-time position in a commercial-wood products business. I lied about my education and told
them that I had warehouse experience. I had already earned a master's degree and couldn't find a job in the High Desert. Where I lived
was rural, and to secure a good job meant I had to drive long dis-
tances in my clunker.

I applied and went to work for the commercial wood products
business as a laborer, earning minimum wage. The commercial-wood
products business manufactured cabinets and like products for existing and new houses. Working at the commercial-wood products
business was like my employment at the glass factory. The difference between working at the glass factory, and the commercial-wood
products business was the sawdust instead of the fine glass particles
in the crack of my butt. Itchy.

The job at the commercial-wood products business was heavy
manufacturing, and the building was dusty, and dirty. I sanded furniture legs almost all day. On occasions, I worked in the field, and
most locations were new housing tracts. As a member of a field crew,
I carried cabinets sometimes up three flights of stairs, and I wasn't as
young as other members of the crew. The cabinets were solid wood
and heavy. I remember some of the individuals carrying the cabinets
on their backs. The situation reminded me of the time when I was
relocating from Hawaii to California while in the military. While I'd
lived on the base, a mostly Polynesian crew came to pack and pick up
our furniture. One individual sat in the truck. When it came time to
move the refrigerator, the crew signaled for the man in the truck. He
was a huge Polynesian male without any shoes. He wore shorts and
no shirt. They strapped the refrigerator to his back, and he proceeded
to carry that damn thing down what I call a difficult flight of steps.
When he was finished with the refrigerator back in the truck he sat.

Anyway, some of the individuals carrying the cabinets up the
stairs reminded me of the individual moving the refrigerator in
Hawaii. After a few days of lifting the cabinets up the stairs, I was
sore everywhere. Although I was in good physical shape, at home,
my muscles ached every time I thought about lifting a cabinet. In
the meantime, I applied to what seemed like over one hundred gov-

ernment and private industry jobs, but to no avail. I kept the applications submitted and all the rejection letters. Eventually, it became depressing, and after reviewing copies of the letters, I threw everything in the trash. I wondered, *If I obtained my doctorate, would things be different?*

After reporting to work one morning, I was assigned to another off-site project and knew I had to carry cabinets up flights of stairs. Before I left, a supervisor called me, and he mentioned that he had a special project. He led me to a silo filled with sawdust that accumulated from the exhaust system from inside of the building where I'd previously hand-sanded the furniture. *Here I go again,* I thought. While working at the glass factory, I had to shovel the residue from the smoke stack scrubbers, a messy situation, but then I'd worn a respirator.

The supervisor at the commercial-wood products business gave me a dust mask instead of a respirator and asked me to shovel sawdust and put it in a bin. I was able to endure the work for about half an hour. I was dirty and itching from the sawdust, and that day was hot in the High Desert, as most days are in the summer. Shoveling that sawdust was labor intensive. At that time, I thought again about the slogan on television and sometimes on the radio when I was younger that said, "To get a good job, one must get an education." With a master's degree in hand and shoveling sawdust, now I started to wonder. Anyway, in the High Desert, late morning, that silo was getting hotter. I told the supervisor that I had to use the bathroom. I was in the bathroom for about ten minutes, cleaning myself. When the supervisor looked out the front door, all he saw were the numbers on my license plate and the dense smoke from the tailpipe of another clunker I'd managed to purchase and piece together. I left the shovel jammed in the midst of all the sawdust in the silo. Oh well, after a few weeks of handling commercial-wood products, I was back at substitute teaching when school started in autumn. The assignments were steady again.

This time, substitute teaching was a challenge. I believed that my status in life should greatly improve, especially after obtaining four college degrees (two associate's, a bachelor's, and a master's). I began to wonder what life would be like if I'd stayed at the navy base job and warehoused bombs and explosives. I began to wonder if my education achievements and the move to the High Desert to buy a home had been the right things to do.

On one occasion, I visited the old neighborhood where we'd lived before relocating to the High Desert. I also visited the community college in Long Beach, California, where I'd attended. I needed to obtain transcripts from where I'd earned an associate's degree. While walking the campus, I remembered the times when I was the only African American or one among the few. Not the case anymore. I also drove by the house where we'd lived at one time. The area where we'd lived had changed as well. Not good or bad, I just wondered what life would be like if we'd never made the move to the High Desert. After all, the intent had been to provide a better life for family and, of course, to invest in real estate.

After my ordeal with the commercial-wood products business, I decided to return to school and obtain a California teaching certification. I was already in the classroom most of the time, so why not become a certified teacher? I applied for classes at Chapman University and was accepted. I began taking classes at night and, during the day, did substitute-teaching assignments. Here I applied for student loans and, from the excess, was able to help sustain us.

After a few courses, I took a general-education class. The individual teaching the class was the principal at high school. One night, he talked to me about teaching opportunities. He said that there weren't many African American male teachers in public school and I should go for it. I thought back to my junior high school days and as previously mentioned, I hope that throwing books in class hadn't deterred the male African American's effort to teach in public school. Nonetheless, the individual teaching the certification class was from San Diego, and although Caucasian, he knew exactly where I was from and said that apparently the neighborhood had changed since his days. He said that I should meet with him and talk about a teaching job. I found that I could teach on an emergency credential as long as I earned six units a year toward my certification. I took his advice and applied at the high school, where he was the principal.

The principal hired me, and I began teaching in November, and the school year ended in June. Because of my degrees in business, I taught business education courses that included keyboarding and computer accounting. I was also responsible for coordinating the work experience program. *Work experience, what is that? Well, at least I'll have a steady income*, I thought. I learned that students in the work experience program earned high school credit for working in a job. For part of the class, I needed to design coursework that helped students learn how to be successful on the job. Something I could've used when participating in that job-training program as a youth. The opportunity to teach business-education classes and work-experience began another important chapter in my life.

Chapter 12

YOU'RE GONNA BE A
TEACHER SOMEDAY!

I continued working on my teaching credential while teaching at the high school. The excess student-loan money came in handy and helped pay our bills. Regardless of my thoughts about an education and a good job, I thought about earning a doctorate degree. *Might as well, and maybe the doctorate degree will propel me into that well-paying job,* I thought. Another reason for pursuing a doctorate or any degree was to prove the naysayers wrong. Yes, years after my sixteenth birthday, I was still striving. However, in my current situation, I still had memories about splinters in my hands from carrying those damn cabinets up flights of stairs.

At this time, I thought about those days living in the hood and having no clue about what life had to offer. I thought about some individuals who might be experiencing the same challenges I'd faced in my youth. I found myself thinking about being an example to some and showing them that they didn't have to remain stuck in their current situations, whatever those might be. Here again, I thought about displaying the never-give-up attitude to my children. Again, they became a reason for achieving in life. However, some might question my tactics at this point; nonetheless, the idea here was to do something to help others. I didn't know that my current situation would lead me to those opportunities and why.

At that time, I also thought back to when my sister had attempted to encourage me to earn a college degree. I remembered how I'd said to her that I was going to make a million dollars distributing cleaning products or investing in real estate. Now I was looking for a doctorate program. Then the competitor in me surfaced. I had a master's degree and I'd passed my sister in educational attainment; however, she was in a program to earn her master's degree. *All right, I'll go for it and be the first person on my father's side of the family to earn a doctorate.* Definitely more education than my sister. She would never catch up to me now. *I will earn that doctorate degree, get me a good job, and then invest in real estate* was my thinking.

Please don't misunderstand me. I love my sister, and she was and is instrumental in my growth as a human being, probably more than she realizes. I remember she was the first one who told me that Santa Claus wasn't real. I was devastated, but looking back, I thank her for telling me the truth. God knows who needs another lie about life to deal with. Because of the devastation I experienced when learning that Santa Claus wasn't real, early in my children's lives, I made sure they knew about Saint Nicholas instead of Santa Claus in addition to stories about the birth of Christ and the commercialization of Christmas. No one with rosy red cheeks was coming down a chimney to bestow gifts on those who behaved. Besides, at that time, we didn't have a chimney, only a small pipe protruding from our roof, and I further emphasized that a jolly fat man couldn't fit down the pipe anyway.

I reviewed state-funded schools and found a program in which I could earn a doctorate degree in property development. In that program, students worked in teams, and the goal was to develop real estate investment property. *Perfect,* I thought. However, for enrollment, the university required that I take tests and earn a minimum score. I began studying for the tests, and the rigor reminded me of the California real estate exam, or the CBEST test. *Too much work,* I thought.

Meanwhile, at the high school, I continued to teach computer accounting and keyboarding classes. Except for the work-experience course, at first, I taught classes with the same demeanor as I had as a substitute, but that approach was ineffective. I needed to learn how to teach students in a nonthreatening manner, and at first, this was a challenge for me. What enhanced my ability to be successful was that eventually, I was able to relate to students and teach according to their level of understanding. This required constant adjusting.

My first-period class was computer accounting, and I had few course materials to work with and had to find a way to teach the class. The first few days, I attempted to teach basic computer skills, but the students were well advanced. I remember students looking at me strangely when teaching. I wanted to do a good job, so I went to the community college bookstore and found a computer accounting workbook. I used the assignments in the workbook, and none of the students knew that they'd completed coursework from a community college textbook. All the students passed the class without difficulty. There were approximately seven students in the class. It helped that all of them were seniors and were motivated to graduate. I was also appreciative of my past and learning something about computers on my own account, which helped me be successful at teaching the class.

The second and third periods, I taught a keyboarding class, which was an exceptional experience. Students completed lessons from a workbook at their own pace. I wasn't a person who could type eighty words per minute, but I taught the fundamentals; after all, I had plenty of practice. While watching students as they completed lessons and typing tests, I chuckled, thinking about the challenges I'd faced while learning how to type. However, I was and am grateful for my experience as a student in that typewriting course, which helped me become successful at teaching the keyboarding class at the high school. Then I realized I came full circle from the days practicing on an electric typewriter, to now teaching a similar course. My experiences also helped me discover how to revise the keyboarding course to enhance learning for students. Sometimes the school principal, the individual who'd hired me, visited the class and complimented me for doing a good job.

In classes, students called me the no-go teacher and knew they had to use the bathroom before class. During class, a pass for a bathroom break was a no-go unless it was an emergency. Before teaching at the high school and while substitute teaching, I had a strict policy about using the bathroom during class. While substitute teaching, I learned that students sometimes made excuses to use the bathroom and then roamed the halls, creating havoc. At first, they knew they could take advantage of the new substitute and now the new teacher at the high school. To circumvent that behavior, at the beginning of class, I made sure students knew that they must use the restroom during recess, passing period, lunch, and so on. For accountability and to decrease classroom distractions, I enforced the no bathroom policy.

In one keyboarding class, a female student asked if she could use the restroom. The student had an attendance problem, and during my time teaching the class, she was present maybe twice. The principal had warned me about the student. After she asked, I said that the time to use the restroom was during her passing period. In a loud voice, she said that she had female problems and had to use the bathroom. She became angry. I relented. From that point on, I never saw her again during that period, nor did she ever return to that class. She pulled one over on the new teacher. Although I gave the student a pass, if something happened to any student during the keyboarding class, I was responsible. I was learning about the nuances of teaching in high school, which was different from substitute teaching.

Teaching the keyboarding class was a success for me. However, the work-experience class was in disarray. I was able to work with other schools that had similar courses, and I revised the work-experience program to ensure that the class accomplished learning goals for students. I also developed curriculum for the class and enjoyed teaching subjects about the world of work. For example, I taught one class where students learned about dressing for interviews. In another class, students learned about completing job applications, and so on. Eventually, the work-experience class became my favorite, and I believed I was positively influencing students' lives.

As the work-experience coordinator, I visited students' work sites and monitored how they performed on the job. I also issued work permits for underage students and monitored their progress on the job and in school. If a student's grades were on the decline, I was responsible for counseling him or her and devised an improvement plan. If there was no improvement, then I could suspend their work permit or permanently revoke it.

Because my existing job was temporary, I applied for teaching assignments at other schools. The school year was ending, and I was excited about the prospects of teaching the next year. The principal and school district commented about the exceptional job I was doing. During the last weeks of the school year, the principal called me into the office. He said that one of the tenured instructors had complained and that he wanted to teach the work-experience class. The instructor was an ineffective teacher and was about to retire. The teacher threatened to file a union grievance. The principal said my temporary teaching assignment was over, but, he would find me a classroom, and I could teach business-education classes. I was upset because I wanted to continue teaching the work-experience classes. Of all the classes I taught, I believed that work-experience was a way for me to give back and help students prepare for employment. However, it appeared that I needed similar classes concerning my work experience. In the meantime, I continued looking for a doctorate program to enroll in while completing a teaching credential.

A few days later, I received a call from a school district close to my house. I'd applied for teaching positions in work-experience, computers, and careers at an alternative-education high school. Students in the alternative-education program typically enrolled because of challenges they faced in a traditional school system, like my dilemma as a youngster; however, I never attended a continuation school. During the interview, I expressed concerns about teaching a careers class. After all, my career path wasn't established, I thought. Perhaps I was already on a career track and just didn't know it. In addition, the person interviewing me said that students in the school might benefit from learning about careers from me, more so than someone who had gone to college right out of high school, graduated, found a job, married, and lived happily ever after. On the way home, I pondered the conversation with the interviewer at the continuation school and thought, yes, students could benefit from learning about some of my trials and tribulations. A few days later, the school offered me the position.

At the school I was currently employed, I politely declined the principal's offer to teach in the classroom full-time, and I finished the school year. Both the school superintendent and the principal wrote letters of recommendations for me. Then I was off to my next teaching adventure.

In the meantime, as mentioned, I continued looking for doctorate programs to attend and believed that earning a doctorate would definitely enhance my career. However, in the back of my mind, I knew that I didn't have the capability to complete a doctorate. After all, I didn't have any money to pay for a doctorate. I applied for several scholarships but was denied. Eventually, I applied for a public-administration doctorate program and was accepted. My start date was the beginning of the school year in September.

Before entering the doctorate program, I had a meeting with my family, and I explained the situation. I communicated the importance of an African American male earning a doctorate. Part of the motivation for pursuing the doctorate was to obtain a better job, I explained. I also spoke about the goal of proving the naysayers wrong and demonstrating a never-give-up attitude. I envisioned getting a good job because of my education. However, I still had flashbacks about carrying those cabinets up the flights of stairs and that sawdust silo. Nonetheless, my family agreed that I should go for it and pursue the doctorate degree.

During that summer, after leaving the teaching job, I was unemployed and I learned that I could've applied for unemployment insurance, but I'd missed the opportunity. No employment, no income. Occasionally, I received a substitute-teaching assignment. From the time I left the last teaching job to the assignment at the continuation school was about two months.

Eventually, I started the doctorate program in public administration. The program required weekend work, and doctorate students alternated facilitating classes, and sometimes we had to conduct team presentations. On one occasion, I had to conduct a presentation, and I was so afraid that I didn't show up. I was also supposed to facilitate a class, but the experience was new to me; therefore, someone in the group took my place. I knew my turn was coming, though.

I had fears about facilitating a class. Although I now had confidence and could return defective items to a store instead of asking my wife and could put up a good argument if receiving bad service, the thought of facilitating a class was intimidating. Speaking in class was already a challenge, and I didn't contribute much and had very little to say. I could do the work, but the presentations, contributing while in class, and networking were challenges for me. Believe me: I wanted to be confident while speaking but I hadn't developed the skill. I felt inadequate because of my inability to communicate openly and wondered if I would ever measure up.

As part of the doctorate program, I attended weekend open sessions in an auditorium in addition to the classes. The auditorium was full, and there was much conversing. Often, I found myself sitting in my car. I worked at listening and trying to learn, but my fears inhibited me. Besides, it was difficult for me to comprehend the subject matter during the conversations. There finally came a time when I had to conduct a final presentation, and I didn't show up. It was the second time this happened. I never returned to class, but I wanted to continue with the program. I spoke with a school counselor and explained my situation. The counselor said that I should've contacted her earlier, instead of waiting until the last minute, and withdrawn from the class instead of failing to show up. That was the end of my doctorate program. The education venture cost me about seven thousand dollars, and I had nothing to show for it other than two failing grades. The situation reminded me of my first classes in the community college wherein I earned two Ds and two Fs. The only benefit from pursuing the doctorate program was that I satisfied the six-unit requirement for teaching with an emergency credential at the high school.

Soon thereafter, I began teaching at the continuation high school. While driving to the school one day, I had a flashback. Years ago, while working at the marine base, I had been driving down the same road to the school district to interview for a part-time janitorial job. At that time, I only had an associate's degree. Keep in mind that the area was rural and the road had one lane each way. As I had been driving to interview for the janitorial job, an older man had been driving twenty miles per hour, and the speed limit was much higher at that time. I proceeded to pass the man on a hill, and I collided with an oncoming car. My fault. Good thing the accident hadn't been a head-on collision. I had avoided that by steering toward the adjacent median. I ran to the other car to ask if the Caucasian female in the car was all right. She'd exited her car and then tried to run, pleading, "Brother, don't beat me!" She'd kept on saying this. I had been dumbfounded.

The situation reminded me of the time I'd been in Hawaii lying in bed with a female I'd met in a nightclub and she'd been crying and asking that I not beat her, which, I emphasize, hadn't been my intention. Not to mention the time I'd been asked to be in a lineup for a rape case while in Hawaii. Recalling the situations mentioned here, I wondered if I had a sign on my back that read, "I assault Caucasian women." Two Caucasian female coworkers on different occasions had said that for six months, they'd been afraid of me. However, both said that after getting to know me, and peeling back the layers that perhaps in their own minds, they'd realized I was a cool guy. In both cases, we eventually became friendly coworkers. Nevertheless, I learned to be cautious, and I understood and understand the challenges some African American men face because of preconceived notions. My father warned me about these situations mentioned here, especially if in the presence of people of other races. Me, as a tall intelligent professional, and now a confident, educated black man who has a presence, I learned to be cautious of individuals who might have preconceived notions and be afraid of me without knowing anything about Ronnie. These can be challenging or dangerous, especially in situations where the dominant population isn't composed of people of color, and or individuals of similar color who may want to impede my success to maintain their in-group status. More on this in book 2.

Anyway, concerning the accident and the female in a frenzy about my beating her, at the same time, two guys in a truck had stopped, they appeared to be construction workers, and because of her frenzy, they approached me in a threatening manner, and there had almost been an altercation. I'd told the guys I was trying to help, and I guess they had been able to sense it and backed off. Soon after, the highway patrol arrived, and I explained the situation. I'd proceeded to the school district for my interview dirty and distressed from the incident. I hadn't been hired for the part-time janitorial job.

Years later now, I was driving down that same road. I thought about what had happened years ago and chuckled. I briefly thought that the female was distraught because of the accident or had watched too many episodes of *COPS* or *The Jerry Springer Show*, and I'll leave it at that. Nonetheless, I was off to my new teaching adventure with the goal of assisting students at the continuation school with career goals and other areas of their lives.

I enjoyed teaching at the continuation school and helping students find ways to obtain jobs, and perhaps careers. I also taught computer applications, careers, bookkeeping, and business math. During the last period of the day, I developed internships for students, and like the work-experience students at the previous school district for which I'd worked, I monitored students in the program.

Like my last teaching job and then at the continuation school, I developed lesson plans and curriculum. However, because of my experience with keyboarding, computers, and associated technologies, preparing for some of the classes wasn't as difficult as it was for others. The computer classroom was equipped with Apple computers, and I had to develop lesson plans for a platform that I wasn't familiar with. For the first three months, I worked six days per week and on Saturdays or Sundays at the school as I prepared lesson plans for the upcoming week.

At the continuation school, some students had behavior challenges. In the beginning, teaching the class was a challenge for both the students and me. More so for the students. Like substitute teaching, at first, my stern approach was successful, and some students who weren't familiar with a structured environment became belligerent and disruptive. Some attempted to sleep in class, and I didn't allow that. Some tried to scare me with threatening looks, and I didn't relent. Sorry, I'm from the hood. In addition, another student decided to make copies of a dollar bill using a high-resolution printer and passed the counterfeit copies around the campus. The student was expelled. One student lit a stink bomb in the classroom; he was also expelled from the school. However, the event reminded me of my misbehaviors while attending school in my youth. I thought back to my school days when I'd made stink bombs out of chicken bones and water. Talk about karma. Now, what I did in the past as an unruly youth was happening to me. Another full-circle event in my life.

Sometimes, female students asked-I assume out of curiosity-if I was married, and my comments directed them to focus on the lessons. Students with inappropriate attire, I sent to the office or threatened to do so. I hate to admit it, but most were females. The principal kept a T-shirt in the office for students who wore inappropriate attire, and I didn't mind sending them to the office. Sometimes, teaching the class was a constant challenge, but soon the students realized I wasn't just there for a paycheck. All along, I thought that if the students realized what was ahead in life, they would pay attention in class, especially when learning about how to find and maintain a job, and perhaps a career. Moreover, I remembered and realized that some of the students faced challenges like mine, some more intense, but I didn't give up on teaching the class with confidence. If a student caused an issue, at first there was a consultation, and if that didn't work, then off to the office the student went. Like the last high school where I was employed, I threatened to call their parents; however, at the continuation school, that threat didn't encourage some students to change their behavior.

As previously mentioned, I also taught a bookkeeping class like accounting, which wasn't difficult because I had experience teaching computer accounting and I'd completed similar courses in my undergraduate and graduate classes. I remember teaching students the accounting equation, which was a challenge, and they asked why they had to learn about bookkeeping. I communicated my experience practicing on a typewriter, which helped increase my proficiency when using a computer and made me more employable. I also explained that the typewriting class I completed sometime ago was the reason I could currently teach at the high school. Some understood and realized that they might one day need the knowledge currently taught at the continuation school.

Teaching the careers and work experience classes were my favorite. I was gratified when students said that they used what they learned in class and landed a job. In the interim, I was learning from teaching the class as well.

As part of the careers program, some students participated in internships with employers in the local community, and I was fortunate to be the coordinator. For example, one student wanted to be a veterinarian. Several times a week during her sixth period, she was able to help in a veterinarian's office, without pay. Another student was interested in child psychology, so she earned some experience working at a day care facility. Students interested in recreational activities worked at a local ski lift. Those interested in the food industry worked in fast food or at a local restaurant. One student worked at a supermarket stocking shelves. They earned school credits for participating in the internship program.

Overall, I was responsible for aligning students' employment with class work. I monitored students' progress in the program and, on occasion, visited them on the job and talked to their supervisors. I resolved work-related issues when necessary. Students had to maintain acceptable levels of performance on the job while completing their schoolwork. During students' tenure in the class, I found that they focused more on school assignments when the course of study centered on their current employment, career goals, work-related aspirations, or some combination of these.

Concerning my career goals, I had several interviews while teaching at the continuation school. Most of the interviews were for career development jobs like my experience working at the two high schools. Nonetheless, I was looking for a job that paid more, and I wasn't sure if I wanted to pursue a teaching career. I needed to make a decision about teaching another year. I was obligated to inform the school's principal about my choice by a certain date. If I signed another contract, I would be committed to teach another school year. Therefore, I continued to interview for other jobs while I contemplated teaching another year at the continuation school.

A factor for my decision to remain at the continuation school was a student who'd enrolled after the school year began. One of the teachers said that the student had a shunt in his brain in addition to other medical problems. The student was intelligent, but his medical challenges prevented him from completing classes in a traditional school system. The student enrolled in the school needing many credits to graduate, more credits than the typical student enrolled in the school. From what I understand, because of medical challenges, the student had almost died.

The student was sort of my buddy, and during lunch, he sat with me. However, I made a point of treating student the same as others. Several times on my breaks, I heard a knock on the classroom door, and it was the student, wanting to chat with me about something or nothing.

I wanted the student to succeed. I knew that he wasn't a quitter. He was a hard worker in all his classes. During the time the student was enrolled in the school, he completed almost an unheard of number of credits toward his high school diploma. To graduate, the student needed to pass a test in the business-math class I was teaching. The student took the final math test several times and he didn't pass. It was the only test preventing him from graduating. It was apparent that the student wasn't going to pass the math test.

After several tries at passing the math test, I informed the student that he had one more attempt to pass the test and that score would be final. I took a tough-love approach and said to the student that if he didn't pass the test, he would need to work harder at math. The student appeared to be disappointed, and I imagine he was concerned about not passing the test. "Perhaps you could come back next year to take a math class or take a class during summer school," I said. Then I thought about the time I was working toward my master's and struggling to pass a course. The instructor had given me a break and said that I had an obligation to help someone who faced a similar challenge and pay-it-forward. I then thought about the student's medical problems and other challenges.

As I gave the student the test, I thought and said, "You have one hour to study for the final math test. Some of the questions may be different, but this is your last chance to pass the test and earn a passing grade in the class." After the student completed the test, I graded the paper. It was apparent that he wasn't going to pass the test. I looked at him with a big smile and congratulated the student for passing the test. I commented about how his perseverance paid off. The student was elated. I never mentioned that the student didn't pass, for I wanted him to believe the efforts were successful. The student graduated that year and was on the honor roll for completing an inordinate number of credits during the short time he was enrolled in the school.

The school year was almost finished when my sister called me. I told her about my experience with the doctorate program in public administration and that I'd dropped out. Both she and I agreed that a doctorate in public administration wasn't a good idea, because my career wasn't heading in that direction. At that time, she was completing her master's at Pepperdine University. Of course, I had to rub it in that I already had my master's, jokingly. She mentioned that Pepperdine University had a doctorate program in educational technology. She also said that my experience in education and working with computers should help me qualify for the program. She sent me the information about the program. I did my research and found that the university enrolled only a few doctoral candidates in the program each year. That wasn't encouraging, and I remembered my experience with the previous doctorate program.

She called me sometime later and asked if I'd received the information, saying again that I should apply. I said, "Me, apply at Pepperdine University? Yeah, right. They will never accept me." She said, "Well, both us of will have a master's. Are you going to leave it at that?" That statement agitated my competitive juices. I replied, "I'll get right on completing the application."

I wrote my letter of intent, and at that time, my ability to write had improved somewhat. In the letter, I communicated my desire for working with computers in the classroom in addition to information about my technological background. I wrote about my desire to help students excel in technology occupations and jobs. As part of the application process, I took the Miller Analogies Test. I was discouraged and thought the application process was a waste of time. Next, the university asked that I sit for a face-to-face interview. I gladly accepted and confirmed an appointment.

The drive to the interview was about one hundred miles to a location in Los Angeles, and the time for my interview was near rush hour. I left the continuation school early and was going to be about thirty minutes late for the interview; I called the university from the I-10 freeway on my newly purchased cell phone. I made it to the university, where a panel awaited. The panel proceeded to interview me, and the first question they asked was about my personal and family life. Before entering the last doctorate program, I had the support of my family. I believed that everything was fine. The panel asked more questions about my personal life than any, and I wasn't sure why. *Shouldn't they be asking more questions about my academic accomplishments?* I thought. I finally figured they wanted to know more about me as a person.

I went home after the interview, wondering why I put myself through the unnecessary drive and the embarrassment. I waited patiently for the rejection letter. In about a week, I received a call from the school's registrar. They called to ask for my registration fee. Disgruntled, I asked why I needed to pay a registration fee and why they were calling me for money. The person said that they needed the funds to finish processing my application. "And congratulations for your acceptance." Today, when I think about that moment, my eyes well up. I was dumbfounded and shocked. *Pepperdine University,* I thought, *what an honor!*

Upon discovering that I was accepted, I celebrated. I sat down with my family and communicated the benefits of the program and that accomplishing the doctorate would be a challenge. I also communicated that after looking at the pictures from previous classes at the university, I assumed I was the first African American male to enter that particular program, and I was right. Three cadres preceded mine, and I was a doctoral candidate in cadre 4. I thought, *How could a high school dropout, someone with a challenging childhood, someone who had financial troubles, someone who had an interesting work history, ever be accepted into Pepperdine?* I then sat down and cried. The tears flowed. I couldn't stop them, and my emotional antics were uncontrollable.

At the continuation school, the school year was just about to end, and the principal again asked if I was returning. However, I was elated about the doctorate program. Still, I wasn't confident that I could finish a doctorate. *Dr. Cubit. Naw!* I thought but proceeded to move forward regardless. Toward the end of the school year, I had to attend a technology camp at Pepperdine, which was a nightly event. Because I was starting a doctorate program, I put earning my teaching credential on hold. For the credential, I finished all the coursework and needed to complete student teaching and the Praxis test, both necessary to earn a teaching license in California. The principal asked again if I wanted to return the next year, and to decrease the pressure for the principal constantly asking, I said yes. In the back of my mind, I was still undecided and knew I needed to make more money than a teacher's salary. Because I had a master's degree, I was earning the maximum salary according to the school district's pay scale. Completing a doctorate degree wouldn't help me as far as earning more money in the school district. Although I said that I was going to return to teaching for another year, I hadn't signed the contract.

For the doctorate program, I completed the technology camp, and I was still thinking about what I wanted to accomplish for my career. I also thought back to that typing class and the nights I spent completing homework assignments and learning about computers. I thought about the time I'd worked at the navy base studying in my car on breaks and at lunch. What about the long drives, attending school, and the decision to relocate? I couldn't forget about the attempts to make a million dollars. In my mind was also the failed effort in the previous doctorate program. I had just known my late arrival to the interview for Pepperdine would disqualify me for the program. I thought about that computer accounting class and the students completing junior-college coursework. I thought about the computer lab with IBM and Macintosh computers. I remember my elementary school teacher saying that I was going to be a teacher someday, and the laughter because of the comments. Certainly,

I couldn't forget about the timing of my sister's call regarding the Pepperdine doctorate program. My thinking was about the naysayers. *Hey, I made it past my sixteenth birthday!* I thought about life and all the connections that had led to my current situation, not forgetting fool's hill.

Importantly, I had a decision to make about returning to the high school to teach for another year. For the high school, I enjoyed working with technology. I especially took a liking to the careers classes and helping students obtain jobs. I remembered the times playing basketball with students, and they were appreciative of the lessons learned on and off the court. I remembered paying it forward to the student in my math class. I remembered the internship student who communicated her appreciation for the experience working in the restaurant, with hopes of future employment in a similar occupation. All of them were "my peeps," for we were from similar beginnings.

About two weeks left in the school year, I gave the principal my letter of resignation, and he was upset. The administration was unhappy as well. I can remember one individual cursing behind closed doors in disgust when he or she discovered that I wasn't returning. I'm uncertain, though, if the individual was disgusted because the school already had plans for me to return and it was necessary to find another teacher or if they were disappointed because the school was losing a good teacher. Anyway, I was appreciative that the high school principal wrote a letter of recommendation that aided in my acceptance to Pepperdine University.

I believed my time working as a K-12 schoolteacher was up, and I wanted to accomplish other professional goals that aligned with my doctorate when completed. In addition, the pay sucked. At that time, I believed I contributed to educating America's youth in the public education system. I hope I imprinted a positive image on everyone I worked with at the school, especially the students. Yet I believed I could do more. Now was time to move on. Teaching in the public education system was personally and professionally rewarding. I suggest that every professional spend one to two years teaching in the public education system.

A student with another year left at the continuation school asked why I wasn't returning. He said, "Mr. Cubit, you're the only one here teaching us. The rest of the teachers gave us projects to do all year. I learned a lot in your class." I said that I wanted to complete my doctorate, and he thought that was awesome. He said, "So then, instead of calling you Mr. C, we will call you Dr. C?" "If I make it," I said.

It was then I realized I had a made a difference for some at that school. Making a million dollars distributing home-cleaning products and earning a gazillion dollars in real estate, that kind of thinking was no longer my focus. I still wanted to make a difference somehow and assist others, especially the disadvantaged, in succeeding in their careers, which sparked an interest. However, I was unsure about my "why." I bade everyone farewell, and the school gave me a card signed by faculty and administrators, and that was the end of my tenure at the continuation school.

Well, you guessed it, back to substitute teaching. I started to think I was going to be a lifetime substitute. Summer arrived, and I needed a job. I went to an employment agency again and lied about my education. I told them I worked at a school district as a laborer. They had an opening in a warehouse picking orders. I began to wonder whether my career, or lack thereof, would flourish. *Perhaps if I stay employed in one place,* I thought. Yet I knew that housing munitions, building missiles, refurbishing tanks, being a newspaper person, and real estate sales weren't for me. I thought, here I was, a careers teacher, and I didn't have a career. I was a doctorate student working at night in a warehouse.

When attending classes on the weekends and at night at Pepperdine, I felt inadequate. Many of my classmates were principals, school administrators, and school teachers with years of experience. Then there was me, the near-minimum-wage warehouse worker. To my classmates, I never clearly communicated my employment situation. Nonetheless, I continued working on my doctorate despite the turbulence I felt within.

At that time, I worked at night in a warehouse for a large discount store. I was waiting for school to start so I could go back to substitute teaching. Then I thought about becoming a school administrator, but I needed a credential. Typically, school administrators have at least three years of classroom experience and have a teaching and an administrator's credential, and I had neither. Earning a credential meant returning to school. Back then, it wasn't possible for me to earn any credential while working in a warehouse and completing my doctorate all at the same time. Therefore, I knew teaching in a school or working as an administrator was out of the question. *Maybe after I finished my doctorate, if possible,* I thought. At the moment, working in the warehouse was the focus, and it was good thing I had experience.

At that time, I had been employed in several jobs and had learned to be prepared for the unknown. While working in the warehouse at night, I didn't have safety shoes on and wore aluminum toe caps held in place by straps. I recall walking around the warehouse, *clickety-clack, clickety-clack.* Eventually, I purchased a pair of safety shoes and kept them in my closet for years just in case. Recently, after keeping the safety shoes for almost twenty years, I finally donated them to a worthy cause. Because my career was in flux for a long time, I kept copies of my forklift license as well. I attempted to keep my real estate license current, but because of extraneous events in my life at that time, it lapsed. I figured that I could always revert to substitute teaching in the state of California if necessary. When teaching those careers classes, I communicated to students that they should always be prepared and create options for themselves. An individual never knows when qualifications acquired in the past or that lone experience might come in handy.

Anyway, in the warehouse, most of the employees were uneducated, in reference to a formal education, and some couldn't speak English, but they knew their jobs. Nevertheless, here I was, a doctorate candidate working on my fifth college degree and earning almost minimum wage. At that time, personal debt was insurmountable, but I had faith that completing my doctorate would advance me into a position I chose in which I could be successful. I was relying on that faith and the message I'd heard in my youth about getting an education and a good job.

At that time, I wondered what was wrong with my work life. Nothing at this point seemed to satisfy my career aspirations. I asked myself, *Was it the establishment, was it me, or was it because of my race?* Why was I unsuccessful with my career or lack thereof? I thought back and remembered a verse in the Holy Bible that states one should be content with his or her wages. Oh, no, not me. I believed there was something destined for me other than being a taxicab driver, warehouse worker, missile and mobile tank repair person, real estate salesperson, real estate appraiser, loan processor, janitor, newspaper slinger, and teacher. *But what?* I asked myself and God.

I continued applying for jobs and, in some instances, excluded noting my qualifications and sometimes even my education. Often, when applying for jobs, I was embarrassed to include my education and dynamic work history. In addition, I knew that if I wanted a better-paying job, then driving fifty or more miles to work was necessary. Importantly, at an interview, an individual reviewed my qualifications and asked me what career path I was on. "What exactly do you want to do?" Jokingly, I wanted to say, "Make a million dollars selling home-cleaning products or selling real estate." I couldn't answer the individual or myself, though. My "why" was unknown; however, at that time, I believed my Higher Power already had the answers to the aforementioned questions, but looking back today, I question if I myself was interfering with achieving my career aspirations.

Chapter 13

FROM MR. C TO DR. C

T he school year started, and I began substitute teaching. I was vigorously applying for jobs in and outside of education. Because I didn't have a teaching credential for public school, I applied at higher education institutions and community colleges.

Substitute teaching seemed more difficult as time progressed. I wanted to do more with my life than substitute teaching, which became a challenge because of expectations for success based on my work experience and educational attainment. I was beginning to understand more about my meaning of success. At that time, my first priority was to find a well-paying job.

After the revelation about success, substitute teaching was still a challenge, and I was hesitant to communicate to anyone about my academic or professional achievement, especially the latter. At this point, it was difficult to accept substitute-teaching assignments. I believed it was time to do more with my life; besides, at that time, I had four college degrees and believed that the expectation for my contributions to society was greater than my existing offerings.

Then I thought about my experience teaching work-experience and careers courses and assisting individuals with employment goals, which was starting to spark an interest. I was discovering that I could affect one's life by helping an individual acquire a job and prepare for a career and perhaps become self-sufficient. First, I needed to start with me.

DR. RON CUBIT

Entering the doctorate program, I was apprehensive. I wondered if I could measure up. I was still somewhat shy and didn't communicate with my classmates much. I was a loner and feared talking in class. However, I enjoyed when portions of our classes were online. I could chat away through the online application.

At Pepperdine, the first trimester was an intensive five classes. Then each trimester began with an eight-day intensive, Friday afternoon and all day Saturday and Sunday, and then every day during the week in the evening. About every four weeks, we came together for Friday through Sunday classes. The rest of the time we spent learning online. The courses contained a blended learning format, and about 60 percent was face-to-face in class and 40 percent was online. Because the doctorate program focused on educational technology, the online portion helped in understanding how to apply technology in the course of learning.

I couldn't afford the doctorate program; therefore, I financed most of it using student loans. I applied for a grant through Pepperdine, and because of our income, it was approved. With the funds, eventually, I bought a larger and reliable car, which was necessary, because during the eight-day intensives, I drove back and forth every day, including the weekends. One way to the school was about one hundred miles, and I drove about a sixteen-hundred miles during the eight-day, thirty-two-hour intensive. I didn't mind driving, because some of my classmates lived on the East Coast and one student was from Canada. Most paid all expenses during the intensives, including hotels and travel. I didn't have much money to pay for the hotels and was happy when I received the student loan and grant disbursements. For some weekend sessions, I slept in my car.

That first trimester at Pepperdine was intimidating. Finding a good job and going to school was a challenge. I had little time for family or leisure. About the middle of my first trimester, my wife and I started having marriage problems. At that time, I discovered things about my marriage that I never knew. Overall, this was a difficult time-driving to school, the challenge of the doctorate program, my marriage, and my employment situation. However, I vowed to com-

202

plete the doctorate program. I knew that if I dropped out, I might not have a chance to earn the degree.

Meanwhile, I applied for a position at a nonprofit organization. The organization needed someone to coordinate a program that helped individuals receiving public assistance (called welfare at that time) transition to employment. I gained similar experience working at both high schools. I interviewed for the position and was hired a few weeks later. The program was funded under the Welfare-to-Work Act, and most of the participants in the program were female.

The drive to my place of employment from home was about thirty miles; however, I was happy about another opportunity to help individuals obtain jobs, maintain jobs, and become self-sufficient. Essentially, I was an administrator for the program without going through a lengthy process to obtain an academic credential.

At my new job, I had an office. I was also seeking to hire someone to teach computer technology courses at night but couldn't find anyone. I developed curriculum for the course and eventually taught the class. During the day, I coordinated the program, and at night, I taught the computer class. Most of the computers were old, and some didn't work. I found myself taking parts from one computer to make a usable one. Finally, the executive director allotted funds to buy all new machines. I did the research and found a source to purchase new computers. I was able to network the computers (peer-to-peer). Typing on that old electric typewriter and those days figuring out how to work with computers and software-not to mention teaching the keyboarding and computer accounting classes were paying off. My next task was to hire a case manager, which I did.

Working with adult learners who were on public assistance was a challenge because some hadn't attended school or applied themselves in a learning environment in a while. The goal was to help them acquire skills to obtain and maintain a job. Most participants in the program had little knowledge of computers. All the participants enrolled in the program at different times; therefore, I set up the class using a model like the one I used in the last high school in which I had been employed. Only three to four students enrolled in the class, and sometimes only one or two were present.

Participants completed a series of assignments before finishing the computer class. Most of the instruction was one-on-one, and using a "drill-instructor" model to teach definitely didn't work. Therefore, I devised a strategy to help those in the class find answers to questions on their own. Eventually, the strategy worked. And the goal was to help students use critical thinking skills for problem-solving. I believed the strategy helped them develop problem-solving skills that could aid in their quest for self-sufficiency.

Here I found myself again in a pay-it-forward situation. To complete the program, a participant had to pass my computer class. There was no way she was going to complete that class. Like the student with the shunt in his brain, she took the test one final time, but it was evident she wasn't going to pass. Well, I paid it forward again and granted the individual a passing grade. Mostly because I wanted her to experience some success in the program, which I believed would transcend to other areas of her life.

Now I was starting to experience worth in working with programs that helped individuals be successful in life. I looked back on my brief days working on the drill field helping individuals acclimate to military life. In other jobs, including those not related to training and development, I was often successful at giving some type of guidance or helping someone learn. It appeared that God was driving me down that path or I was beginning to find my "why" or my "why" was finding me. Perhaps I was finding a meaning behind my grandmother's comments about fool's hill, that I wasn't finished climbing, especially in relation to my career.

I continued working on my doctorate degree and borrowed money from student loans. In the back of my mind, though, I still believed that one day the investments in real estate and my ability to advance on the job would help make the payments. At the center where I was employed, I started working the night shift teaching the computer class two nights per week. We needed money, so you guessed it-I was a substitute teacher during the day. In my little spare time, I worked on earning my doctorate. My marriage was distressed, with little hope of reconciliation. I moved out of the place where we were living and found a studio apartment. My challenge with my marriage was affecting my ability to perform on the job and complete the doctorate program, but I forged on.

Just before finding a place to live on my own, we had a garage sale and sold all our belongings. I wanted to blame the doctorate program and my sporadic employment status. My wife at that time and I attempted counseling, but nothing helped. It seemed that we weren't committed to making the marriage work. Maybe we were more concerned about our personal endeavors than about reconciling. Remember: at that time, we had three children, one about to graduate from high school, another in high school, and one in junior high.

Because of my personal challenges during the second trimester, I failed a class. Performance in other classes declined as well. During my interview for Pepperdine, the professors reinforced the importance of a stable family life while completing the doctorate program. In addition, the challenge with completing the coursework was demanding, and the issue with my marriage was taking a toll on me. On one occasion, while I moved items out of the house to my own place, an assignment was due that day. I sat on the floor in that empty house, logged onto my class, and completed the assignment while sitting on a bare floor. That was tough. Because of my performance in the doctorate program, a committee counseled me and communicated that if the trend continued, perhaps I should consider taking a hiatus and continuing later. I attempted to defend myself but realized that the challenge I faced was my fault. Yes, I was revisiting fool's hill. During the counseling session, the professors said that I had to repeat the class that I failed. However, I was determined to succeed despite it all.

The current situation at Pepperdine and the comments from the professors were more serious than portrayed. Today I'm fortunate that I didn't drop out. I do believe the professors were concerned about my situation but they had to follow university protocol. The intervention reminded me of the time I was in the Marine Corps while on the drill field and was counseled about my performance. However, this time, the outcome was different. I went home, found my handgun, and loaded it. I didn't know what I was going to do with it. I was in tears and wanted some relief. It was here that I made a decision. I figured that God made everything happen for a reason; therefore, I must forge on.

I continued working at a nonprofit organization, and I saw an advertisement for a quasicounty agency. The line of work was like my current job, and the announcement displayed that the individual would be responsible for coordinating a program that helped homeless individuals attain self-sufficiency. Reading the job description, I learned that the candidate must have the ability to speak in public and facilitate group sessions. I wanted to perfect my presentation skills and thought, *What an exceptional opportunity to accomplish this!*

I applied for the job, and someone in the human resources called me stating that I'd forgotten to submit a document; therefore, my application had been rejected. I wrote the company and explained that the paperwork was included-I really needed the job. I was hired and was now the programs specialist for the quasicounty agency. My job entailed working with service providers in the county that helped the homeless. My experience in the social services arena was starting to grow, a far cry from real estate-related jobs or selling cleaning products. The job also included fieldwork, which I enjoyed. In addition to my new job, I continued working part-time at the nonprofit organization until they found a coordinator. They finally hired the person that I hired to be the caseworker. I continued working at the center at night, teaching computers, and I quit substitute teaching. I didn't mind because I taught only a few days per week anyway. The job at the homeless coalition paid more and provided health benefits, something my previous employment at the nonprofit job didn't.

One day, the executive director of the homeless coalition approached me. She was an attractive African American female. She said that an employee with the same last name worked in a different department. I said that yes, she was my soon-to-be ex-wife (with emphasis). I had the hots for the executive director but knew that a relationship would be difficult in that employment situation. I don't believe she knew my hanker for her and I don't believe the feeling was mutual.

African American females managed both the quasi county agency and the nonprofit agency. I was blessed with these extraordinary working relationships. For me, their professionalism was something I've yet to experience in the workplace.

Those were interesting times. I was still working on my doctorate, and I changed jobs three times. I relocated twice, which challenged me in completing the doctorate program. While working at the homeless coalition, I began focusing my doctorate program on situations that applied to my job. During this time, I asked the coalition to help me with my education and provide tuition assistance, a stipend because what I was learning at Pepperdine was job related. However, they allowed me release time for classes, which was helpful during the thirty-two-hour intensive. I was now progressing in the doctorate program and needed to think about what I wanted to research for my dissertation. I also believed that after graduation, job opportunities would flourish.

A policy course at Pepperdine required a weeklong field trip to Washington, DC. During the trip, the goal was to meet policy-makers and politicians and then explain what the doctorate program at Pepperdine University entailed. The objective was to explain to politicians the effectiveness of using technology for teaching and learning, with hopes of gaining support for any upcoming legislation concerning this. Using technology for teaching and learning was somewhat innovative at that time. Missing the trip could postpone completing the entire course and the doctorate program.

While completing the doctorate program, I faced financial challenges as well but found a way to pay for the trip. At that time, I had a checking account with a thousand-dollar overdraft protection, and I used money from my paycheck to purchase my plane ticket. I was able to pay for the entire trip using the funds from the overdraft and my paycheck; however, I owed my bank one thousand dollars. I was able to reduce some cost for the trip because a few of us shared a room.

The trip to Washington, DC, was eventful and informative. Some of us took a picture with Senator Barbara Boxer. As a group, we met with an assistant secretary of education from the Office of Civil

Rights. A student and I took pictures with Senator Dianne Feinstein. Years later, I looked closely at that picture and realized the zipper of my trousers was open. In viewing the picture, I thought, *Damn, can't you get at least one thing right?* Every time I see that picture, I laugh. Anyway, I had doubts about earning a doctorate, but I kept plugging away.

Working at the homeless coalition was a new experience for me, different from any job I previously held. My goal was to make the coalition a centerpiece of the homeless programs in the county. However, in the meantime, I continued to apply for government jobs, this time for positions as a workforce professional instead of real estate-related jobs.

Continually working for the homeless coalition, I was involved in several projects. As part of my doctorate program, I learned how to build websites. I developed a website for the coalition, which was used to communicate with service providers for the homeless throughout the county. Those technological skills continued to work for me, which I attribute to that first typewriting class. Next, I facilitated meetings that included service providers for the homeless throughout the county. I remember the first session and preparing for the meeting-man, was I nervous! However, because of my preparation, the first meeting was a success. I was determined not to fail. With time, membership in the coalition, particularly for the Care Faire, doubled, and then tripled.

A first task for the homeless coalition was conducting meetings for a Care Faire. The Care Faire was a one-day event designed to serve the homeless throughout the county. The objective was to provide services for the homeless such as eye exams and glasses, showers, clothes, food, and coffee from a well-known brew house. Haircuts, veterans' services, and access to other county services were available as well. At the onset, the committee for the Care Faire wasn't well-formed. To gain support for the Care Faire, it was necessary for me to speak at meetings. At that time, I was still uneasy about speaking in public and knew I needed to improve my speaking skills. Prior to the event, extensive planning took place.

To plan the event, it was necessary that I facilitate biweekly meetings. It was also necessary to advertise the event, and to accomplish this, I appeared on public television twice. For the first television appearance, I remember waiting in the green room and then proceeding to the stage. While I waited for the cameras to start rolling, the show host provided some directions and stopped in midsentence and asked if someone was knocking on the door. *No, those were my knees knocking in fear.* Just kidding. I did all right and was more confident during the second appearance on TV. I felt special when coworkers said they'd seen me on television. I was proud then because an electronic billboard near the freeway had information about the Care Faire, and in a marquee were my name and contact information. Me, the former hood rat. Sometimes when I remember events like this, I get emotional.

Coordinating the event was an undertaking. During the Care Faire, I had an opportunity to roll up my sleeves and solve problems. The event was a success, as noted by the local newspaper. I was proud, and like teaching at the alternative-education high school, with the help of the coalition, I'd believed we made a difference in the lives of many that day.

Working for the coalition was interesting times. As previously mentioned, my wife at that time was employed there, and several times, she visited the office. Her workstation was nearby, and we saw each other. We tried to reconcile, but at that time, challenges prohibited it. In hindsight, the inability to communicate with each other, stress, debt, and career pressures were contributors. In California, I think they call it irreconcilable differences. I didn't help the situation by dating someone who also worked at the coalition.

While at work one day, I received a call from the Department of Labor, Employment Training Administration regarding a job for which I'd applied. The position, once again, was for a federal government job. This time, the job was for a workforce development specialist. The individual on the phone explained that if hired, I would work with programs that helped disadvantaged individuals achieve and maintain employment. The position was in San Francisco, California, and I would have to relocate. I learned that I had to accomplish the move using my own resources. I was happy because I would be working with programs that helped disadvantaged individuals find and maintain a job and then achieve self-sufficiency. Keep in mind that I was about to complete the coursework portion of my doctorate program and then start my comprehensive exam en route to completing my dissertation. My children were living with their mother and her boyfriend, and my wife and I were headed in different directions, so I decided to relocate to San Francisco alone if hired.

Then the professors at Pepperdine mentioned that we should start thinking about completing the dissertation. For my dissertation, I was contemplating researching technological systems for collaboration within an organization and exploring the effectiveness of technology for learning. However, in the back of my mind, I was thinking about the career-development programs I worked with and helping disadvantaged individuals. For my dissertation, I thought about how I could mesh systems for learning and helping the disadvantaged. Then I thought about when I had been a participant in a job-training program in my youth. How might I structure a similar but successful program differently?

In addition, I wanted to find ways to enhance programs for disadvantaged individuals and believed that working for the federal government might be a good platform to accomplish this. *Could I make a difference?* I wondered. *The individual from the hood who had challenges adjusting to life? Could I help young people, specifically people of color, who faced challenges like mine in my youth?* I completed my master's and researched ways to manage a diverse workforce. *How can I help? How could I contribute?* I could be a superhero, like Spider-Man, my favorite. I believed the job in San Francisco working for a federal entity would aid me in fulfilling my goal to help others. At that time, it appeared that my "why" was evolving and aiding my ability to traverse fool's hill.

I interviewed for the job in San Francisco and visited the office. The executive director at the homeless coalition discovered that I might be leaving. The individual who'd interviewed me for the job in San Francisco knew somebody at the county agency and inquired about me. The individual whom he called wasn't on my reference list. The individual who gave the reference was a good friend of the homeless coalition executive director.

One day, the executive director for the homeless coalition asked to meet with me in her office. This was the first time she'd asked to meet with me. During the meeting, she bluntly asked if I was leaving. I was dumbfounded and shocked, and I wondered how she'd found out. I needed to give her an answer quickly, and I decided to confess. I said that I'd interviewed but hadn't received a job offer. She asked if I would take more money to stay. For me, it was too late; I had made my decision to take on the new challenge in San Francisco if offered the job.

The Department of Labor, Employment and Training Administration offered me the position in San Francisco, and I accepted. I was excited about the opportunity to work with job-training programs for the federal government. I thought the situation was ironic because in the past, I applied for several federal jobs in San Francisco for realty specialist positions but had never received a reply. I realized the realty specialist position for the federal government wasn't meant to be. The executive director asked me again about the job in San Francisco. I was waiting for my final two weeks to submit my resignation notice, but she kept asking. Finally, I gave my immediate supervisor at the homeless coalition my resignation notice and I gave the executive director where I taught the computer classes at night a resignation notice as well.

I hated communicating that I was leaving the homeless coalition; I appreciated the professional working environment created there by the executive director. I wondered now, since she wasn't my supervisor, if perhaps I could ask her out on a date. I was too shy to act, though, and I thought I already knew what the answer would be. At the center where I taught computer applications, I appreciated the professional working environment the African American executive director created there as well. Concerning my fool's hill journey and finding my "why," I owe a debt of gratitude to both African American females.

Before relocating to San Francisco, as I was ending the coursework for my doctorate and transitioning to the dissertation phase, I looked back at my work experiences: teaching at a high school in a rural area and coordinating the work experience program; working as a career education coordinator; teaching in an alternative-education high school; establishing work internships for youth; managing a work experience program for individuals transitioning from public assistance; and coordinating a program for the homeless. Then there was the move to San Francisco.

Before making the transition to my new job, I drove to San Francisco several times looking for a place to stay. I was concerned about the cost of housing. On some visits to the San Francisco Bay Area, because of the high prices of hotels, I slept in my car. At that time, I had a large SUV and could manage. Then the technology boom was at its height in the San Francisco Bay area, which drove up the cost of housing, including rent. At that time, there were fewer places to rent than the number of possible tenants, and I had to compete for a place to stay. Because of the competition, to rent, I needed an excellent credit rating, which I didn't have. I saw an advertisement in the local paper for a room to rent and drove across town to submit an application. I spoke with the landlord, and he showed me the stack of applications of possible tenants. I asked for an application and commented that I was going to look for places close to my job, and if my search was unsuccessful, I would return the application. I knew because of my credit rating, completing the application was going to be a waste of time. Anyway, I had faith that moving to San Francisco to pursue a career helping others was the right thing to do.

I still needed to complete my doctorate classes, and after the last class at Pepperdine that Saturday, the entire cadre participated in a farewell dinner at a fancy restaurant in Marina Del Rey, California. At that time, my car was loaded, and I was ready to make the transition to San Francisco. The following Monday morning, I had to report to work. When I left the job at the homeless coalition, they held a surprise party for me, though my leaving was supposed to be a secret. I recalled that when I left my last federal job, they'd held a barbecue and I didn't show up. *Why celebrate my leaving?* I thought. For the doctorate program, I still needed to complete my comprehensive exam, and I believed I would accomplish that after relocating.

I left the farewell dinner with my cadre mates from Pepperdine. My car was loaded, and I said goodbye to my classmates, for it was our last time together. As Pepperdine classmates, we endured about two years together. I said goodbye to everyone, and I was off to San Francisco. As I drove to the San Francisco Bay area, steering wheel in one hand and a map in the other, the situation reminded me of the time I replaced that Japanese car engine-a repair manual in one hand and wrenches in the other.

I arrived in the Bay Area late and had trouble finding a place to stay, so I slept in my car. I looked all day Sunday for a place to stay, to no avail, and slept in my car again. The next morning, I called my job and said that my first day in the office would be Wednesday of that week. During the call, my supervisor told me that I would be traveling to Portland the next Monday. I spent most of the day Monday and Tuesday looking for a permanent residence. It was a challenge because I didn't have good credit and I had no job history or references in the San Francisco area. I paid for a hotel until Monday because I knew I would be leaving for Portland. On Wednesday, I reported to my new job in downtown San Francisco. Every morning before reporting to work, I packed my belongings in my car and headed to the train station. I didn't want to leave anything in the hotel room, for my personal items were all I had, and everything was in storage in California. I worked a couple of days and was introduced to everyone in the office. Monday, I was off to Portland and stayed there for about a week.

Sometimes I slept in my car. Mostly on the weekends, though. By this time, I was a pro at car sleeping. Because I couldn't afford to rent a place to stay, I decided to find a room to rent. Global positioning satellite (GPS) wasn't available at that time, so I bought maps, and off I went.

I could write a book about the challenge of finding a place to stay. Some of the property owners wanted to conduct a credit check. Some had lifestyles that didn't align with mine, and some wanted first and last month's rent and a deposit, which was way beyond the amount of funds in my pocket. One house was so filthy I wanted to offer to help him clean it before leaving. One house had too many cats-no, thanks. In an affluent neighborhood, I inquired about a room, and the individual started licking their lips-no thanks and no offense, I hope. Another individual looked like Uncle Fester from *The Addams Family*, and his mate looked like Grandpa from *The Munsters*, and I was waiting for someone to emerge from the back and say, "You rang?" At that house, I had thoughts of the fava bean couple when selling brushes door-to-door, and my tires screeched as I pulled away.

Throughout my search for a place to rent, I stayed in shabby hotels. On one occasion, like the time we'd lived in Long Beach, California, one hotel had food coming out of the shower drain. I wondered where my life was heading. *Here I go again.* At that hotel, I couldn't take my shoes off, because the carpet was filthy. I made sure to leave the window cracked, for sometimes the stench was unbearable. At one hotel, a well-known chain, there was a security guard at the gate. Another security guard canvassed the area as well. I later found out that someone had been shot and killed at the hotel. While staying at one hotel, I developed a sickness-unbearable coughing, fever, and nasal congestion. At the hotel, I couldn't sleep on the sheets. I had a tough time but continued writing my comprehensive exam for my finals at Pepperdine despite the challenges.

I stayed in sleazy hotels for about four weeks and was about to run out of money. I had to wait for about three weeks before I received my next student loan disbursement. I had to find a way to make it or return to Southern California and ask for my job back. I finally realized that renting a place of my own wouldn't work and decided to rent a room in someone's house. I had a few dollars and began looking, or soon I would be stranded, out of funds, and without a permanent place to stay.

Eventually, I moved into a house with an owner and two male occupants. It wasn't my preferred living situation-in fact, I hated it. The location was about sixty miles from my job. During the workweek, I drove about ten miles to the train station, which took about an hour in the unbearable traffic. Then I had an hour's train ride to my job. That one-hour ride was instrumental, for I used the time to review research materials for the comprehensive exam and soon-to-be dissertation.

I continued working on my doctorate despite my transient situation. Every weekend, I went to a different library to conduct research for my comprehensive exam. Afterward I ate dinner and then went to the movies. Sometimes, to break up the monotony, on the weekends, I went to a jazz concert or a concert in the park. The San Francisco Bay area was home to many jazz musicians and was an exceptional place for concerts. Working on my comprehensive exam and other activities was a way to block out the challenges, including the undesirable living conditions. However, I was adamant about making the transition to the San Francisco Bay area work.

It was time for my first Thanksgiving while living in the Bay Area, and I was on my way to Southern California to have dinner with my girlfriend and family. I bought flowers and was going to ask her to marry me. I called her on my cell, and I don't remember how everything started, but the conversation went awry. The heated conversations were consistent, and today, I look back and realize the challenges I faced at that time probably contributed to my negative demeanor and escalated the arguments. Anyway, I hung up the phone, left the freeway, and found a place to park. Then I changed my phone number. I eventually drove to California and spent that Thanksgiving with my father and family and gave the flowers to my daughters. That was the last I heard from my now ex-girlfriend. It wasn't until approximately fifteen years later that we briefly connected on Facebook. I do hope to see her again someday as a gesture of friendship. Back in the Bay Area, now I was surely by myself and in unfamiliar territory in many ways.

My job in San Francisco required that I travel. I liked the job, especially working with the job-training programs for the disadvantaged. Here again, because of my background, I was assigned projects that had a technology component. One was non-formula-funded grants for labor market information (LMI). I assisted states with developing technology applications to deliver LMI to the public. For LMI projects, I was assigned the states of California, Arizona, Nevada, Hawaii, and the territory of Guam. Except for Guam, it was interesting traveling to those states and working with LMI. In that capacity, I made sure that the states performed according to any agreements. Then I believe I'd found my "why" for life and the importance of that "why." That "why" involved assisting those less fortunate to acquire and maintain jobs. As part of this, I was realizing how the power of education was affecting my life and could help others. Where was fool's hill now?

I was also assigned several earmark grants for technology-based, or computer-based, job-training programs. Again, I owe this to that typewriting class and working with that electric typewriter and banging on those keys in the wee hours of the morning and on the weekends. In addition to the experience exploring how computer technology works. For the earmark grants, I had the opportunity to work with public and private organizations entities and gain an array of experience. For one grant in Arizona, on a review, I visited the grantee and all the sub partners-one of those was Boeing.

The grantee and I drove to the Boeing training site. The representative from Boeing arrived with a model aircraft in his hand. The aircraft resembled a passenger jet and a helicopter with wings in the normal position and a long propeller on top as well. We introduced ourselves, and the Boeing representative placed the model aircraft on the table. He said that the model aircraft was something he carried around and that at the last staff meeting, he'd placed the model on the table. The topic of discussion during the staff meeting had been how to eliminate drag if the aircraft was in flight and how the propeller on top should be positioned. The goal had been to find a way for the aircraft to take off like a helicopter and fly like a jet. Another objective had been to decrease the time an aircraft was on a runway and, by that, decrease flight delays. We spent some time conversing about the aircraft. Then I proceeded to ask questions about the grant and the job-training program. Periodically, we gravitated back to the conversation about the aircraft, and after fifteen years, I believe I have the answer. Anyway, I was content with my career at that time, and visiting all the companies that helped individuals become self-sufficient was exceptional.

At that time, my employer, the Department of Labor, developed a cadre of online tools that the public could use to conduct career searches, find a training school, develop a résumé and more. The application was called America's Career Kit, an online application. I was trained in Washington, DC to use the Career Kit, then was designated the regional contact for the application. I traveled throughout the region and conducted workshops and training for the application. I had the opportunity to present at national and regional conferences and conducted workshops at small and large organizations. Thank God, literally, for the experience gained from presenting at the homeless coalition. Imagine that, someone who walked several miles from National City to the Greyhound bus station downtown, sometimes through the barrio, because I was too shy to use public transportation. Now I was conducting training and workshops before audiences. Certainly, now, I didn't need my wife or brother to return items to the store for me, although that shy person sometimes resurfaced.

Concerning my doctorate, all courses were completed, and I passed my comprehensive exam. I was now at the dissertation phase. The question now was, What shall I write my dissertation about? *Something about technology to change the world,* I thought. I created a topic and asked an African American professor to be my dissertation chair. Why? Because I believed she would be sensitive to the proposed topic. I wrote my topic paper and thought I had met the dissertation chair from hell. I couldn't believe her demeanor and antics. I continued working on my dissertation topic paper, and she didn't respond to my email messages. Unbeknownst to me, she no longer worked for the university, and her disappearance was unexpected.

At this time, I endured challenges: financial difficulty, contemplating a divorce, being without a female companion, relocating to an area where the cost of housing was astronomical, and a new job. Not to mention the thought of completing a doctoral-dissertation. I was at my limit psychologically, and informed the university that I was taking a hiatus. I was now among the "all but dissertation" (ABD)-those who completed classes but not the dissertation-and I suspect the number of ABDs in total to be astronomical. I know many who completed the coursework but not the dissertation and never achieve that doctorate. Anyway, I just needed time to adjust to my new surroundings, and a break would serve me well. I was tired, mostly mentally.

Here, I went to my doctor for a physical and wasn't happy with the results. I had always kept myself in excellent physical condition. He asked me if I was taking digitalis, a heart medication. I said no. He took another electrocardiogram and quickly said that I needed to see a specialist for testing. Next, he asked how often I took my hypertension medication. I said never, because none had ever been prescribed for me. I didn't believe what the doctor was asking, because I ran five to six miles per day. I lifted weights for tone and did calisthenics regularly. Most times, I ate balanced meals. I had stopped smoking and hadn't had a drop of alcohol in seven years. Besides the ailment I endured during my move to Bay Area, I was rarely sick. Typically, doctors asked me, "Why are you here?" because I was in good physical shape for someone my age. This was a difficult time in my life.

The doctor scheduled me to see a heart specialist, and I was afraid. What made matters worse was the appointment was two weeks away, which didn't help my blood pressure situation. To monitor my blood pressure, the doctor asked me to take periodic readings. I needed to check back with him in a few weeks.

The time came for my heart examination, and they asked me to bring running clothes. Two weeks went by, and because of the way things were going, I regressed to the negative. By then, I was thinking that I needed a heart transplant. I wanted to inform my children, but I was apprehensive about the unknown. In the heart specialist's office, they connected me to machines and a breathing apparatus. I jogged on a treadmill, walked for a while, ran for a while. Periodically, the doctor checked the readings on the machines, and the event reminded me of the intro to *The Six Million Dollar Man*, but believe me, I didn't feel like one.

After the exam, he asked me to get dressed and met me in another room and explained the results. Was I afraid! Sitting down, he explained that my heartbeat might be abnormal for some, but for me it was normal. I was happy and said that maybe my heart had been broken so many times, a point of dry humor. My comment was from relief and perhaps nervousness, and I don't know why I said it. He just looked at me and said that he would send the results to my doctor, and then I realized that my "broken heart" comment was inappropriate for a heart doctor. Nevertheless, I was relieved. Here I came to realize the impact of extenuating challenges that an individual faces in his or her life, and how such challenges can affect one's health.

I went to see my doctor to discuss the result of my heart exam and to give him the record from my periodic blood pressure readings. Throughout the month, my readings were abnormal except for about four days. He asked what took place during those four days. I thought back and determined those four days to be the time when my daughters spent time with me in the San Francisco Bay area. Here I stress (pun intended) the importance of family. The doctor prescribed medication for the blood pressure and explained how to control it, and I was on my way.

Anyway, I knew that the longer I procrastinated about completing my dissertation, the more likely it was that I would stay in the ABD status. The chances of becoming Dr. C diminished. Then I decided on a dissertation topic. Instead of something that wouldn't be of interest, such as education and technology to save the world, so to speak, I decided to do research on job-training programs.

At that time, the Department of Labor, under the H-1B Immigration and Nationality Act, section 101(a)(15)(H), funded technology-based job training programs to offset the reliance of foreign labor in technology-based occupations. I had the opportunity to work with several grant-funded programs under the H-1bn Immigration and Nationality Act, which allowed employers in the United States to employ temporarily foreign workers in specialty occupations. Since I had an opportunity to work with technology-based programs at the Department of Labor and was already working with several under the H-1B Act, I decided to write my dissertation about technology-based job-training programs that assisted the disadvantaged in obtaining and maintaining a job. After all, I had been a disadvantaged youth and participated in a job-training program; I had experience working with job-training programs as well. Why not research and write my dissertation about something that might make a difference, something of interest to me and perhaps others? After deciding on my topic, I contacted individuals with whom I had worked in the past and explained the goal for completing my dissertation. All of them thought my topic was an excellent idea, and what a connection!

Still, I didn't have a dissertation chair so I contacted the university. When I had been completing a course in the doctorate program, a Caucasian female, a mature, ex-nun English major who lived in Lakewood, Colorado, mentioned that if she had an opportunity to work with me, she would push me to bring out my best. I asked her to be my dissertation chair, and she accepted. She set some parameters, and I was off to writing my dissertation. At that time, we formed the dissertation committee as well.

Believe me: the dissertation was tougher than the doctorate coursework, and my chair pushed me. She had this six-foot-two African American male constantly in a state of submission, and the entire three years were humbling. Some chapters I sent to my chair for review up to six times. Sometimes when she returned them, I wanted to scream, but I bit my lip and said, "Yes, madam, will do." In comparison to all the other things in my life, the dissertation was the most challenging. Forget about having a relationship. I went through three during the dissertation process.

Conducting the research for the dissertation was challenging but fun. I had an opportunity to review research studies about job-training programs for the disadvantaged, and everything was related to my new job. I was researching and writing like crazy, and my dissertation chair said, "Stop. You need to do a pilot study to determine the feasibility of your research topic." I said to myself, *What do you mean a pilot study?* I needed to get this thing, the dissertation, finished, completed. She explained the purpose of the pilot study, and I said, "Yes, madam." I conducted a pilot study and interviewed disadvantaged individuals in a job-training program. Fortunately, I was able to conduct the pilot study at a place I'd worked at previously. As a way for me to give back, individuals participating in the pilot and dissertation study earned twenty-five dollars.

During this time, my youngest was finishing her last year in high school. However she was struggling, and my wife at that time and I feared that she might not graduate. My daughter was focused on other activities instead of completing her studies and earning a high school diploma. When my first son and daughter graduated from high school, my ex-wife and I were still together somewhat. For the first two children, not finishing high school was unfathomable, and both parents could focus on their completion. Unfortunately, my youngest didn't have the luxury of two parents in the home working together in her interest. I wasn't going to allow my daughter to face the world without at least a high school diploma. No, she wasn't going to mirror Dad's high school experience. *No class reunion or prom for her,* I thought.

I submitted a request to my existing employer to telework from the High Desert in Southern California, which was approved. The agreement stipulated what I must accomplish while working at home, and I appreciated the effort from the organization. I packed my things, and off, I went.

I teleworked from Southern California and physically reported to the office in San Francisco periodically. An advantage for the organization was that I was able to work with grant-funded organizations in Southern California, which minimized travel cost for the Department of Labor. Concerning my daughter, I picked her up from school every day; she studied and completed her homework at my place, and I took her home at night. On the weekends, I picked her up and she studied and slept at my place. On Sunday, she studied only a half-day. As part of the process, her teachers gave me a report every Friday, and I dropped in on her classes unannounced.

Then I thought about a comment from my grandmother. Once, she saw how I was raising my children, she said, "Daddy Ronnie, who would've ever thought?" "Boy, I'm so proud of you." Other than the teachings in the Bible, I never did have a foundation for parenting, but I vowed that my children wouldn't experience the challenges I faced while growing up. Then I thought about those comments about making it past my sixteenth birthday. Those comments and my past were drivers for me to be successful at parenting.

My daughter was approaching her final months in high school and was struggling with her math class. If not successful, she couldn't walk with her graduating class. I wanted that for her so bad. I didn't want her to experience what I had in my youth-no prom, no high school graduation, no class ring. Today, when I hear individuals comment about a class reunion, sometimes I wish I could experience this, especially the family-oriented events. I graduated approximately three years after the individuals with whom I went to high school. Though I did graduate, I wanted all my children to experience the benefits of attending a high school and graduating with a class.

For her last class, my daughter needed a C to graduate but didn't pass the class. However, on her own, she went to summer school and earned her high school diploma. I'm so proud of her, because she didn't give up. Who knew how that challenge and overcoming it might change her life and that of others? I once heard someone say that C students, or the ones who struggled and succeeded, typically changed the world, and the A students who didn't have serious life struggles and didn't struggle in school might not have as big of an impact.

While teleworking from Southern California, I often reported to my job in San Francisco. Most of my colleagues asked how my dissertation was progressing. I do believe some asked in jest, as if I was never going to finish. However, I was progressing at a rapid pace. At every visit, before greeting me, I was asked about finishing my dissertation.

Finally, I was at a point where I'd completed all the chapters and was about to defend my dissertation. I was nervous as hell because my dissertation defense was a public announcement at the school. However, I was thrilled because only a few people were present. After defending my dissertation, my committee said that I needed to change a few things. *What do you mean add a learning component?* I thought angrily. I bit my lip and proceeded to make the changes Afterward, I submitted it, and the committee accepted my final dissertation. I was almost finished-publishing was next.

On one visit to the office in San Francisco, it was business as usual for me. Keep in mind, I never told anyone that my dissertation was complete. During that visit, we were in a training session, and an individual publicly asked about my dissertation. It was that one individual who always had a smirk on her face when asking. I looked at her and said, "All finished, except for editing my chapters. Practically a doctor now." I believe most individuals were happy for me.

I returned to Southern California and continued to prepare my dissertation for the final version, which the university had to approve. Here, I appreciated that my dissertation chair was an English major. Writing the final version took only a few months. For some, the final version takes a year or more. In addition, I did appreciate that my dissertation chair pushed me like she did. At that time, I was appreciative of all the versions of the chapters. However, the greatest gift delivered by my dissertation chair, because she knew something about my background and the struggles attaining my doctorate, was when she said, "Dr. Cubit, you're a success story. Continue on." Every time I think of the conversation, I can't contain myself, and the tears begin to flow like they are flowing right now. That meant so much to me, especially coming from her.

Graduation was an important day in my life. My mother was no longer with us, and neither was my father. However, my step-grandmother and stepfather flew from Ohio to attend the graduation and ceremony at the Pepperdine campus in Malibu. Those in attendance were my new girlfriend, my soon-to-be ex-wife, my sister, and two of my children. We toured the Pepperdine campus and we could see the Pacific Ocean from a high elevation on campus. Then I understood why the Wave is the mascot for the university. That campus was beautiful, more so than I could imagine. Enjoying the beautiful campus and the ambience of everything that day, I was proud of myself but was still in disbelief. *I did it.* The event for me was spectacular.

One day, I was at a store that I frequented, and the cashier asked why I never smiled. I wanted to say "Mind your own business" and "I have nothing to smile for." I cracked a complimentary smile and proceeded to accomplish the task of the day. At home that night, I thought about the interaction with the cashier and asked myself, *What do I have to be thankful for?* and *Why should I smile?* One time, someone asked me if I was happy. I said yes, and then she said, "Tell your face about it." *What the shuck!* I thought. Then I thought about my life and the challenges I'd faced. I thought about those in my youth who weren't as fortunate. From that moment, I thought I should be smiling every day. I should have surgery and affix a permanent smile on my face like the Joker in the *Batman* comic books. That smile would be especially important in times when I'm focused on a task and my facial expressions displayed a serious demeanor, which was inherent and a learned behavior. However, I'm working on smiling at all times, which creates a good feeling inside. Nonetheless, that graduation day at Pepperdine, the smiles wouldn't stop. I was elated.

That day was hot, and Pat Boone was one of the speakers and singers. All the doctoral candidates were sitting in the front row, and from my cadre, only one other person graduated that day. The entire underclasses received their diplomas and walked across the stage, and then it was our turn, the doctorates. All the doctoral candidates donned their robes, but when we walked across the stage individually, the dissertation chair placed the hood around the candidates' necks. The master of ceremonies called my name, and I didn't know if I was going to be able to handle the hooding ritual. I was nauseated and dizzy. I needed to do this and walked across the stage, shook the president's hand, and waited to be hooded. My dissertation chair couldn't make it, but I remembered her words: "Dr. Cubit, you are a success story." A member of my committee placed the hood around my neck, and briefly I thought about my sixteenth birthday years past. I could hardly contain myself as I'd walked across the stage and to my seat. However, I don't believe anyone knew how the event affected me. *Fool's hill, where is my placement now?*

For my graduation after-party, I reserved a hotel suite near the Los Angeles Airport and invited family and friends. I couldn't believe the number of people that showed up. Folks from previous jobs and friends, and I thought, *Wow.* An individual with whom I worked at the nonprofit organization attended and said that he'd seen how dedicated I was in obtaining my doctorate and mentioned that he was pursuing his master's. Years later, after he earned his master's degree, he reinforced how I'd influenced his academic achievement. I still feel guilty about not attending his graduation party. A best friend, Margaret, attended and gave me a money clip with "Dr. C" inscribed. I cherished that gift, until one day, I noticed it missing after a person installed my cable TV, but her gesture was commendable. My children attended the after-ceremony event, and eventually, my youngest daughter appeared, for she missed the graduation ceremony. Also in attendance were my stepfather and step-grandmother. That was my day, and I deserved it.

Chapter 14

IS THE GRASS TRULY GREENER

I continued working for the Department of Labor and was getting bored. I liked job-related traveling, and I enjoyed training others. On one occasion, I was able to help a community college develop curriculum for disadvantaged students. The college received a grant from the Department of Labor, and I was the federal project officer responsible for monitoring the program.

I conducted a site visit at the college, and the coordinator responsible for the program talked about the challenges teaching disadvantaged students. She said several students weren't comfortable working with technology. Some of the students were of color and had been out of school for a while. Most of the instructors at the school were Caucasian. I provided technical assistance to alleviate the challenges of teaching this special population. When doing so, I remembered the advent of conducting research for my doctorate, and students saying that they learned by performing a task, physical movement, a kinesthetic learning philosophy, more so than direct instruction or lecture in the classroom. I also related my experience working for a nonprofit organization and teaching a computer class and how the approach helped me reach more students. In addition to working at the continuation school, I communicated the need to work with students at their level and to remember that everyone has a different learning style, and perhaps a project-based learning approach in addition to revising the entry and exit strategy could help. During my next visit, she wanted to give me a hug and said that changing the course structure helped reach more students, which led to an increase in course completions.

I was approaching my four-year anniversary at the Department of Labor and was seeking a management position. However, I believed that my current employer didn't have the capacity to retain me after I earned my doctorate. I believed advancement opportunities were limited. Moreover, I wanted to discover what my experience and doctorate could do for me. At that time, I was still teleworking and living in Southern California, and the office wanted me to move back to the Bay Area. I didn't want to relocate and remembered the exorbitant cost of housing in the San Francisco area. I was living in Southern California in the High Desert. The rent for housing was cheaper, and I was close to family. At that time, I wanted to work closely with programs that had an immediate impact on participants as opposed to my role as a government official providing technical assistance or oversight. I also wanted to venture into teaching at colleges and universities.

Eventually, a university offered me an adjunct position teaching a careers class at an army base. I mentioned to my supervisor that I was going to teach a careers class, and the organization was concerned about a conflict of interest. A supervisor said that I couldn't use my federal position to influence the public or for personal gain. I said that teaching at a university bore no connection to my federal position. Anyway, I took the teaching position, my first at the university level. For students in class, instead of addressing me as Mr. C, they now called me Dr. C, a title that a student at the continuation school professed for me years earlier. Teaching part-time at a university was an exciting experience. However, concerning my full-time job, I wanted to venture into management or obtain a position in which I could have more responsibility. I began applying for federal jobs for management positions and had a few interviews. Apparently, earning my doctorate didn't help.

The time came for a promotion, and I submitted an application for the job. If I were promoted, the extra money could help defray the cost of my moving back to and living in the San Francisco Bay area. My supervisor hinted that I should interview for the position and gave me a date to return to the office. The day of the interview, I took a flight from Southern California. While sitting in the foyer waiting for my turn, I said to the receptionist that I declined the interview and took a flight back to Southern California. A few weeks later, I resigned a third time, leaving the federal government because of the perceived inability to grow professionally. I now had a secure job, and because I was a veteran, I didn't have to worry about a reduction in force or layoff. In addition, I had a doctorate. Surely, I could change the world. I was facing "the grass-is-greener dilemma." Nonetheless, at that time, I didn't know what the future had to offer, but I was willing to take the risk. Well, you guessed it-back to substitute teaching, which was short-lived. Fool's hill, where am I at this point?

I interviewed for a training-and-development position at a casino in the Palm Springs area. The individual who interviewed me had a PhD and was the human resource director. I was excited about the opportunity to work for an organization in the private industry, and I wanted to experience new things about teaching and training. The interview and the application process at the casino were intensive, more so than the hiring process for a federal government job. I understood the intent behind the hiring process because the organization generated millions of dollars and had to be sure that employees weren't theft risks. I noticed that some individuals were hired and forced to resign or quit once the report of investigation for the background check came back. Eventually, the casino offered me the training-manager position. I loaded a rented truck, and was on my way to the Palm Springs area in Southern California.

I was now working for an organization in the private industry. I was excited about the opportunity to develop a training-program. However, the pay was less than I'd expected, but I believed the experience would advance my career. At least I had a management title. In addition, the health benefits, in my opinion, surpassed those provided by the federal government. From the time I left the Department of Labor until the time the casino hired me was about three months.

I was now improving a training program for the casino, and the first thing I developed was a training-needs assessment. The goal was to discover the need for training throughout the organization. During the process, I discovered the need for required training, such as sexual harassment, and enhanced performance. In time, I was able to revise the new-employee-orientation program. At first, the new-employee-orientation was a one-day event, and I expanded it to two. Several employees said they feared attending the two-day event, but after the sessions, many said the orientation was the best they had experienced. "We weren't bored" was one of the comments I received. I developed sexual harassment, customer service, team-building, communications, and diversity training to name a few. All the training had a positive impact on the organization. The company owned a building near the casino. I was able to take an unused building full of junk and convert it into a training center. Instead of using the auditorium in the casino, I conducted all training at the newly converted center.

I gained valuable experience, and a major accomplishment was facilitating team-building sessions for senior managers in departments throughout the organization. An accomplishment that I was most proud of was the development of the excellence in leadership program. This was a six-week program for new supervisors. The program had facets of classroom instruction, project-based learning centered on problem-solving and team-building sessions. As part of the program, and in order to complete the training, individuals in teams developed strategies to solve an actual problem at the casino. For the evaluation of the final project, I assembled a team comprised of employees, managers, members of the board of directors, and customers who frequented the establishment. Everyone throughout the organization, including customers, was involved. I coordinated meetings in which we developed strategies to evaluate the projects. The entire event was a tremendous undertaking.

For the final presentation, teams competed for a monetary prize, but the motivation was also to win the competition and be recognized as the initial team that won the first annual excellence in leadership team competition for beginning managers. The event was held in a large auditorium and was wholly successful. I believed the event and the effort made a difference for that organization. I was proud of the contribution.

Working for an organization in the private sector was different from working for the federal government. Again, I was faced with unwelcomed advances like sexual harassment. In the first incident, I received a call from one of the gaming managers. She asked me to come by her house for dinner and a drink. I mentioned to her that our department was meeting for a drink at night and she was welcome to join us. At first, I was unaware about her intentions but later understood. Later I found that another individual who was just hired at the casino did accept the invitation and had dinner with her. In describing what took place during dinner, he had a smile on his face. Anyway I wasn't attracted to the individual, and besides, she smoked cigarettes. In 1994, approximately ten years prior, I smoked my last cigarette and vowed to never date anyone who indulged in this. To date, I've honored both of those goals. She managed one of the largest departments, and soon after, she prevented employees from attending training sessions, and attendance declined drastically. She was well connected and, I believe, had some influence over my supervisor, and I was left without recourse. Thinking back, I should've had relations with her (I want to use a different word here that starts with F) just to remedy the situation.

In another situation, a black female had the hots for me, and there was constant pressure to date her. Every time we passed in the hallway, she commented about what a good woman she was and why I didn't make an effort to date her. To make matters worse and intensify the situation, on one occasion, she and others were invited to have lunch with members of my department including my supervisor, the human resource director, and another manager. Throughout lunch, all she did was make advances toward me. Not only was I pissed, but I was also confused by what took place, and I communicated my resentment about her advances. What made matters worse was that all human resource managers did was laugh. Because of the situation, I took the rest of the day off and internalized my displeasure concerning the situation.

In the situations mentioned here, I wanted to say to both females making the advances that previously, I was involved in two workplace relationships; both weren't advantageous and affected my performance on the job. In both situations, I wanted to quit my job, but things worked themselves out. Because of those prior experiences, I feared workplace relationships. However, toward the end of my employment at the casino, I relented and started dating someone in my department, which, I believed, cancelled my stance about workplace relationships. This didn't alleviate the challenges I faced with the two females at the casino. In addition, the African American female seemed overwhelmingly vengeful, and she was a manager in the dining facility. I made sure not to dine there when she was on duty.

Working for the casino bureaucracy was different from employment for the federal government. Previously, I mentioned the experience developing the off-site training center. As noted, the casino was in the Palms Spring area, the summer was hot, and the training center didn't have adequate air-conditioning. I found two portable air-conditioning units at a building supply store. I submitted a requisition to purchase the units on a Wednesday, and by Friday, the organization had a check waiting for me to pay a vendor. The quick turnaround time was something I hadn't experienced when working for the federal government; the same held true when purchasing training supplies or submitting a request to attend a seminar. At the casino, the time between submitting a requisition and receiving the materials or services seemed almost instantaneous.

While working at the casino, I revised the existing newsletter, which evolved into a successful communication tool for the organization. It was an ongoing challenge to find ways to encourage employees to read the newsletter. To increase awareness, I walked around with a camera, interviewed employees, and asked departments to submit articles. My task was to edit the content and use a publishing tool to create the newsletter. Sometimes I wrote an article about employee development and training. If I published the newsletter later than expected, employees called to ask when the next one was going to be circulated. Employees especially liked the crossword puzzle, and the solutions to the puzzle were based on articles in the newsletter or something related to the casino. Employees who submitted a correctly completed crossword puzzle within a few days earned free show tickets or free meals from the restaurant. The "Who Am I?" section was a big hit as well. That section featured a frame without a face and a big question mark. The content in the article below the frame gave personal and employment-related facts about an employee. Those who guessed correctly who the employee was earned prizes and had their names featured in the next newsletter. The next month featured a picture of the individual. The "Who Am I?" section was a way for employees to learn something about coworkers. Overall, having fun and asking employee how to improve the newsletter were essential to its success.

The newsletter, the new training facility, and the expanded new-employee orientation were accomplishments. Developing training for diversity management, sexual harassment, team building, customer service, and monitoring the results of the training, to name a few, all had positive impacts on the organization. In addition, facilitating team building sessions for senior managers and the development of the "excellence in leadership" were successes for me personally. Not bad for a former hood rat.

Believing that I was doing an excellent job, I thought it was time to ask my supervisor for a raise. It took me about a week to generate the nerve to ask. I thought back to when I worked for the federal government and raises were almost automatic-a benefit, I now realized. The day came for me to ask for a raise, and my supervisor said that he had to ask the board of directors, and he said that I was deserving of one. About a week later, he called me into the office and said my request was denied. About a week earlier, I'd received a call from a local community college about a job. I interviewed for the position as director of a training program some time ago. The community college offered me the position.

I served my two weeks' notice and proceeded to my new job. While working for the community college, about a month later, I found that everyone at the casino received an annual bonus. As I calculated, my bonus and an automatic raise would have been approximately eight thousand dollars. I figured I would recoup the loss in about a year from my new job; still, eight thousand dollars in my pocket at that time would have changed things for me. Had I known, perhaps I would have made a different decision about leaving the casino. However, the challenges presented by the two females were enough for me and helped make my decision to leave. A lesson learned here was that the grass may not always be greener, and if transitioning to a new position, know the details before leaving the existing one. I later discovered that my supervisor at the casino took another job soon after I'd departed and said that a deciding factor was the inability to duplicate the programs I'd created.

Around that time, I experienced personal challenges that affected me, and perhaps I wasn't thinking clearly. Apparently, I was still searching for that ultimate employment situation in relation to my "why." I wanted a job in which I could use my knowledge, skills, and abilities.

Another challenge was attempting to reconcile with my wife; however, I quote B. B. King, "The thrill is gone." During an attempt to reconcile, she communicated to me information about my children and their perception of me, and I wasn't happy. Here I note the importance of communication with children when a husband and wife part ways. Sometimes what husbands and wives say, in the heat of a moment, the children shouldn't hear or be privy to what was said. Especially if something during the conversation is taken out of context. I really stress caution here. Anyway, I should've considered the source. Soon after the failed reconciliation, I decided to file for a divorce and hired a lawyer. Meanwhile, my stepfather was in town, and my sister said that they were coming to visit. I thought that was odd because no one ever visited me. They opted to visit and stay for a few days. The first night, we had an opportunity to talk, and the next morning, I cooked breakfast for everyone.

After we had eaten breakfast, my sister said that she wanted to talk to me about something but, before that, we should pray. While we prayed, thoughts of the past were on my mind. After finishing our prayer, she said that my father wasn't who I thought he was and my real dad was sitting across from me at the table, the individual I thought was my stepfather. She then proceeded to present evidence but didn't really know the truth because my mother and the person I believed to be my father took the information to the grave with them.

I was in a state of confusion, disbelief, and anger. Immediately flashing before my eyes were the times that my father hadn't fulfilled his promises to my brother and me, the times I spent with family members on my father's side when I'd thought their attitudes toward me were distant. I thought about my children and what was ingrained into their belief system. Next, in a flash, I thought about when my ex-wife said that she was pregnant and how I fashioned my life so that my children wouldn't grow up without a father. I thought, *How could someone know he was my father and not step up and claim me?* At the table, I asked my stepfather why. He said, "That was what we did back then." I asked my sister and my stepfather to leave. I said, "Pack your stuff and get the hell out of here, shucking assholes and liars." Every time I think about that event I get emotional.

This was a crucial moment for me. I called my partner who had experienced a similar challenge in her life. Next, I called my brother, and we analyzed what my sister had said, and both of us thought, *No way.* Both my brother and I are over six feet tall, and the person who now claimed to be our father was, on a good day, five-foot-three. How could this be? Unless there was a recessive gene somewhere. We are much darker than him. Our hair is nappier than his. The claim didn't add up but created confusion in both our lives, but we remained in disbelief. Then I remembered a comment from my mother about a remark I made about our hair in jest. I wished our hair wasn't so nappy, and what my mother had said. I didn't know what my mother meant at that time; perhaps she was saying that my lineage wasn't as it seemed. My brother and I knew there were ways to find an answer but we were reluctant because both of us feared what we might find.

Soon after my sister and stepfather delivered the news, I abruptly left my position at the community college. Another reason was that position involved sales, and you know my experience there. The day of departure, I must've driven five hundred miles, no destination.

Time to think. Once again, I didn't have a plan to progress in my life, but I still knew my "why" for employment. Was leaving that job a fool's hill mistake?

At that time, I believed everything was a lie. Getting a good education and an excellent job was a lie, and the job I'd just left didn't help. Again, I wasn't looking for a handout, and I worked hard to overcome the challenges of life, earn five college degrees, and transform myself. The failed marriage, divorce, and the legal challenges from that didn't help. My children and what I believed was betrayal made matters worse. What about Santa Claus? All lies. Now I was faced with what I believed was another lie: for years, my father wasn't who I thought he was. *Is there a God?* I thought. I was able to overcome the challenges of the hood, but this was too much! *What do I need to do to find peace of mind in my life?* I was in a state of despair.

Eventually, I checked out. After abruptly leaving my job, I didn't answer my phone or respond to emails. Except for my partner at that time, nobody knew my location and couldn't contact me for three years. I didn't care what was going to happen next. I needed a break from everything and everybody. This was a crucial time for me. I reverted to subconscious acts and binged on unhealthy food and salty stuff, like times as a youth in the hood when faced with stressors. *Will the quarter-size blemishes on my body return?* I thought. Then, I completely ignored my physical fitness activities, and the absence of this caused additional stress in my life. I gained about thirty pounds. Thinking back, I'd yet to realize how I contributed to that dilemma in my life and I also thought about my past. Was I in the belly of a big fish, like Jonah in the Bible because he didn't adhere to what God had planned for him? Perhaps I should've never left the navy base and moved to the High Desert. The answers to these questions evaded me, and I believed the promise of a better life eluded me as well.

Chapter 15

OUTDOOR CLASSROOM?

At that time, I was despondent and didn't know what was in store for me. This time, substitute teaching wasn't an option. Moreover, before leaving the job at the community college, I'd applied at several colleges and universities for adjunct online teaching positions. Before leaving my last job, a college hired me to teach online technical communication courses. Soon after, another university hired me to teach career-management courses. A third contacted me to teach education and introduction to college courses. Teaching online became my full-time job. I was somewhat my own boss. No brick-and-mortar buildings, no office, no supervisor watching my every move. Thank God for my college degrees, especially the doctorate, because some of the learning institutions preferred that classroom instructors have an advanced degree.

Nonetheless, now I was busy teaching and sometimes working more than sixty hours per week. For about two years, I managed to teach courses online at three universities. Then I contracted with a fourth, and I was responsible for facilitating introduction-to-college classes in addition to technology for business courses. At one time, my workload for the four institutions was sixty-three students, which was unfathomable. For some universities, I taught two to three classes at a time. I was in survivor mode. I was also in a limbo state, but I wasn't giving up on my dreams. My girlfriend at that time said that I wasn't in survivor mode but that I was a survivor who always managed to find a way regardless of the challenges I faced. I managed to function as a teacher for approximately four years. My girlfriend at that time was instrumental to my success as well.

As previously mentioned, as an online instructor, I didn't have a supervisor. Occasionally, someone from one of the colleges or universities contacted me when a student complained about his or her grade. I kept good records, followed protocol, treated all students equally, and never lost a protest. As long as I managed the workload for each class and was able to complete assigned tasks and submitted grades on time, I was my own supervisor. Then, a favorite class to teach was career management, and I was in my element. During the class, I was able to relate my experience about the world of work to include discussions about the balance of work and life. As an adjunct professor teaching career classes, I had a job, but my career appeared to be in a state of flux, and I resembled that expert mechanic who drove the worst-running car in the neighborhood.

I realized that I could teach courses anytime and anywhere, so I bought a new laptop. I also purchased a device that allowed me to connect to my classes wirelessly anywhere and anytime. Sometimes at a park. Sometimes in my car. Anywhere! One time, my girlfriend and I took a trip to Canada. We took turns driving. When it was her turn to drive, I connected to my classes. Sometimes we went camping, especially in places that provided access to the internet. During those camping trips, I was able to teach my classes.

Eventually, I decided to explore if I could teach classes from the outdoors or in the wilderness. I always wanted to devote time to exploring the wilderness, and I remembered when I was in camp while in the sixth grade and the passion I'd felt for the outdoors. Now was the time to explore that passion. Ergo, the technological side of me kicked in. I thought, *Why not teach my classes wherever I wanted, even if in the wilderness?* I decided to go for it.

I purchased a satellite dish for my internet and solar panels and a wind generator for energy. I also carried a backup generator. During the day, the wind generator and the solar panels powered the batteries. If my batteries were low at night, I fired up the generator. Off I went, sometimes weeks at a time, to isolated areas, grading papers, accessing the internet to chat with students, or checking my email. If anyone happened upon me in the wilderness late at night, my camp-site resembled Las Vegas at night. Sometimes I almost depleted my food supply, and had to travel to the nearest town to resupply. Often I stopped at a local truck stop and took a shower.

I purchased high-security locks and cables and figured out a way to latch everything to a tree. Eventually, I bought a portable solar shower unit, one that used propane to generate hot water. Sometimes I took my golf clubs, which I never used, and practiced hitting balls while in the wilderness. Often in my underwear or in the nude, of course with sandals, and ashy legs. Each time I smacked that golf ball when in my birthday suit, I thought, *Ahhhhh, freedom in more ways than one!* Sometimes the music was blasting; while listening to old-school jams, I would be dancing my ass off, sometimes under the moonlight. Warm nights and a campfire smoldering in the background.

During the day, most times I listened to smooth jazz. I also purchased a hammock for naps. There I was, a black man in the wilderness, sometimes in the nude, grading papers, teaching classes, hitting golf balls, dancing my ass off or riding my mountain bike.

On one occasion, I was enjoying myself when I heard a vehicle approaching. To access my location, one had to drive on a rough dirt road. Therefore, I could hear vehicles approaching from miles away. I decided to put on some clothes, and in the vehicle was an African American forest ranger who drove to my location in order to replenish the toilet paper in the outhouse. I was shocked, because he was the first African American forest ranger I'd met in the wilderness. I hadn't thought they existed. However, he was more shocked than I was, and when he saw me, he asked, "What the shuck you doing out here, man?" He thought I was conducting CIA operations or researching. He looked at my setup and said that black people didn't do shit like this. I said I typically do shit that black people don't do. We started talking, and he said that he was amazed that sometimes individuals shot the outhouse for which he was replacing the toilet paper. I had noticed this before, and I said, "You mean someone shot the shitter." We both laughed and then talked for about two hours. I showed him my setup; he was impressed and perplexed. He left, and

I assumed my position with bare-minimum clothing and continued hitting those golf balls. Before that week was over, knowing that others frequented that location on the weekend, I packed my "Beverly Hillbillies" vehicle and found another location less frequented by people. Sometimes when I camped in less-secluded areas, individuals stopped and asked to look at my setup. Some had questions, and often cars slowed down, looked, and then sped away.

I continued to teach classes online. I was mobile, and I changed locations frequently. Using my outdoor setup, I had the opportunity to teach classes from places like San Diego, Petaluma, Canada, the beach, the mountains, and the desert. For one holiday, I was camping in the Mt. Pinos area of Southern California, and my girlfriend and her daughter decided to join me. I gave them the location, and they met me at a gas station and then followed me to the campsite. They were in awe of the beauty of the location. After unloading their gear, I decided to be adventurous, and we went for a ride. After taking a detour, we found a biker bar in the middle of nowhere. We dared to go in to have a drink. We sat at the bar, and carved in the wooden bar were some interesting symbols. We didn't care. We ordered shots of tequila anyway. While sitting there, we could hear gunshots in the distance. As we were leaving, I met the African American forest ranger, the same one I'd spoke with while he was replenishing the toilet paper in the gunshot shitter. First, he commented about my being fully clothed, and I wondered what my girlfriend was thinking after that comment. Then the ranger said that drinking at that bar shouldn't be a problem. We returned to our campsite and after my girlfriend and her daughter returned home, I loaded my gear into my vehicle and was off to my next location in the Mt. Pinos area in California.

Chapter 16

DO BLACK PEOPLE HIKE?

C amping and anything outdoors became my passion, perhaps a way to block out the challenges I was facing. Camping in isolated places was and is my favorite pastime. At that time, I owned a large SUV and packed everything inside. I even had camping gear on the top of the car. My SUV resembled the vehicle in *The Beverly Hillbillies* without the chair on top. Attached on one side of the luggage rack was the pole for my wind generator. My girlfriend always laughed at me and was amazed at the amount of stuff I could pack into the vehicle.

Now that I had accomplished the camping goal, I decided to venture into hiking and then backpacking. I was off, into the wilderness on foot, which was a new experience. In my youth, I always had an affinity for the outdoors. Besides youth camp, my other experience enjoying the outdoors was finding a hill with dried weeds and taking a piece of cardboard and sliding down the hill on the slick vegetation. Sometimes it was a challenge trampling down the weeds, though. A favorite place to go weed-sledding now is the 805 freeway in Southeast San Diego. In the hood, at certain times of the year, while riding in the car, one could see several trampled weed-sliding hills.

Anyway, in the beginning of my outdoor hiking experience, I purchased attire and equipment from a well-known department store. Since I was in the military, I had some gear, and I managed to start with that. I thought, if the gear was useful while in the military

240

then, it should be useful now, and the department store items should be sufficient as well. Wrong, wrong, and wrong. Eventually, I discovered that gear purchased from well-known outdoor suppliers was and is far superior to the military gear or department store items. In addition, I subscribed to a well-known backpacking publication and conducted searches on the internet, which helped as well. Discovery about outdoor hiking through trial and error was a challenge.

During my first few hikes, I looked like a militant on the trail, and some individuals were hesitant when approaching me; some were definitely confused to see an African American male hiking, sometimes in desolate areas. However, I found my new joy in life. While hiking, I was able to see sights that I'd never imagined seeing while living in the hood, or camping. I was obsessed and experienced some of the best times of my life while hiking. After gaining experience, I took on the more-challenging trails, and the sights were more spectacular; fewer people frequented those areas, which I didn't mind. I bought a camera and became what I call a shadow photographer. In those pictures, if the sun was in the right place, my shadow was always in the background. I found peace from hiking.

Now I decided to enhance my outdoors experience and venture into backpacking. My first backpacking trip was with my female partner. This wasn't a real wilderness experience; however, it was a memorable one. The first was a trail near Laguna Beach, California. My backpack was overloaded, and I carried some of my gear from camping in a tent or car. The weight in my backpack was almost unbearable. On that trip, we backpacked to a campsite about three miles from the trailhead. We set up camp near a mountain bike trail. Every day, we left our campsite and hiked to the beach. Some days, we left the campsite and hiked to the car then went to the store.

The area was overwhelmed with field mice, which were a nuisance, and therefore, snakes were abundant. While hiking, we saw evidence of snakes, as they crossed the dirt paths. At night, we heard coyotes howling at the full moon. Under the moonlight, we saw a cricket-like creature climbing up and down the outside walls of the tent.

As previously mentioned, this was a rewarding experience; however, I wanted to spend more time in the real wilderness. I started watching all the wilderness survival shows such as *Survivorman, Man vs. Wild*, and *I Shouldn't Be Alive*. Watching television shows in addition to reading books and magazines helped me develop the framework for my backpacking adventures. I learned what not to do if facing dire situations while in the wilderness. I made sure I was prepared for most situations. I wanted to experience the most challenging experiences outdoors, and time in the Marine Corps increased this desire.

I was now in the planning stages of my first backpacking trip in the wilderness, and I picked a strenuous trail. In a popular magazine, I discovered an article about a trail near Apache Junction in Arizona in the Superstition Wilderness. I attempted to find trails in California; however, during the winter, most of them were inaccessible, sometimes because of inclement weather. I checked the weather for the trail in Arizona and found that the area would be dry and hot during my backpacking adventure. I then bought a GPS and marked my waypoints along the trail. I also uploaded a map in my GPS device. I practiced using the device on day hikes. Except for my backpack, which I recently purchased and still use today, everything was practically new. I was off to the wilderness on my first backpacking trip. During that first backpack trip, my goal was to spend three days and finish the thirty-five-mile loop, of which I had already mapped the coordinates.

My backpack must've weighed seventy-five pounds. On the way to Arizona, about a four-hour or more drive from my location in California, I had a flat tire on my almost-bald tires. I changed the tire and I was excited and apprehensive because I knew nothing about my destination. When I arrived at Apache Junction, I checked into a hotel, left my personal items, and was off in the morning to the trailhead.

On the way to the trailhead, I was in awe of the beauty of the place and its scenery. When arriving, I asked if I could park my car at the trailhead, and the security guard said that it was okay. I had a long climb up a hill, and on top was a cross. I started my descent into the canyon and heard the water rushing in a creek a few miles away. It took me about five hours to get to my first campsite, and today, that hike is only about two hours. It was starting to get dark, and I needed to relieve myself; it was my first real experience taking a number 2 in the wilderness. I was nervous, and I was fearful that a snake or Gila monster was going to bite me in the ass. I looked like a nervous animal, looking here and there. How do you spell *relief?* And I was all right after the initiation was complete. During my first backpacking trip in Superstition Wilderness, Boulder Creek had plenty of water, and I was able to use my brand-new purification apparatus.

Here was my first night in the wilderness, and I was scared shitless. I thought a bear or a mountain lion was going to attack me, I went to sleep. Let me rephrase, I *attempted* to sleep. One item I always carry even if on a day hike is bear spray, and I only had to use it twice-and not on bears. That first night in the wilderness, I raised my tent next to some bushes, and while I was sleeping, the wind started to blow. I thought the vegetation brushing up against my tent were animals, and I was blowing my whistle most of the night. Several times, I shouted to scare the phantom animals away. Eventually, because of the water consumed during the day, I needed to relieve myself. The cacti, in the shadow of the moon, looked like creatures, and I wanted to take off running in my thermal underwear.

I probably slept two hours that night and woke to find icicles on the inside of my tent hanging from the poles. Because of the condensation inside the tent from my body heat and the cold air, icicles had formed. The next morning, I prepared my breakfast using the heavy stove I used for car camping. I took a few minutes to practice using my slingshot in case I became stranded and needed to eat a bird or something. I was off with my heavy backpack. I never found my route, and following the path on my GPS was useless. I took a wrong turn but was able to find my way, thanks to another backpacker who was hiking with his dog. I explained to him my backpacking destination, and he said that I was way off. He also said that he feared he would read the paper the next morning and find that I was lost or had met my demise in the wilderness. I thought it was cool that he was backpacking with his dog. I was in about two days and exhausted from my backpacking experience and I never found the route. It was then I planned my exit.

On the way back, I became confused and thought that the trail had changed, and I needed to find a way out. I decided to ditch my gear and climb over a ridge, which I thought was the lowest point and the nearest exit. I proceeded toward the descent and became somewhat anxious about what was taking place.

At that time, I remembered being lost in the woods while in Oklahoma and another time in the Marine Corps. While I was on the big island of Hawaii, a group of us, all marines, decided to bushwhack to the top of one of the volcanoes. Yeah, right. No gear and no water. Nevertheless, we decided to climb that volcano. After we had hiked up the side of a mountain for a time and viewed the hills and dells, we realized that hiking to the volcano wasn't possible. We headed back, and again, like the outdoor trip in Oklahoma, I knew the best route to return to camp. Everyone took a different direction than I did, and here again, I was alone, finding my way back. Unlike the situation in Oklahoma, no dog to follow this time. While in Hawaii and finding my way back, I happened upon a wild turkey. While I was lost in the wilderness, for me, some things seemed larger than they actually were. Nonetheless, that wild turkey seemed like it was ten feet tall. I took off running one way, and the turkey took off running in the opposite direction. Here we have one turkey in its natural habitat and one turkey lost in the woods, *again*. An advantage in Hawaii: although I didn't have a trail to follow, because of the elevation, I could see the base camp as I made my descent.

On the big island of Hawaii, most of the terrain was volcanic rock, which we called lava dogs, and some were razor-sharp. Well those military boots were demolished like those "roach-in-the-corner killers" I destroyed while lost in the woods in Oklahoma. Does history repeat itself? This time, there was no father to yell at me, though. However, during the hike in Arizona, not only was I scared because I was lost, I also remembered the fears when lost in the woods in Oklahoma and Hawaii, which didn't help. At that time, I hadn't developed the ability to remain calm, gather myself, form a plan, and proceed to find a way out.

I remembered something while watching a survival show or reading an article: when lost, stay on the trail. I descended from my climb, proceeded back to the trail, followed it in the opposite direction from which I'd arrived, and sure enough, that was my way out. I finally made my way back to my car; however, some of my clothing was destroyed. My shirt was torn. My cotton pants were ripped from my knee all the way to my crotch. I took the items back to the store, and they refunded my money. Nonetheless, I had fun-and vowed to return. Because of the challenge of finding my way out and the potential for a catastrophe, I bought a personal locator beacon, which I carry with me on all four-wheel drive excursions, hiking and backpacking trips, and wherever I travel in general.

Before summer, I returned to Arizona to backpack two times, and each time with improved gear. On one occasion, because I didn't want to burn any living vegetation, I lugged a five-pound fire log, the sawdust type. I never had a chance to burn it and ended up taking it home. My backpack was heavy during that trip. It wasn't until about my fifth trip, approximately three years later, that I was able to finish the route I'd originally chartered. Now I know the trails in the area like the back of my hand but always chart my route, carry a compass, and take a map. I was in my later years in life on that first backpacking trip. Never too old, folks.

Currently, I backpack in that area once a year during the holidays. During my descent and exit, I look at the place I chose as my exit during my first hike, when I was lost. I believe if I attempted to climb out through the course I first chartered when I got lost, I probably wouldn't be here communicating my experience. Now, the Arizona area is a favorite place to backpack, and each time, the experience differs. At the higher elevation, I was dusted with snow flurries one morning. Sometimes the climate is so hot that I take my shirt off while backpacking. However, at night, the cold can be unbearable, but usually, I'm prepared for extreme weather conditions. On one occasion, I experienced a flash flood and had to wade in chest-high water to exit. That was a scary experience, especially hearing the thunder and lightning at night. One night, I had an intervention with a skunk. That night, I was sitting around the campfire and heard commotion in the bushes. I switched my headlamp to the red lens, and out of the bushes, I saw the animal's eyes reflecting the red light from my headlamp.

Finally, I switched the light to normal vision, and the skunk continued to gallivant in my direction, which looked like a friendly manner, and it appeared that the animal's tongue was hanging out the side of its mouth. Finally, I stood up to make myself appear larger, and the skunk took off. I threw a rock in its direction to let it know that my reach extended beyond the campsite. What did I do that for? Skunk-booty smell all night.

Anyway, in Arizona, with each backpacking venture, I dream of experiencing a journey with my son first and afterward, with my son-in-law, and grandsons. I believe they would find the same peace as I do, and I do believe they and anyone can learn much about themselves in the outdoors, including self-discipline and overcoming challenges, and about the joy of nature's beauty. I hope I can experience a backpacking trip with my son and family before I meet my demise.

While backpacking, I take the adventures seriously, no music, no cell phones, no computers, or anything to alter my mentality. This enhances the beauty of the experience. Listening to nature and the surroundings creates a peace. Especially at night, while sitting around a campfire tired from backpacking all day. Sitting on a log or a pile of rocks while cooking dinner-peaceful. I usually end my day at 9:00 p.m., depending on the location, and am up at 6:00 a.m. after several late-night pissing interventions.

Since my first backpacking trip, I've had the opportunity to partake in backpacking trips to California, Arizona, Utah, and Colorado. Sometimes I'm gone for one to two nights or as many as ten days. However, Arizona is special to me. I backpack in Arizona at the end of every year, and several times spent Christmas and New Year's backpacking there. Spending time there at the end of the year serves as a point of renewal before the beginning of a new year. I experience challenge and change with each backpacking experience. In 2014, I blew my Achilles tendon on the first day, which has been a recurring injury since my time in the military. However, I was able to survive by taking an exorbitant amount of pain medication twice per day. By day 4, I was fine and managed to backpack forty-five miles on that trip. This was the first time I tumbled three times on the same day, and in one incident, a tree limb almost flung me into an accumulation of jumping cholla cacti, which would have been devastating. However, that trip was one of my most enjoyable, and I learned so much about myself.

Besides Arizona, one of my memorable backpacking trips happened along the Pacific Crest Trail (PCT) in California. I was going to backpack about a 150-mile section. I was off, and I told my partner that I would call her and she could pick me up at a different location from where she dropped me off. I hiked in about five miles and ran into areas heavily impacted by snow and ice. I met a couple of backpackers, and they mentioned that they had MICROspikes, or crampons, which allowed them to hike a trail in icy conditions. At that time, I didn't have MICROspikes and had to turn back. I called my partner, and she picked me up. However, I was determined to finish the backpacking adventure, and in a few days, my partner dropped me off at another location. At that point, I had never backpacked for an extended length of time. Typically, I backpacked somewhere and stayed for a few days and then returned, perhaps a forty-mile round-trip. Here I would be out for longer.

While hiking or backpacking, the fears that challenge me most are snakes and heights, especially when climbing high elevations and then looking down into a canyon, knowing that if I fell nothing would stop me from tumbling. On one of my first hikes, I remember turning around and returning to my car because of the fear of heights. I finally gathered the nerve to finish that hike and vowed to never turn back because of heights. Today, I chuckle when I hike that trail; the fear today isn't the same as it was during that first hike. Does the fear of heights still exist? Certainly. However, I learned and am still learning how to overcome the challenge.

While hiking the PCT on that 150-mile journey for one section in Southern California, I was faced with a decision. I was on part of the trail, and when looking down, all I could see was the valley below and, in some places, a stream. There were no ledges and nothing to stop me if I fell. The entire time on that ridge, I was in my fear-of-heights state. In some places, parts of the trail were missing and I had to jump over a canyon to continue. When beginning that section, I was faced with three options. If I turned back, I would break a promise to myself; therefore, I only had two options. One option was to proceed, and another was to be taken out in a helicopter because I had frozen on the trail. I proceeded. To make matters worse, night was approaching, and I wondered if I had to sleep standing up on the trail. Eventually, I found a small area in which I could bed down for the night. Was I tense! I hoped and prayed that the trail would lead me to the end of hiking on that ridge early the next day. Now I can probably hike that part of the trail in less time, but then, because of the challenge I faced with heights, taking my time was essential.

Up in the morning, I didn't prepare breakfast. I unwrapped a couple of energy bars, put sunflower seeds in my pocket, and was off. Briefly I hiked on the ridge, which finally disappeared, and I was on flat land. However, that was short-lived, and I was on that ridge again. I backpacked several miles and passed what was a hot spring, and a few day-hikers were there. I came to an oasis, a beautiful place, had lunch, and drank unfiltered water from a free-flowing spring. I figured, at that elevation, there was nothing above that could pollute the water, and I was right. I proceeded and was approaching the High Desert section of the trail, and the sun graciously heated the rocks. Not only did I have the height to contend with, now there was also the heat. Finally, backpacking that ridge was over, and I approached an area with trees, a pond, and flowing water. Because of the elevation and backpacking that ridge, now I know why the trail has its name, the PCT. The heat challenged me and I dived in water and didn't care about the pollywogs and wiggly, protozoa-looking creatures that gyrated back and forth to propel themselves or the other junk in the water. I just wanted to cool down. Soaking wet, I took out my water-purification system and attempted to use it. It malfunctioned and almost exploded from the soot in the water and the pressure from the clogged unit.

When hiking or backpacking, I always carry two or three ways to purify water. Typically, I carry either a SteriPEN, or a Katadyn water treatment system, my trusty water-purification tablets, and a way to boil water, if necessary. Recently, I purchased a water-pu-rification straw but haven't used it. While on the 150-mile back-packing journey, because my water-purification system wasn't oper-ational, I reached in my backpack and grabbed my water reservoir. I then grabbed a sock that I used to filter the water that contained the pollywogs and wiggly, protozoa-looking creatures that gyrated back and forth to propel themselves, and then I dumped a couple of water-purification tablets in my water reservoir, and off I went. In addition, before I continued backpacking on that ridge-what felt like Mt. Everest to me-I met a couple. They said that they never used mechanical devices to purify water and carried a vial of bleach, which was cost-effective. *Perhaps next time,* I thought.

Next, I had to overcome my fear of snakes, which is something I might never accomplish. Prior to hiking the PCT, I probably saw two snakes while on trails or backpacking. In the past, while hiking Southern California, I heard several rattlers in the bushes but didn't see any snakes. The last sound I want to hear is the ungodly rattling sound in the bushes. On my trek along the PCT, I was always on alert for snakes. I saw a few, some lying across the trail in the morning, try-ing to warm themselves. Because of their cold-blooded nature, they couldn't move. Therefore, I had to go around or jump over them. On one backpacking venture on the PCT near Whitewater, California, in a twenty-four-hour period, I saw three snakes, which was unusual. A gopher snake of about five feet slithered across the trail. The gopher snake looks and coils like a rattlesnake but rarely attacks humans. While I was resting on the trail during a strenuous climb, a very fast snake slithered past right in front of me, less than a foot away. I had never seen a snake move so fast. On that same day, I was crossing a creek and jumped to the other side near what I thought was a twig. Less than twelve inches away was a baby rattlesnake, and I was for-tunate it didn't strike. Since snakes rely on the ground vibration to determine if something is in close proximity, I believed the vibration from the water passing over rocks confused the snake, which is likely the reason it didn't strike.

I still have bad dreams about snakes and might have one tonight after writing this. In the Marine Corps, sleeping in a two-person tent,

I awoke late one night to relieve myself. Climbing into my sleeping bag, I thought a flap inside was a snake. In the early morning, I shouted, "Snake!" and tore down the tent; the marine who shared it with me didn't wake up. The next morning, the platoon leader asked what happened to our tent. Another marine said that he'd heard a commotion early in the morning. There I sat, next to the partially erect tent, with bloodshot eyes from the lack of sleep. I'd prefer never seeing another snake again in my lifetime. What amazes me here are the fears I developed in life that didn't exist previously (snakes and heights). I examine situations like these constantly.

In examining my fears of snakes and heights, I thought back to my younger days and remembered that on occasion, when we'd lived in Ohio; a gang of us was in a different neighborhood, and to get home, we had to cross a train trestle. The trestle had two sets of tracks, and if a train approached, we jumped to the other side. We were fortunate that two trains didn't cross the trestle at the same time. Nonetheless, this trestle crossed a major river and was high off the ground. If one fell, he or she certainly plunged to a frigid death in the river. We crossed that trestle, and my fear of heights never came to mind.

When backpacking along the PCT, an individual might encounter the good deeds of an angel. An angel is someone who goes out of his or her way to help backpackers. Sometimes angels leave a cache (pronounced "cash"). A cache is something that an angel leaves containing things like fruit, bread, water, snacks, you name it. For example, I learned that one individual, or individuals, used a team of mules to deliver water to one cache. The angel risked life and limb to deliver the water over rough terrain so that backpackers along the PCT could quench their thirsts when backpacking the dry and desolate area. One time, an angel, a Caucasian female, saw me heading back to the trail and offered me a ride. I was on my way back from a resupply in Big Bear, California. I looked like a derelict and knew I was funky. She stopped and asked me where I was headed, and I told her that I was hiking the PCT but eliminated part of the trail. She said, "I can't let you do that," and took me back to where I exited the trail. I was fortunate that she did, because I would have missed a beautiful part of the trail. For me, her actions were recompense for the time I was in a car accident and all the female said was "Brother, don't beat me! Brother, don't beat me!" or the other challenging situations I faced because of Caucasian females. Sometimes situations cancel themselves out or come full circle. Thank you angel.

While on that 150-mile backpacking adventure, I happened upon one cache, and there was a chair recliner and a window frame. The window frame was positioned to capture a vivid view of the terrain. On the trail, one could sit in the chair and look through the window and capture that view. The chair was filthy, and I refused to sit; however, I was able to enjoy the view from the window frame. That cache had and provisions, more than any I'd experienced. I found it amazing that people went out of their way to resupply caches for individuals backpacking the PCT. Nonetheless, some caches were advertisements for hostels, places backpackers could rest, obtain a shower, or buy some provisions, of course, for a fee. Sometimes around the caches, one had to be aware of snakes, especially the caches that had fruit. At one cache, a big snake lay there but took off when I approached.

The morning after leaving the area with the pollywogs and wiggly, protozoa-looking creatures that gyrated back and forth to propel themselves behind on the 150-mile PCT journey, I approached an area that had biting flies. They buzzed around my head all day, and fortunately, my headwear had a flap in the back that prevented the flies from biting my neck. That was a hot day, and the flies bit any exposed skin-any. I used insect repellent; however, I believe they had become immune to it. The constant buzzing around my ears became nerve-racking. When I stopped to rest, the biting flies were at their worst and seemed like they always managed to find a place to bite. On one occasion, I had to relieve myself and had to constantly fan my ass to keep the flies from biting. Eventually, I ended that part of the adventure and was running low on water. I found a murky pool that had more pollywogs and wiggly, protozoa-looking creatures that gyrated back and forth to propel themselves. Eventually, night was approaching, and I was exhausted and needed to find a place to camp. Backpacking around a last bend in the trail at dusk, I happened upon a campsite right on the banks of a well-known lake. What a tough two days! But the view at my campsite and the ambience around the lake was my reward.

I finally ended my 150-mile journey and was proud of myself for the accomplishment. On that journey, I created the motto, "the trail always provides," and that truth is valid today. During the 150-mile journey, I overcame mental and physical challenges, none I had never experienced in life before. I thought, not bad for a middle-aged black male from the hood. I completed parts of that same trail after the 150-mile journey, and on one hike, I met a gentleman who was backpacking all the 2,650 miles of the PCT. He was sixty-three years old and having problems with his feet. He stopped at the hot springs near a section of the trail and stayed there a couple of days to soothe his feet. He said that the year before, he'd backpacked the entire trail with his son. I communicated my goal to hike my favorite trail with my son. He said, "I hope you accomplish your goal, and I do believe the experience is something you'll never forget." The 150-mile journey increased my love for the outdoors, and I haven't stopped experiencing it since.

After I finished the 150-mile trek, most of my gear was destroyed. After I left the pollywogs and wiggly, protozoa-looking creatures that gyrated back and forth to propel themselves, my shoes were wet and began falling apart. For one boot, I wrapped the toes with duct tape and those department-store-bought boots were soaking wet and felt five pounds heavier. My shoes made a squishing sound with each step, and I looked like Frankenstein. In addition, the tips of my hiking poles were worn and almost gone. I keep the hiking poles for memory of the 150-mile journey. My pants had holes everywhere; good thing I carried two pairs. The aforementioned validated my creed to spare no expense when purchasing gear for the outdoors.

On one occasion, I backpacked in the Sinkyone Wilderness in Northern California, one of the most beautiful areas to backpack to. Bears frequented the area; therefore, the regulations required that I carry a bear canister. In the bear canister, I placed my toiletries and food, which I'd previously placed in Ziploc bags. When using the Ziploc bags, I always used the freezer bags, which were, in my experience, more durable and useful than other storage bags, but they were somewhat heavier.

In Sinkyone Wilderness, I backpacked the area during the time when ticks were at the heaviest, and the rangers said that I should use insect repellent. I was two days into my backpacking trip and was setting up camp when I looked down and saw ticks everywhere. I relocated my camp to another area. It was time to climb into my tent, bed down, sleep, and it was then I felt a sting near my abdomen. Sure enough, a tick was digging into my skin. I took tweezers and removed the tick, placed it in a moist napkin, and then in an empty medicine bottle. After my backpacking adventure, I drove 70 miles out of my way, 140 miles round-trip, to the health department in Eureka, California. I left the tick in the moist napkin for examination. The health-care person said that they would analyze the tick to determine if it had the Rocky Mountain spotted fever disease. About seven days later, I received a letter stating that the tick was free of any diseases.

Anyway, to expand backpacking experiences, during the winter of 2014, I backpacked in the mountains of Colorado, in a colder climate and in snow. What had I been missing all these years? My résumé now includes backpacking in the desert, in the mountains, in forests, along the ocean, mixed terrain, and many weather conditions.

Today, I know how to decrease the weight of the content in my backpack without sacrificing comfort or safety, which can be a good thing if hiking miles or days if backpacking. Do I claim to be an expert backpacker or hiker? The day I entertain that thought, I believe I sacrifice safety and pleasure when experiencing the outdoors. There is always something new to learn while experiencing the outdoors, and adverse situations can be unpredictable, and I believe no one can prepare for the unexpected. However, I do believe an individual can prepare to minimize the impact of the unexpected. On top of that, my respect for heights, snakes, and the outdoors keeps me safe. I still have much to learn, and someday I plan to backpack the entire PCT, approximately 2,600 miles; the Appalachian Trail, 2,200 miles; the Colorado Trail, approximately 500 miles; and the Continental Divide Trail. I now have a picture of the Machu

Picchu trail and the ruins in Peru on the wall in my bedroom, and my goal is to hike or backpack that trail as well.

I continue to find those challenging outdoor experiences and push the limits. When hiking or backpacking, sometimes I experience the challenges of the cold, the rain, and the heat. Now I understand the idea of "I've Been to the Mountaintop," in the speech by Dr. Martin Luther King, Jr., and the mountainous ventures of Jesus Christ and Moses. I can only imagine the life-changing dynamics they endured. Each time I return from a venture into the mountains and wilderness, I'm a different person.

Recently, I backpacked a few days in Canyonlands in Utah. It was hot and there was no water except for the Green River. I backpacked down several gorges, and on the way, I was able to extract a small amount of water from rain puddles. I happened upon two individuals near a truck, and they were camping inside. I approached them to ask if they knew of any water holes. They were startled and asked, "What the shuck, how did you get down here, man?" I explained, and they were somewhat in disbelief. They said, "Ain't no water here, man, and over there is the Green River, but it's not accessible." They felt sorry for me and gave me a gallon of water. I could see the Green River in the distance. However, when approaching; from a cliff, the water wasn't accessible. Believe me: it was scorching hot that day. I looked at my map (stresses the importance of always carrying one) and found that I was near a drainage ditch, so I followed it. While in the drainage ditch, I began seeing pools of water. Finally, there was the Green River, and what a beautiful sight! I wanted to camp there, but never do I camp in a drainage that leads to a river. Plus, when setting up my camp away from the river and returning for water, there were signs of snakes. No way, Jose. My fear of snakes prevented my camping here.

I camped under a lone tree for a few days, taking day-hiking trips and enjoying the area. Sometimes I heard families canoeing down the Green River, and while drawing water, I made a point to wave at them. My gestures were friendly, and I wanted the families to note that, yes, African Americans do experience the wilderness. They must've wondered how the hell I got there. While backpacking back to my car, here again I was challenged with heights, and in some areas, when I looked down, it reminded me of that backpacking trip on the PCT and on that ledge for a day. I wondered if hiking the PCT in that same area, I'd face the fear of heights. The scenery while backpacking in Canyonlands, Utah, was amazing.

On a recent trip while I was in Arizona, upon my return, the security guard for the parking area approached me and said that they were beginning to worry. I was out for about five to six days during my traditional year-end backpacking adventure. I said that typically, I backpack the area during the holidays and leave my itinerary on my dashboard in plain view, with contact information for my relatives. He said that typically, people backpacked there and left their cars for one to three days and almost never as long as I did, which caused some concerns. From that point on, the conversation transitioned to sports, football teams, and whatever else. The overarching fact is that it was a valuable experience. I'd never had an opportunity to talk with that individual, but my return from backpacking provided an opportunity for him to learn about me and I him. A reason that I love venturing in the outdoors is because you never know what you're going to discover. Which, for me, increases my excitement for the outdoors.

So far, individuals have been friendly during my hiking and backpacking trips, and I extend the same friendliness. I have yet to encounter individuals with ill intentions, and most are helpful. One never knows when he or she might need assistance. Some individuals stop and ask questions. Once while hiking, I was cornered by two senior females, and they asked what seemed like fifty questions. I thought they wanted to throw me down on the trail and start humping me. The trail was narrow, and I had to turn sideways with my backpack on so I could continue my hike.

It is my experience that many people of color don't hike or backpack. I've probably seen one African American male while hiking. I've yet to happen upon one African American female while hiking. While backpacking, though, I've yet to see one male or female African American backpacker.

While I was on that 150-mile PCT trek, a male hiker of dark complexion, perhaps from a suntan, walked past me, and after a few feet, he yelled, "Sir, I'm sorry to ask you"-and he moved closer-"can I take your picture?" I asked why, and he said, "Hey, man, you're the first African American male that I ever encountered while backpacking." I said *yes*, and another backpacker was passing, so he asked that individual to take our picture together. One other occasion, while backpacking the PCT, I reached my resupply point at the post office near Big Bear, California. The clerk in the post office asked if I wanted to have my picture taken to hang on the wall. First, I said that I didn't want my picture appearing on any post office wall because I wasn't a fugitive. We both chuckled. She said that typically, when individuals reached that resupply point, they had their picture taken to hang on the wall, highlighting a significant achievement. She then said, "You'll be the first African American ever." I grinned and copped a pose (slang for simply posing). I then asked, "Which is my best side, my right or left?" while sticking my chin out. She took my picture and gave me a pebble with the year inscribed on it, which I still have today.

I've experienced other situations on the trail that lead me to believe that hikers or backpackers may not be used to seeing African Americans in the wilderness. I was hiking in Colorado on the Beaver Brook Trail once. That day, I hiked an "out and back" from the saddle to the other trailhead and back. While hiking back, I was on my descent, which displayed a magnificent view of Longs Peak, when a couple saw me and said, "What the shuck," and almost took off running. I was hiking near Eldorado State Park on the Walker Ranch Loop and stopped to eat my lunch in a shady area. Hikers and mountain bikers used that section of the trail. Typically, bikers and hikers look down at the trail, especially if it has rocks or other obstacles. Well, while I ate my lunch in that shady area, somewhat high in the rocks, a lone biker passed, looked up, saw me, and almost went over the side. That was a sight to see, the mountain biker making that correction after realizing my presence. I might've startled him.

In another venture near Fort Collins, Colorado, I was hiking in one of the natural areas and decided to sit on a rock and have lunch.

A lone runner approached that section of the trail. He looked up and saw me and then said, "Oh, shit." He made the sign of the cross on his chest and then clasped his hands in prayer. Then he said, "Thank God. I thought you were a mountain lion." I wanted to say, "Man, I look nothing like a mountain lion." I find some of these experiences comical. However, I do realize the seriousness of what I mention here because some may react differently from others, especially in uncommon situations on the trail.

As previously stated, I learned much from the outdoors and hope people of color can experience the same. I've found that individuals in the outdoors are accommodating and friendly. Nonetheless, I recently watched a television series, and the show was about fourteen men stranded on an island for thirty days and needing to work together as a team to survive. Several were African Americans. During the last episode, I was disheartened that none of the African American men survived the thirty-day challenge.

Because America is becoming more diverse, and the majority in ten years may be the minority, an understanding of and appreciation for the wilderness is important among people of color, especially among the younger generations. Remember: the younger generation will be the ones voting on key issues. An understanding of issues concerning our wilderness and enhancing the preservation of it may come from those in the majority or those who have an appreciation for the environment and the outdoors.

The outdoors increases my appreciation for nature, which overlaps with other areas of my life. The discipline, patience, planning, and control of emotions in challenging situations while in the wilderness transcend to other areas of my life. I also experienced slips and falls that could've been devastating. The outdoors provides constant growing and learning experiences for me.

In addition, nothing angers me more than venturing into the outdoors and seeing trash or campsites that had rusty cans and old bottles. Sometimes if trash is near the place that I camp, I throw it into my fire. For campfires, I never burn anything living. I've learned to appreciate the outdoors, for one day, I may not be able to enjoy those pleasures.

And I'm blessed with interesting situations while in the wilderness. Once, in Arizona, I met a family with young children, and they used llamas to carry their gear. I took pictures and had an opportunity to stop and talk with the family. I met a female from Australia on the PCT. I believe in packing in and packing out, that is, taking all my trash with me, never leaving a trace, and preserving everything that I touch.

In retrospect, I had a valuable experience talking to the backpacker with whom I'd taken the picture when we crossed paths while on the trail. Another couple who kept a vial of bleach was between jobs and hiking the PCT. We had time to communicate. I saw another man with a long beard; he was backpacking the PCT without shoes. Not to mention the good conversation I had with the female angel who picked me up in Big Bear without reservations. All of these exceptional experiences because of my joy of backpacking.

Once on that 150-mile PCT trek, I hiked to a partially enclosed area and ladybugs were everywhere. The sun was partially shining through the trees, and some of the insects glistened. I would never have seen that in the hood. When facing challenging times in my existing life, sometimes I mentally draw upon the many wonderful experiences while hiking, backpacking, and camping, especially the times in the nude, dancing and hitting the golf balls. I also think about how my son, sons-in-law, or grandsons might experience peace while in the outdoors. I also think about my children when they were younger, which provides some entertainment, and sometimes I solve the world's problems and mine as well. Outdoors, my goals for life consume my thoughts as well.

Chapter 17

THE RECONNECTION

Eventually, I reconnected with my family, and I do believe my separation from them challenged relationships, especially with my son. If love exists, mending fences, so to speak, can be accomplished. The process takes time. I love my children to the depths of my heart, and I hope that they realize this. Although we faced challenging situations, I do believe I raised respectful, intelligent, caring, loving, dynamic, diverse-thinking, and responsible, children-among many other positive attributes.

During the separation from family, in addition to the outdoors, here I had an opportunity to explore and connect to me. I ventured into other pastimes that included gardening, cooking, watching the food channels, and watching a female-centric movie channel. All these helped me explore my softer side. Something I had yet to accomplish. A female I was dating said what attracted me to her was my business dress and professionalism, my ruggedness while in the outdoors, my bad boy presence, and my softer side. Nonetheless, the separation from my family, enhanced awareness of the importance of those in my life. Family. I thank God for the challenges in life that led me to the experiences mentioned here.

Soon after my reconnection with my family, I received a phone call. The person on the phone said, "You were successful during your interview, and we would like to offer you a job as an education specialist working with the United States Forest Service Job Corps job-training program for the disadvantaged." The program is designed to assist disadvantaged students while they earn skills in civilian conservation occupations. I believed I was about to fulfill my dream. I thought, helping disadvantaged and inner-city youth in earning skills to work in occupations that support the United States conservation efforts, the outdoors, what an opportunity! I would be responsible for helping students with the education components of the program, helping them earn a high school diploma or a GED. Driver's education, English as a second language, testing to enhance critical thinking skills, were components of the education programs as well. I thought back to the time I attended camp as a disadvantaged youth, my love for the outdoors, and now I had the opportunity to work with the Forest Service and inner-city youth. I also thought about my tenure as a disadvantaged youth and how education enhanced my life. I thought about my dissertation and how I tailored it toward programs for disadvantaged youth. I thought about all the programs I worked with that helped the disadvantaged. I thought about the student at the continuation school with the shunt in his brain. I was excited about the opportunity and took the job.

Because I wasn't a federal employee at that time, I paid for my relocation from California to Golden, Colorado, where the position was located. My girlfriend at that time was instrumental in helping me make the transition. We packed a U-Haul truck with my belongings, and off we went. It took us a few days to drive to Colorado where the job was located. I discovered that my first day on the job, I had to fly to Kentucky to visit a Forest Service Job Corps center. I was happy about the opportunity.

I missed my flight and was unable to travel with other members of the team. They finally met me in Atlanta, Georgia. I slept well that night and was excited about the challenge ahead. My first day on the Job Corps center as the education specialist for the organization, a male African American student approached me in tears and said, "Can you help me? The teachers and staff in the education department don't understand me. They just don't get it."

Oh, shuck, I thought, and that intervention with that student resonates with me today. Reconnecting with family and what takes place in my career from this point forward is still being written, in book 2, especially the event that led me to the shabby motel.

Chapter 18

THE INFLUENCES

Today, I continue to forge a connection with family and those who cross my path by whatever means; I contend that everyone has an influence, whether positive or negative. A motto for me, as communicated in my dissertation, states, "Because you entered my space, be it love, family, employment, neighbor, education, spiritual, or religion, etc., may your days be brightened and may our relationship be heightened."

Concerning influences, first, I communicate the obvious, and that is God. Am I a person who preaches fire and brimstone? No. However, I have a personal relationship with my God and appreciate the guidance and, especially, the challenges in my life. I'm not going to give examples here, but I do have reference points, some subtle, and for me, the challenges and rewards indicate that my Higher Power exists. Just read the content here. The many times I faced situations that could've caused death. The times I broke the law and wasn't arrested. I do believe, if I were institutionalized in jails or prisons, I might not have written from this mind-set.

However, I understand that individuals face challenges more difficult than mine, and for whatever reason, they may not be able to tell their stories. I do believe my God preserved me to communicate for some, especially those living within challenging social systems, to include disadvantaged individuals.

I've not attended church for some time; however, I've read the Bible from cover to cover several times. I do believe my Christian upbringing provided a foundation that rooted and grounded me based on the teachings in the Bible. Although I now live Colorado, my church home is in Diamond Bar, California, and my pastor is an individual who started in a Safeway store. I identify with the challenges he faced early in life, and I do appreciate a teaching ministry versus a preaching ministry. Like a verse in the Bible that states, "How will they learn without a teacher?" I learned much from that ministry. In addition to the teachings in the Bible, the affiliation with my life experiences adds to my personal relationship with my God.

Another influence and lifesaving experience was my enlistment in the United States Marine Corps. Although I was someone from the hood, I struggled acclimating to a military life, and the marines contributed greatly to what makes me who I am. Yes, I still have some of that military demeanor, especially when it comes to personal appearance, organization, some discipline, and keeping myself in good physical shape. One regret is that I didn't have the tools to better serve in the military and my country as well. For a while, there I was, what they called a shit bird, and I lacked the tools to be effective, which could be good or bad, depending on the perception. It was a valiant effort on my part, but the experience is an accumulation of what makes me, and I appreciate the time spent in the marines. I saw a commercial on television about the United States Marines Corps, and the narrator said that wherever there are battles, you'll find a United States marine. This statement stays with me. I thank the Marine Corps for instilling that never quit part of me, which becomes the story of my life as I traverse fool's hill.

I recall graduating from boot camp and watching the film. The film commentator said, "you gave us a child, and we made him a man." No females in boot camp during those days. Although I faced challenges adjusting to the military, graduating from boot camp was a proud day for me.

More so, I make no excuses for my life experiences. However, I did serve almost eight years in the military and earned an honorable discharge. I was selected for drill instructor school and earned noncommissioned officer status. If not for the military, I don't know where I would be today. Because of my time in the military, I earned my high school diploma and was stationed three years in Hawaii. After discharge, I was able to go to college using the GI Bill, buy a house using a VA loan, and have preference when applying for federal jobs.

Nevertheless, my heart goes out to today's youth, especially the disadvantaged and wanting to volunteer to enlist in the military. Those without a high school diploma, such as myself some years ago, may not qualify for entry to the armed services. Especially in today's technology-based military. Perhaps the military should consider an enlistment for those without a high school diploma who score high on the entrance exams. If enlisting, the individual should be under contract to earn his or her high school diploma in the first two years. Strategies like this could help change an individual's life.

Another influence for me were the many supervisors that I was blessed with in the world of work, some good and some terrible. I can write a book about the many supervisors I worked with and the pleasure and displeasure of working with some. I could also write a book about the challenges a professional African American male faces when supervised by some of the same race and some of other races.

Nevertheless, I do appreciate the two African American female supervisors who provided me a challenging but professional work environment-one individual with whom I worked in a quasi-county agency, and the other an executive director in a community-based organization. For both organizations, the charge was to help the disadvantaged or those striving to achieve self-sufficiency. Those organizations previously mentioned provided a work environment that aided in enhancing my career. In addition, I learned so much from the challenging supervisors as well, mostly while working in federal agencies. They enticed me to write this book and book 2 in the draft phase. Thank you!

I can't discount the education institutions that I attended. Combined these include four junior colleges and three universities. I appreciate the patience demonstrated during my coursework, and most of all, the critical-thinking skills I developed. Once upon a time, I couldn't think my way out of a paper sack. I believed my education, compounded with life experiences, age, maturity, and divine intervention, assisted in heightening my critical-thinking skills. Most of all, the education institutions provided a framework for me to develop these skills.

When going to college, I remember sitting in classes not understanding what the teacher was saying. I just couldn't comprehend. *What the hell are they talking about?* I thought. The ability to decipher and retain information was underdeveloped. I had to read some documents ten times, and still gained only a partial understanding of the content. Today, I can read, decipher, provide viable input, and critique almost anything. I believe intelligence and book knowledge can be contributing factors to a level of success; however, wisdom derived from divine intervention provides the ultimate level of successes. If I had a choice, I prefer wisdom versus book knowledge or intelligence. Nevertheless, I believe a combination of wisdom, intelligence, and what one learns formally or informally can provide a well-balanced approach to experiencing life. However, I do believe the confidence attained from achieving my level of education enhanced my ability to confront some challenging life situations.

I can be a viable contributor to meetings, a class, a public forum, and so on. Now I have the ability to solve issues through writing rather than through adverse or violent means, which I was accustomed to in the past. Because of this, I now subscribe to Benjamin Franklin's thought that the pen is mightier than the sword and, I add, more powerful than stupidity.

While highlighting how education affects my life, I must take into account the assistance and motivation I received from my fifth-grade teacher. I still have the letter she wrote to me, which touches my heart every time I read it. My dissertation chair greatly influenced my life as well. From both my fifth-grade teacher and dissertation chair, I believe their desire to help me was sincere and divine. Concerning my dissertation chair, I hope that one day she realizes how she helped change my life. I remember mentioning to her that I wasn't sure about situations in my life. The mature ex-nun Caucasian professor at Pepperdine said, "Ron, you stay right where you're headed, and don't deviate from your goal." That message caused me to forge on and served as a platform for me to complete my doctorate. The communication between my dissertation chair and me further enhanced my belief to never give up regardless of the pressure from the nay-sayers. The situation reminds me of content in the first motivation book I read by Napoleon Hill, which communicates that stickability is ability. I can never repay the debt of gratitude I owe to my dissertation chair.

I can't discount my parents, for they had a tremendous influence on my life. My grandmother in Ohio, I still think about her and try to mimic her laugh. Her forgiving and understanding heart serves as an example for me to follow, and she cooked the most fantastic and delectable cakes. After all, my grandmother gave me the inspiration for the title of this book.

Concerning my parents-good or bad, because of my upbringing, I was determined to raise my children different from what I'd faced. I do appreciate my parents for my base in raising my children. Forgiveness is bliss. If I can't forgive, God may not forgive me for my transgressions, and rightly so. I must remember that I'm charged with imbedding a forgiving heart toward my parents, and I ask my children to bestow the same on me. I hope my children continue to enhance the lives of their offspring, which can lead to an enriched quality of life for my lineage and society.

Don't misunderstand me, I love my parents. Given their experiences in life in the civil rights movement, their demeanor could've been different. I once asked my mother about an experience while attending a basketball game when the Houston Rockets were the "Daygo" Rockets. I attended the game with other disadvantaged youth as part of a program. All the individuals in my group were African Americans. While we were standing in line, some in my group punched the Caucasian boys that passed by. I didn't understand why, and I knew these were violent acts. Upon returning home, I told my mother about what had taken place at the basketball game. She said that they probably hadn't liked what those boys were wearing. Later in life, I understood why the violent acts took place. However, I do appreciate my mother's effort to smooth the situation over. Nevertheless, I was well educated about the differences in race; however, the thought of hating someone or disliking someone who was different was left up to me. I attempted to instill the same in my children.

Folks, remember you only have a set of parents; take care or fix the relationship, for one day, someone may receive their calling. Based on my experience, I can say that one doesn't want to ever be in a state of "I wish I had." Those with living parents, cherish the relationship you have with them.

Another family member I wish I could talk to today is my sister Beverly. She died too early and left us with many unanswered questions. I wasn't the model brother, and she was in a special education class. We called them Eddies. I was insensitive at that time, and we as a family lacked the resources and understanding necessary to care for her. I believe the school system at that time didn't have the capability to educate her either. Now as an educator, thinking back makes my heart heavy. Nonetheless, I do remember Beverly's heart. I just wish I could've made life different for her. I want to talk to her at this stage of my life. I have so much I want to say to her. I pray that I have the opportunity to sit down and talk to her one day. Today, I want Beverly to know that I'm all right now and that I miss her dearly. I want to give my sister a hug that lasts for days. I never want to let her go, not only in the physical sense but in my heart as well. *I love you, Beverly.*

I wish I had an opportunity to talk with my sister, grandmother, mother, and father, all of whom are deceased. I want them to know who I'm today and that I'm all right. I wish I could give them a heartfelt hug and tell them how much I love them. I would never let them go. I want to tell my mama how I applied our motto, that only the strong survive. I want to thank her for the times she helped me, but because of my state of mind, I failed to recognize the effort it took to bail me out of situations, some when I was an adult. Now I understand more about the challenges she faced in life and how I added to her problems. Mama, I thank you so much and can't wait until the day I can see you again, because I miss you so much!

Sometimes I believe that because my sister and mama left us so early, I might be angry and must be cognizant about how I relay those expressions to females with whom I have close relationships.

Recently, because of the absence of my mama and sister in my life, I asked that God remove any heartfelt challenges I face. I hope that someday I can see them again and catch up.

My married life greatly influenced me. I'm not married now but I do appreciate my first and second wives, especially my second wife for my children. Looking back, I have a different respect for females and relationships because of marriage. I do appreciate the challenges and the good times as well. Both of you helped me become a better person more than you might realize. Thank you, thank you.

My brother the now-ordained minister, you survived the shenanigans of your older brother. I love you, man, to the depths of my heart. We experienced so much, and I know you, bro, and understand, especially when it comes to employment and family. We ran a close race concerning the number of jobs held. My eldest sister can fit into this category as well. A correlation may be the transient nature of our youth. For example, if I begin to feel uncomfortable in any situation, including where I live, the car I drive, and sometimes, regrettably, the relationships I have with females, I gotta go! In addition, besides the challenges we'd faced in the hood. I inflicted some punishment on my younger brother. But I do believe that paid off-he didn't take crap from anyone.

He excelled in football and in the classroom. My brother would fight if he felt someone was taking advantage of him, which is a benefit of having an older brother; after all, what role does the older brother serve other than making the younger brother tougher? I remember one time when we were in elementary school my brother was in a fight with few boys and was stabbed in the arm with a pencil and had a piece of lead imbedded in his arm that had to be removed by a doctor. He still kicked ass though. Anyway, forge on, bro. You have the tools inside of you to accomplish anything in life. I didn't have the advantage of an older brother. Perhaps I'm better because of this. I remember in school, as I mentioned in this book, how an individual used his older brother to confront me and punched me in the face. I wonder if that same individual still relies on his brother to handle life battles now. For the younger brother's sake, I hope not. However, my brother stood alone and didn't need that kind of support except for that one time in elementary school. On your own, you excelled beyond that. Most of all, I love you, Darnee, and would die for you.

Because my brother and I endured some of the same challenges, I understand our transient mindset and our relationships with females. Males typically seek relationships with females who resemble their mother. However, I do understand you, man, and thank God I have someone who understands me as well. I do apologize for the introduction to smoking cigarettes, though. I overcame the challenge of smoking some twenty-odd years ago, and I hope you've done the same. If anyone can give an accounting of some of the situations in this book, my brother can. When we visit, he reminds me of stupid things I did and I've forgotten. When my grandmother passed, we had an opportunity to connect while both of us were in Ohio during the funeral, and there were several times when we were riding in the car he said, "Remember when you did this or that over there?" One event was at the VA and involved the geese eggs and another was throwing an axe at someone's feet then running in the house laughing. *Oh, shuk,* I thought, *I did that.* Two of my children were in the car at that time and I had to divert the conversation. Most of all, I know that I can depend on my brother to trade blows concerning bald-headed jokes. To my brother, forget you, you bald-headed gerbil with a hyperactive gallbladder! Love you, man.

I can't overemphasize how my eldest sister influenced my life. Her direction was instrumental in my attempting to finish high school, joining the military, and entering Pepperdine University. There was a time when we talked on the phone for hours. I do believe the message about who my real father was somewhat separated us. For someone who was a single parent and faced domestic violence, she excelled. I remember the times when you faced domestic violence and I didn't recognize you after it happened. Your courage to leave that relationship and raise three responsible children while earning two college degrees and then obtaining a third, your master's, requires noteworthy mention. Then teaching in school districts where some would decline employment! I admire my sister for overcoming those challenges she faced.

As I recollect, domestic violence was prevalent in the hood. In some cases, the female was the perpetrator. However, back in the day, some instances of domestic violence went unreported. The last thing a black person in the hood wanted was the "popo" showing up at the door because the relationship between those in the hood and the popo was, in some instances, adversarial.

Today, I understand how some instances of domestic violence can surface, especially in the hood, because sometimes the environment allows it to persist. Individuals who may believe they are oppressed, are in poverty, and have one parent in the home-usually the mother-are angry because of injustice. Tradition, drugs, generational adverse social conditions, and other unfavorable socio-economic conditions can perpetuate domestic violence. Because of the domestic violence that existed in the hood and in the lives of those close to me, some, especially men, and I mean some, adopted the trait because of the generational prevalence. Do I condone acts of domestic violence? Absolutely not! But I do understand how the act can persist. I was married to someone who experienced domestic violence before we were married, the result was unfortunate, and I end here with that. Enough of that negative content.

For me I tend to be too easygoing. I don't like conflict, and I'll run the way Joseph ran from Potiphar's wife in the Bible. My I "gotta go" transient nature might resurface as well. Importantly, some of the experiences I mention in this book taught me to be careful.

My sister gave me advice about enlisting in the Marine Corps. Great advice. Although I struggled finding myself, the Marine Corps helped save my life. My sister also gave me advice about enrolling in the doctorate program at Pepperdine University. At that time, she was earning her master's at Pepperdine University, and she did graduate, and a fantastic accomplishment considering her beginnings.

Importantly, I'm fortunate that my sister is still alive. One day, we had a family outing at Mission Bay Beach in San Diego. I must've been in the third or fourth grade. This was one of the few outings when the entire family was together, including my father. My sister as she sang a Christian song about taking one-step, decided to venture into the water, took a step too far, and fell off an underwater shelf.

She started screaming and splashing because she couldn't swim. All my father could do was watch and yell "Somebody get her!" in his fourth-grade manner of speaking. A Good Samaritan, a Caucasian male saved her, and thank God. Losing my sister would've been devastating. After all, as the younger sibling, I wouldn't have had anyone to call names and to make angry. More importantly, I would have missed the positive experiences she bestowed in my life. My sister has a dynamic story to tell, and I hope she does someday.

My sister, earned an associate's degree, bachelor's degree, and then a master's degree from Pepperdine University while attending school part-time, sometimes at night. My eldest sister serves as an inspiration for me. An additional highlight here is that she raised three children who, are well-rounded, responsible, tax-paying citizens and always family. I love my sister and would give my life for her. Again, directly, she has a profound effect on my life.

I saved the best for last. My children have influenced my life more than I think they realize. Because of my children, I stopped smoking cigarettes some twenty years ago on my birthday. Today I despise cigarettes, I can't stand the smell of cigarette smoke. I cringe when I see someone driving in a car with the widows up and smoking a cigarette with a child in the car. If I ruled the world, I would draft legislation, and anyone caught smoking in an automobile with a child present would be fined, heavily. Think about the damage the smoke can cause to a child's respiratory system, and the child doesn't have a say about what's happening to their health. For eight years I didn't drink a drop of alcohol at all in or out of their presence. I went cold turkey because I wanted to set an example for them. Am I perfect? Not by a long shot. I remember my pastor saying how a society, when creating statues or humanlike figures, constructed them with an imperfection; perhaps a toe was missing or there was some other blemish. The reason for this is that only God is perfect. I assume the thinking was, how could man, a term used in the biblical sense, or how could humankind, create something perfect? I've yet to discover a perfect individual. Only God bestows perfection.

I make no excuses. I did the best I could in rearing my children, considering the tools I had. One day, I hope they realize the same in raising their children. My goal was to be a responsible parent and be involved. Yes, when they were in school, I visited their classes unannounced. At home, they couldn't watch television until about 8:00 p.m. and all homework had to be finished. On weekends, there were no cartoons until chores were accomplished, and they knew their assignments. When I see my children interacting with theirs today, I heave a sigh of relief and denote that perhaps some of the goals I had for them came to fruition.

In addition, I attempted to provide a framework in which my children could flourish. My son played sports, and we attended most of his games. My daughters participated in gymnastics. I tried to reward them for accomplishments and defended them at school when I believed the teacher was wrong. I remember on time the bus driver dropped my daughter off at the wrong location in a rural area. Was I upset! The school's superintendent and principal knew who I was after that ordeal. Most of all, no matter the situation, I never said that any of my children needed to see a psychiatrist, unlike the message for me in my youth, especially if they did something uncommon, which children tend to do.

When punishing, I did so without anger and made sure they understood the reason for the punishment. Yes, they were spanked, but never out of anger, because I believe in the Bible verse "Spare the rod and spoil the child." However, a few Christmases ago, my son and I had a conversation about spankings. I said that today I'm not sure spanking is a good tool for punishment or behavior modification, because if improperly administered, the act can represent violence. Today, I have mixed emotions, but the threat of spankings worked for me, I think. Keep in mind that spankings weren't always the method to motivate my children rewards and recognition worked as well. For example, when my children earned good grades we celebrated; we put the exceptional school assignments on the refrigerator for all to see. Picking them up for lunch and returning them to class was another strategy. Pick them up at school and go for ice cream. Be creative. If my children accomplished an exceptional goal, I picked them up from school unexpectedly and took them to an amusement park for the day. Believe me, it was more effective than punishing.

Nonetheless, consistency of application, including corrective action and recognition, served as the ultimate guiding principle when raising children in the Cubit household. Recognition and corrective actions were applied equally, depending on my children's stage of life. However, the rolled-up sock fights, the horseplay, the runs around the school track, and other things were fun as well. Especially memorable were long drives to Oklahoma and Ohio, always stopping at the same rest stop in Texas and watching them in the playground and capturing that experience on video. Nonetheless, at the end of one trip I blew it when someone opened a can of tuna in the enclosed automobile. On another trip, when visiting a national monument, I stressed the importance of preserving the area and leaving everything intact. However, I did remove something during that visit and returned it during the next trip.

During that same visit, we were miles away from the national monument and I thought I had lost something. We drove miles back to the national monument and I continued my search. My daughter asked me what I was looking for. I said my sunglasses. She said they were on my baseball cap, which was on my head. Parents sometimes aren't perfect. I dropped something one time and my daughter while young said, "I didn't know dads dropped things."

On one occasion, I noticed that cookies were missing from the cookie jar. I asked who took the cookies, and no one confessed. The children were on restriction from everything until the cookie bandit confessed. I wasn't upset about the cookies missing, the dishonesty is what I was trying to teach them. I encouraged them to just tell the truth because honesty with oneself was important. Finally, my youngest confessed. She received her punishment in addition to a lecture about truth and honesty. My heart goes out to parents today, and with the laws that children seem to know and all the other issues they face in society, all I can say is, I'm fortunate. By the way, in the spirit of honesty I now confess, I was the most frequent cookie thief in the house. My children probably know that. That cookie jar was clanging late at night, and I remember the sound. Whatever!

One tool I used in rearing my children was references to my past as a child. I remembered the things that caused my parents grief, and I decided that my children weren't going to experience the same. In raising my children, I had a plan from day one. I quote Stephen Covey here: "Begin with the end in mind." I wanted my children to experience life without prejudice or apprehensions. Today, they have friends from diverse backgrounds, and I'm so proud to see their understanding and sensitivity concerning others. However, they possess an awareness of social conditions that may affect their lives. I remember having a conversation with my son after the first time he experienced someone following him around a store for no reason. He was confused, despondent, and experienced other feelings including anger. That was a heartfelt conversation. I don't take all the credit, for my children's understanding of social conditions, because for most of their childhood, both parents were in the home.

Now I get the biggest hugs from my children, especially my son. Why? Because that was what I gave to them. As a parent, I believed it was my duty to create an environment for my children to flourish. I learned so much from my children. One can't imagine. My son's dedication and honesty. I remember how, as an adult, he told me something that they used to do when their mother and I were away. I thought I was going to hear something dreadful. After he told me, I chuckled internally but was relieved; however, I was inspired that he was honest and wanted to reveal a situation to me. What he said was very different from what my brother and I used to get into when my parents were away.

When my son was a toddler, it took some time for him to utter his first words, and when he did, all he could say was "Whoy." I was like, *What the hell do you mean by* whoy? It seemed like an eternity before my son said his first words. He was attending preschool and about to enter kindergarten. I was worried that he might not be able to talk. Here I learned patience. Now in his adult life, you can't shut him up, and like me when I was younger, he knows everything. I do appreciate his courage in intelligently conveying his worldly views and supporting those beliefs. I love my son's free spirit.

I used to hide in the house from my children until they could find me, sort of a hide-and-seek game. One day, we couldn't find my son for what seemed like hours. I started to get concerned and had thoughts of abduction. Finally, he popped out of the clothes hamper in the bathroom like a jack-in-the-box and said "Surprise!" with the widest grin, and I'll never forget that face. At that time, I experienced anger when he startled me, then relief, and then laughter. I find that only children can entice a parent to experience so many emotions at once.

I'm so proud of my son. I bought my daughters a piano, a small one. He took that piano and learned how to play it himself. He did the same with a guitar, all self-taught. He took that guitar and developed a skit and performed at some of the well-known comedy stages in Southern California. I believe he met his girlfriend and now wife at one of those performances. He's not like me, no smashing the trumpet or El Kabong with the guitar. His patience to learn how to play those instruments on his own makes up for my inability to do so, sort of. I thought he should explore that natural talent for music further, but it's his choice.

At one time, I exposed my son to the military as an option after he graduated from high school. I took him to the recruiter and introduced both of us. He took the ASVAB test and scored amazingly high. The recruiter said that my son could pursue any military career he wanted. That recruiter came to my job, and almost begged me to help him enlist my son in the military. He said that discovering a person of color who scored high on the ASVAB was a treasure.

I believe my son thought, "We already have one individual in the family with that military disposition, we don't need another." One of the best times I spent with my son was when I volunteered to be a youth basketball coach for two years. He excelled in the sport but was cut from the high school basketball team. He signed up for track and field and broke some school and division records in the high jump and long jump. I say that if I were his coach, perhaps he would have excelled in basketball in high school. Destiny differed, but I enjoyed my time coaching his basketball team for two years and sponsoring a team for one year.

My first daughter is more like me in comparison. I used to be grouchy in the morning and could see some of that in her. My first daughter has to be in control, like yours truly, but she hasn't been lost in the woods. Some thought my daughter wouldn't amount to much. The mother-daughter issues at that time didn't help. Because we share similar traits, I knew she was going to be all right, and in time, she was going to impress us. Eventually she had many accomplishments in school. When she was in grade school, her name was in a marquee for student of the month. Everyone who drove past saw her name. Someone called me and said that they saw her name on a marquee in front of the school. I drove by, and sure enough, there was her name. I thought, *All right, when driving by the next day, I'll take a picture*. Wrong. The next day her name was gone. Lesson: take every opportunity to record your children's success.

My eldest daughter displays a never-give-up attitude. One day, we went to a park, and instead of playing in the sand or with others, her goal was to climb the slide not from the stairs but from the opposite end. Children went down the slide, and she waited until they finished, and then she continued with her goal of climbing the slide from the opposite end. In comparison to others, this was a long slide. She kept trying and failed several times. After about two hours, when I mentioned that it was time to go, on her last attempt, she finally made it up the opposite end of the slide. She had this big smile on her face, and at that time, her cranium was twice as large as her body. And her comment, "Daddy, I made it!" resonates with me today and serves as a reminder for me to never give up. I sometimes remind her, whenever she faces a challenge, about the slide.

Now, about my youngest daughter. Some say that parents tend to favor the baby of the family. Come on, we all have the inclination to do so. However, my goal was to distribute love equally. I don't believe that love for children have degrees or preferences. I already communicated the situation about the cookie jar. In addition, I do believe my youngest daughter has a forgiving heart. Besides, I remember, when going running for exercise, she used to follow me on her bike with those little ashy legs, her snotty nose, and slippers. Sometimes I ran in sandy areas, and I remember stopping to wait for her as she pedaled her bike. Never did I help her because the goal was for her to catch up on her own. Keep in mind that if my daughter had been going to fall off a cliff, of course I would have helped. However,

I hope the subtle lessons learned, such as the bike-riding adventures, would teach her how to be persistent through challenges she'd face in life. Earning her high school diploma was a perfect example of that.

In another incident, my youngest daughter and I went to the store. She purchased some treats and sat in the back of the car. She said that the intent was to save some for her brother and sister. Later down the road, I heard some crunching in the back seat. So much for saving some for her siblings. I joined her in devouring the treats. In another incident, my youngest and I were driving back from Oklahoma and were near Albuquerque, New Mexico. While I was driving up a steep hill, we were entering a snowstorm. I shifted my view through the front windshield back and forth because I couldn't see. She said, *"Turn on your wipers."* Duh! One Father's Day, she gave me a CD by Luther Vandross, and the main song was "Dance with My Father," and it touches my heart when I hear the song. Not so much the song's content, but the meaning. An event I will never forget is the drive to Oklahoma and Ohio with my youngest daughter and her friend. We camped all the way up and back. While in Colorado, we hiked up an enormous hill and her friend saw a snake, which was interesting. We took several detours and one was a visit to George Washington Carver's monument. In addition, I had fended off the boys in Oklahoma, but I will never forget the entire adventure. Many memories and lessons learned from all my children, and recalling those at times often serves as relief when I face challenging times.

I have a thought that when I get to the pearly gates and Saint Peter reviews my life history, especially my younger days, he'll comment, "Wow, these issues in the past may deny you entry into heaven." Then Saint Peter reviews my children's record. He glances back and forth between the two records then mentions, "You get a reprieve. Get your ass back down there, and do more good."

Why do I deserve a reprieve? The Bible states, "Ye shall know them by their fruits" (Matthew 7:16) King James Version.

I earned a reprieve because of my children, but remembering my reprieve is only a chance to forgive me for all the dumb things I did. I thank God for blessing me with the ability to raise responsible children who have the opportunity to improve societies for generations to come. When they were young, I created a living portfolio for each child with everything from hair from the first haircut to school assignments and gave it to them once I believed each was responsible enough to keep the information current. Nevertheless, I still have their report cards. With considerable thought, I include a letter, verbatim from my son, and registered by all my children on my birthday, which he posted on Facebook:

Hey, Pops,

I want to take my time out to say a few things on this day.

There have been times in my life where I wonder why I am the way that I am. I have even been questioned by my wife as to why I do things a certain way; or why my demeanor seems somewhat stern and straightforward when it comes to my personal endeavors. Often times, I take on tasks without requesting help from anyone else. It seems that I have always been this way, but I couldn't even fully pinpoint the origin of some of my characteristics as a man. As a child, I never understood the dynamics of being a parent. I never understood why you did things in the way that you did them. I could never grasp the concept of how a parent must be stern with children in certain matters that would seemingly be a small issue. It wasn't until I was in my early 30s when I realized that being a parent is one of the toughest jobs that any person can have.

I realized that some parents grew up with no parents of their own, and they had to do the best that they could to raise children without a point of reference. I also realized that some parents do everything in their power to provide their children with a life that differs from their own childhood because they want their children to have a better life.

Daddy, I want to let you know that even though there were times we didn't see eye to eye, even though there were times I tried to challenge you, even though there were times I was angry with you, I want you to understand that I understand. I understand that I can never know the full capacity of what you have suffered through your life, but you did everything in your power to shield me and my sisters from those sufferings. I understand that it is hard to raise a man of color in this society, but you prepared me to be aware of those things that I would face in my adult life. I understand the times where you would show me how to do things once and told me I was on my own after that. These things helped shape me into the man I have become today.

So when it comes to bringing up the next generation, whether it be my nieces and nephews (blood or otherwise), my goddaughter, or my future children, I will never forget the life lessons that were imparted to me during my childhood. I will never forget where they came from. I will never forget the sayings, like, "Hey, boy, it's business before pleasure, understand?" or "Hey, man, remember it takes a man to be responsible, that's why I call you man." I will never forget the legacy of where we come from, and I will never forget to wear the Cubit family crest with pride, dignity, and honor. In all this…

Happy Birthday, Dr. Ronald W. Cubit, a.k.a., Pops.

Love,

Leishan, Lealani, Lahina

Parts of this letter remind me of the times my children were responsible for getting in the car by themselves and then fastening their seatbelt without my assistance. I was patient and just watched until they completed the task. I wanted my children to learn how to do things on their own. They were required to use a dictionary instead of asking me how to spell words, effectively complete assigned chores, and do their homework. The goal was to help them learn to be self-reliant. I note here a prize, for any parent, is what they impart to their children and to realize how, what they learn helps them develop into a responsible person. I make the statement that a parent's love can be bestowed and realized in the content of their children. I thank God and my life experiences, for assisting me in accomplishing this. However, I'm proud of what I accomplished in parenthood, and I love my children and their potential. The obligation to raise children of color was challenging, and many times, I wasn't Ronnie. I had to do what I thought was necessary to rear my children, sometimes, it was very uncomfortable. Could I, would I, or do I want to venture down that path again? It's an opened-ended question. Better yet, NO. Now, I have a different relationship with my children. I demand fatherly respect and that other side of me can surface if necessary, but that has yet to happen, and I hope it doesn't. Now, my children have the opportunity to experience a different side of me, Ronnie. My grandchildren are exceptional and being a grandad is my reward.

In addition to my children, some who influenced me were and are individuals who, in my youth, said that I wasn't going to amount to anything. Thank you! I constantly defer to my youth in this book hoping that some reading this exposé come to realize that he or she doesn't have to remain stuck in their current situations especially if it is unfavorable. However, sometimes finding a way out may not be evident. Do something and fail. I believe there are three prisons. One society creates, such as brick-and-mortar ones, socio-economic conditions, and so on. The second type is prisons created by others, the negativity, preconceived notions, the I-am-more-powerful-than-you attitude, and the prejudice. Get the point? And third are the prisons an individual creates. Inhibitions, fear of failure, ignorance, "yeah, but it was their fault," "the woman made me do it," and the unwillingness to change. I believe the third prison is the most detrimental because it creates a gateway for the others to exist. Fortunately, education and the experience of educating myself has been an outlet for me. What is yours? Referencing the quote at the beginning of this book, what is your "why"? Find your "why," and your world will definitely change. I promise.

I'm not the president of the United States but plan to run for office after publishing this book. Just kidding. However, I didn't live up to those predictions that I wouldn't make it past my sixteenth birthday. In addition, I tip my hat to some who said that the CBEST, real estate exam, and master's degree were out of reach for me and that a doctorate was too difficult to accomplish. I proved them wrong, in addition to those in the military who attempted to stymie my efforts or career. In those employment situations where I wasn't part of the "good ol' boy network," these situations sparked a fire for me to forge on and prove the naysayers wrong. To those with whom I had a relationship and they wanted me to be someone else, in addition to those who tried to change my personality-ha ha. Other sources of encouragement were and are the individuals who attempted to hold me back because of my race, my stature, and their dislike of me for whatever reason. To the individuals mentioned in this paragraph, I thought about extending my middle finger to all of you, but the action doesn't demonstrate a good example for my children and grandchildren, nor does the action display a forgiving heart. More so, I learned that what others think about me is none of my business.

In addition, throughout my life, I had people who helped me, I believe, through divine interventions. Here, too many to mention, and some of these individuals are of different races, nationalities, and sexes. I do believe these individuals had a genuine interest in helping me. I thank you for your motivation to help, and I'm grateful for your support. I'm not Saint Peter, but I do believe that if there was a doubt concerning your entry into heaven, the saint may take an extensive look at your record as well.

One day, someone asked who served as a role model for me. Sadly, I couldn't think of anyone except for God and the teachings in the Holy Bible. Another includes Dr. Martin Luther King, Jr. Besides the individuals mentioned in these writings, I couldn't think of anyone who served as a true role model. Someone after whom I could pattern my life or with whom I could network. I didn't have the luxury of a role model, and the only individual who came to mind was me-with a caveat: *I'm not perfect!*

I'll state, I'm not the same person I was fifty, forty, thirty, or ten years ago and have experienced a metamorphosis. My mind-set is altogether different. The Bible speaks of repentance, ridding oneself of the things of the past, turning face from those sins. I profess that here, regardless of public opinion, which doesn't matter, because God knows what is in my heart. However, I must forge on in the hopes that someone reading the content here changes his or her life. Although I have prejudices, I love life, the world, and everything it encompasses.

Chapter 19

TO BE CONTINUED...

In concluding the story of my life at this point, I communicate some of the challenges that I faced while making the transition from one stage to the next. The process wasn't easy. In this book, I note how I sometimes created obstacles that impeded my success. Sometimes the obstacles were conscious. However, I note that sometimes the obstacles were unconscious. Looking back, I cringe today at some of those memories and situations I thought were the norm. Whether the acts were conscious or subconscious, I must move on. Every memory presents opportunities for me to learn and grow interpersonally.

I'm not proud of many instances described in this book. However, I wouldn't be describing the content here if it weren't for those experiences that created *me*. I challenge everyone to examine those situations in life that, in combination, make the essence of an individual, if for no other reason than to enhance one's life, and perhaps the lives of others.

In this final chapter, I continue thinking, which sometimes gets me in trouble. Often, I recall teachings in the Bible and ask myself, *If I had an opportunity to talk with one individual other than Jesus Christ, who would that be?* Immediately, I think about Jonah because of the challenges he faced, especially while he was in the belly of the big fish. If it were me in the belly of the fish, during the entire event, I'd be hollering for Mama like I used to when, having moved to a new neighborhood, I was being chased by the older children, probably because I said something to antagonize the situation. Anyway, because of the challenges Jonah endured, I bet I could learn much from him.

Sometimes I find myself in the belly of a big fish, especially if I don't use my God-given talents. I realize my comments in the introduction chapter of these writings indicate a belly-of-the-fish situation. Staying in the shabby hotels and sleeping in my car were challenging situations. Perhaps I needed those situations to motivate me to forge ahead in life.

The challenges I describe in the beginning of this book in that shabby motel prompted me to finish this book, which I started in 2004. I now state that within these pages, I often communicate my motivation because of the naysayers in my life-those who said I wouldn't make it past my sixteenth birthday. Now that I conclude these writings, I realize the importance of writing this book for me, and not the naysayers. Do I have anything against those naysayers? Not at all; they provide some motivation for me. Nonetheless, I encourage everyone to take on a similar challenge in detailing your life, and if so, what would you say? What is your recollection of the hills, dells, and plateaus you faced? Write it for yourself, and leave publishing as an option. I've found this writing journey to be therapeutic. I laughed, cried, and found some revelations about me and about life. Most of all, I hope that others reading here benefit from the content in these pages, whether an insight to understanding or to help others, holistically. I felt an obligation to write this book because of the blessings in my life: "For unto whomsoever much is given, of him shall much be required" (Luke 12:48, 21st Century King James Version).

"Use it or lose it" is a motto for me. Many times, I didn't adhere to God's chosen path for me. When that happens, I believe I experience a belly-of-the-big-fish situation. I'm not a saint, but I do believe I experienced challenges similar to Jonah. When the fish spits me out, I say, "Okay, God. I get it," but I still get in the way sometimes. I should always remain in the belly of the big fish until I relent to God's chosen path for me. I must be receptive to the divine messages.

While in the semblance of the belly of a big fish, did I like being there, or do I have a fetish for that place? Hell no! A poor choice of words, but looking back, I realize the challenging experiences enhanced my personal growth. Today when experiencing the challenges of the belly of the fish, my goal is to endure the situation, because in the end, I will be all right.

Knowing what I know about me now, earning a million dollars through whatever means may not be in my best interest, especially if my subconscious demons surface. I know for a fact that if I had been successful playing sports and earned a big-time contract, it would've written my death sentence, and those who said that I wouldn't make it past my sixteenth birthday would be picking their teeth with a toothpick and saying, "I knew the [N-word] wouldn't amount to anything. He had it all and shucked it up."

I do believe my challenges in life shaped me, though, to a degree, yet I still have a ways to go, and I hope perfection never appears on my résumé. However, I like my place at this stage of life and know I need improvement in many areas. Perfection is my goal but may never be my state.

In reading the content here, it seems like the character here, me, was a constant shuck-up. I would trade the actions described in this book for complacency any day. I think, *What would life be like if I continued driving that taxicab years ago? What would life be like if I were still warehousing missiles? What would life be like if I never pursued my education? What would life be like if we hadn't moved to the High Desert? What would life be like for my children?* I can't answer these questions. However, I ask myself, *What would life be like if I hadn't?* That is the ultimate question for me.

I didn't have a clue how my actions in life influenced another. In the past year, unexpectedly, three individuals told me how I influenced their life in a positive way. I hadn't a clue how my actions had an impact on their lives.

I'm thankful for becoming a success at failure. In my life, I always took the indirect route and the difficult path, and sometimes I was lost in the wilderness. I never settled for complacency: the Marine Corps, obtaining my doctorate, taking jobs that enhanced my public-speaking skills, writing my memoirs. I don't believe my spirit allows me to take the well-traveled road. Most of all, I do have some regrets, and would change a few things if I could, but I don't apologize for the path I've taken. However, my heart goes out to those whom I might've hurt and those whom I might've helped; I hope my actions balance out.

Yes, I've had many failures, but I believe I am a different person because of them. I love my time in the outdoors and the challenges in my life that led me to this. Perfection isn't a slate for me because it limits growth. The journey as much as the destination shaped me. The "why."

I relate a situation about an associate who said that his or her life was boring. I asked if he or she was ever in trouble in school. The person said no. Traffic tickets? He or she said maybe one. Any other situations where you experienced issues, broke the law? The individual said no and that life was boring, including the music the person listened to. I said, "Tomorrow, go slap your supervisor, and before that, run a red light in front of a police officer. Then fart just before you roll-down the car window and the officer leans over and says license and registration please. Then maybe you'll have a different perspective in life because you did something out of the ordinary and had to overcome the challenge." That person looked at me, turning his or her head side to side several times like a puppy trying to figure out things. "Just kidding," I said. Then I said that he or she should feel fortunate about his or her life, and I am sure he or she has influenced someone, positively including me. I say here I'd rather be in my shoes rather than his or hers, because if both of us lost everything and were despondent without support, I wonder who would survive. However, I can relate to the words of musician David Bowie: "I don't know where I'm going from here, but I promise it won't be boring."

In looking back at most of my life, I realize there wasn't a boring moment. I'm almost hesitant here when I write that I'm fortunate that my life wasn't perfect. Again, I'm fortunate to be alive and have the ability to communicate here. I still make mistakes and may have another twenty or so jobs before I meet my maker. I still see myself as an individual from the hood trying to figure things out.

Here I rephrase the Starfish Story by Loren Isley. An individual walked along a shoreline and noticed the many starfish stranded on the beach. The individual proceeded to throw the starfish in the ocean. An individual walking on the beach saw the person throwing the starfish in the water and said, "You can't possibly make a difference throwing these starfish in the ocean. There are so many." The individual throwing the starfish in the water picked up one, tossed it in the ocean, and then said, "I made a difference for that one."

I hope you experience success at failure. I believe I accomplished a goal if only one person benefits from the content in this book. Whatever my fate, I never quit. Most of all, I believe the quality of my life isn't based on the goals I didn't achieve but on the disparity of what my life would be like if I didn't attempt. During a seminar I attended, a speaker talked about a poem by Linda Ellis called *The Dash*. When an individual dies, their headstone displays the date when he or she is born and when he or she dies. Between those dates is a dash. That dash indicates what an individual accomplishes in his or her life. Good or bad. What will your dash represent? I am proud to have a dissertation in the Library of Congress and now this book. Shall I live forever? Here I quote Ben Franklin: "Either write something worth reading or do something worth writing."

I still find real estate investments intriguing. I buy my home-cleaning products from the store, but I appreciate the experience gained from my goal to be successful at it. However, based on my experiences, I now believe I have a responsibility to continue helping people become self-sufficient in addition to striving for what is right and doing things the right way. Behold I found my "why," or my purpose in life, as communicated by Mark Twain at the beginning of this book. Better yet, my "why" found me, and I discovered the meaning. Today, regarding my thoughts about fool's hill, I'm still trying to figure out my status, but I want to rename that hill. Perhaps in the next book I reference fool's hill, but I intend to write a different story. Most of all, I hope you find your "why" and experience the hills and dells that contribute to its meaning.

Success to you,

Dr. C.

Special Acknowledgments

(In No Apparent Order)

God (of course)
My Grandmother Gladys
Dawn S. Wilson (thanks and always)
Dr. M. Stimac (Dissertation Chair)
Ms. Lane (At That Time My Fifth-Grade Teacher)
Mother, Margaret
Father, John
Stepfather, Richard
Sister Beverly
Brother, Daroll
Sister Vivian
Pepperdine University, GSEP
Long Beach City College
Victor Valley College, California
Chapman College, California
Southwestern College, California
Cerritos College, California
University of Redlands
United States Marines Corps (Semper Fi)
Spider-Man
AWay Corp
Spotlight 29
High Desert Lodge No. 107 (Fraternally)
Chaparral High School and Students

Barstow High School and Students
Victor Valley Elementary School District
Apple Valley School District
Hesperia School District
Margaret Rochelle (always a friend)
The United States Department of Labor, San Francisco (ETA)
NCNW Bethune Center in Rialto, California
Community Services Department, San Bernardino, California

ABOUT THE AUTHOR

D r. Cubit, a.k.a. Ronnie was born in California and lived in Southeast San Diego (Daygo) and lived for a short period in Dayton, Ohio. Ronnie is an outdoor person and enjoys hiking, backpacking, camping, four-wheeling, and spending time in his recreation vehicle. Ronnie loves music (smooth jazz, old-school, classic soft rock), and his trail name is Mr. Music. He also enjoys cracking some tile a.k.a. dancing for some of you. He believes in keeping fit however, nachos can be his downfall. Ronnie enjoys wielding a green thumb, making people laugh, and can burn in the kitchen sometimes. Ronnie is still a devout Los Angeles Chargers (formerly San Diego Chargers), San Diego Padres, and Los Angeles Lakers fan. He currently resides in Englewood, Colorado.

Ronnie was labeled a disadvantaged African American young person. He attended a job-training program for disadvantaged youth and if defined today, was among the hardest to serve. Ronnie was a high school dropout and later in life earned his diploma. He now has a doctorate from Pepperdine University. Ronnie also has a master's degree and a bachelor's degree, both from the University of Redlands. He also has two associate's degrees (Victor Valley College and Long Beach City College) and, in the past, completed classes for his teaching credential.

In *Fool's Hill*, Ronnie communicates how God, education, family, and other things helped change his life and that learning in any form can be rewarding. Ronnie has extensive experience in teaching, training, group facilitation (see http://www.foolshillthemeaningwhy.com/more-info/) scroll to Speaker Opps, and workforce development in the public and nonprofit sectors. He is currently employed as a workforce development specialist, education specialist, and spent time as a center director in a government organization that helps disadvantaged youth acclimate to life and employment. He was a professor at five universities or colleges and his work experience includes teaching in public education. He served nearly eight years in the United States Marine Corps.

Ronnie has three fantastic children and six outstanding grandchildren. In *Fool's Hill*, he states that his children positively changed his life. Based on his experiences, Ronnie aspires to help others avoid the pitfalls of life, which is his reason for writing *Fool's Hill*. He believes that anyone can overcome life's challenges. His mantras include "Forge on," "UCAN2," and fraternally, "Success to you."

Dr. Cubit A.K.A.—Mr. Music

Important links

Dr. Cubit's website: http://www.foolshillthemeaningwhy.com/
Dr. Cubit More Info: http://www.foolshillthemeaningwhy.com/more-info/
Book 2: http://www.foolshillthemeaningwhy.com/book-2/
Dissertation: https://www.learntechlib.org/p/123449/